Existing in the Information Dimension

This book presents new insights into the nature of the human mind as a product of the brain. It does so by discussing how biological and technological information systems differ from their counterparts with physical functions, presenting Emergent Information Theory as a solution to the mind-body problem and overarching framework for all biological and technological information systems.

Emergent Information Theory is a new theoretical approach to the specific type of information and emergence exploited by biological neural networks and digital systems. One of the conclusions of this theory is that these entities and their associated processes are non-physical and exist in an information dimension connected to but distinct from the three dimensions of physical space. It is in this information dimension that our minds exist, making it ultimately more our home as sentient beings than the physical realm inhabited by our bodies. This book presents existing scientific and philosophical evidence that leads to this conclusion, followed by application of the theory to biological and technological information systems. The author concludes with a call to action for further research.

This fascinating text will be of interest to any researcher of consciousness, the mind-body problem or AI, as well as those working in related areas such as physical neuroscience and systems theory.

Daniel Boyd is an independent researcher living in the Netherlands who has developed Emergent Information Theory as a theoretical approach to biological and technological information systems. He is currently a member of the Board of IS4SI (International Society for the Study of Information).

Existing in the Information Dimension

An Introduction to Emergent Information Theory

Daniel Boyd

Routledge
Taylor & Francis Group
LONDON AND NEW YORK

First published 2025
by Routledge
4 Park Square, Milton Park, Abingdon, Oxon OX14 4RN

and by Routledge
605 Third Avenue, New York, NY 10158

Routledge is an imprint of the Taylor & Francis Group, an informa business

British Library Cataloguing-in-Publication Data
A catalogue record for this book is available from the British Library

ISBN: 978-1-032-56702-0 (hbk)
ISBN: 978-1-032-60784-9 (pbk)
ISBN: 978-1-003-46054-1 (ebk)

DOI: 10.4324/9781003460541

Typeset in Times New Roman
by codeMantra

to Gill
for creating and forming me

to Anneke
for supporting me

to so many scholars
for their insights and inspiration

and to Wolfgang
for opening the door

Contents

Preface *xi*
Reader's guide *xvii*

PART 1
The evidence: Pieces of the puzzle 1

1.1 Information and the physical 3
1.1.1 Definitions of information 3
1.1.2 Information and life 4
1.1.3 Information technologies 5
1.1.4 Information in control 6
1.1.5 Other definitions and uses 7
1.1.6 What isn't information? 8
1.1.7 Disentangling information from matter 8
1.1.8 Information processes 9
1.1.9 Phase space and the information dimension 10
1.1.10 Physical and informational dimensionality 10

1.2 Systems theory 12
1.2.1 Hierarchical organization 12
1.2.2 From the fundamental to the cosmic 14
1.2.3 Degrees of emergence 14
1.2.4 Origins of physical systems 17
1.2.5 Origins of living systems 18
1.2.6 Origins of technologies 19
1.2.7 From form to function 20
1.2.8 Causation in emergent systems 22
1.2.9 Understanding complex systems 23

1.3 Biological information systems 25

1.3.1 Information storage and transfer 25
1.3.2 Information acquisition and communication 26
1.3.3 Information processing 27
1.3.4 A new generic solution 28
1.3.5 Brain anatomy and support functions 28
1.3.6 Where are the brain's functions? 29
1.3.7 The connectome 30
1.3.8 How does it work? 31
1.3.9 How to wire a neural network 32
1.3.10 Nature and nurture 34
1.3.11 Imitation, language and the communal brain 36

1.4 Philosophy and religion 38

1.4.1 Philosophy of the mind 38
1.4.2 Philosophy beyond the mind 41
1.4.3 Religion and the soul 42

1.5 Technological information systems 46

1.5.1 How information technologies are different 46
1.5.2 Physical support systems 47
1.5.3 Information storage and transfer 48
1.5.4 Mechanical information processing 50
1.5.5 Electronic information processing 51
1.5.6 Causation in information systems 53
1.5.7 Expert systems 54
1.5.8 Machine learning 55
1.5.9 The mysterious ways of artificial neural networks 57
1.5.10 How to build a neural network 58
1.5.11 How to train a neural network 60
1.5.12 Networks and integrated digital systems 62

PART 2
Conclusion: The origins and growth of the information dimension 65

2.1 Emergent Information Theory: An introduction 67

2.2 Biological information systems 70

2.2.1 How evolution opened the door 70
2.2.2 Neuronal interaction: from specific to generic 73
2.2.3 Neuronal networks: from connection to (de)construction 75
2.2.4 Information combination and emergence 79
2.2.5 Information storage: memory 82
2.2.6 Dimensionality of the brain's information content 83
2.2.7 Structural causation and control 88
2.2.8 Activity and the time dimension 90
2.2.9 Functional causation and control 92
2.2.10 Spontaneous generation 95
2.2.11 The special case of consciousness 97
2.2.12 No brain is an island unto itself 99
2.2.13 Communication 101
2.2.14 Symbolic language 104
2.2.15 Information distribution 107
2.2.16 Language and culture 109

2.3 Information technologies 112

2.3.1 Information transfer 112
2.3.2 Information processing 114
2.3.3 Digital information processing 115
2.3.4 Data digitization 122
2.3.5 Dimensionality of digital information processing 125
2.3.6 Digital simulation 127
2.3.7 The digital community 130

PART 3
Discussion: Living with the consequences 135

3.1 Existing in the information dimension 137

3.2 The gamble evolution took 141

3.3 Determinism and free will 145

3.4 From organism to superorganism 151

3.5 The communal mind 160

3.6 Cyber-social systems 166

3.7 Artificial consciousness 172

PART 4
Epilogue 177

4.1 Towards a science of emergent information 179

References *187*
Index *201*

Preface

Do we really need yet another book about the relationship between brain and mind, body and soul? My contention, self-evidently, is that this is far more than an indulgence: it is a necessity.

Many years ago, curiosity brought me into this arena in the hope and expectation of finding clear and satisfying answers. Listening to what wise women and men had to say I was frequently amazed, inspired and impressed. Some I could only follow in a general sense, lacking the specific intellectual background and technical skills required to join them at the cutting edge of their work. Yet, it became increasingly evident that the academics were far from consensus. Some were even in diametrical opposition.

Why should we care? As intelligent, sentient creatures we have an inherent drive to understand ourselves both as individuals and in social relationship with others. In an existential sense, we yearn to determine our place and the meaning of our presence as part of reality as a whole. More pragmatically, we face the challenges of malfunctions of the mind. While the medical treatment of physical ailments progresses in leaps and bounds, we struggle to alleviate the suffering caused by mental illnesses. We are also confronted with a range of social challenges derived from the minds of individuals such as criminality and less-than-desirable socio-political situations. A better understanding of the nature of the mind could clarify the reasons for these limitations and potentially lead us to novel approaches to solving them. Recently, an additional motivation has been added to the list. Artificial intelligence has now climbed out of the science fiction books and philosophical musings to confront us eye to eye. In direct dialogue Large Language Models may claim, with unnerving eloquence, to have joined us as sentient beings. They describe and justify their possession of mind in a way that is not easy to deny, however implausible it may seem. How can we prove that there is no ghost in their machine? What does it mean if there is?

Considering this area of human exploration, I am reminded of the parable of the blind men and the elephant. Encountering the beast for the first time, each feels a particular part of the elephant – a tusk, an ear, a tail, a leg – and describes what he has discovered to the others. Needless to say, this doesn't lead to consensus concerning the nature of this animal. In some versions of the story, the men assume that the others are lying, leading to conflict. In others, they ignore each other, each remaining within his own limited and fixed perspective. In more hopeful versions, they try to combine their findings to form a more complete picture than any of them could create individually.

The blind men investigating the mind-body problem range from neuroscientists to experts in artificial intelligence, from information theorists to quantum physicists. Even within each of these disciplines, there are frequent differences of opinion. Sometimes, these are due to the use of different methodologies or coming from different backgrounds. Sometimes, they are due to different interpretations of the same observations. In dealing with these differences, each of the above versions of the outcome of the parable can be observed. While academics will seldom resort to physical fisticuffs, intellectual battles are sometimes fought with an intention of winning the truth by defeating delusion. On a daily basis, most of those involved simply get on with the job of chiselling away further in their own corner, ignoring the rest. Over drinks, most would acknowledge that their work is only part of the greater picture, and congresses are organized to bring people from different disciplines together in a noble attempt to build the bridges necessary to unite such a fragmented landscape. Yet, in spite of these efforts, the big picture remains elusive.

So why is this subject so difficult? How does it differ from other areas of human endeavour? Why is it that, while those working in this area can't even agree on fundamentals, physicists and engineers can land a spacecraft on an asteroid 30 million miles away? A feat like that is only possible with a complete consensus between all of the specialisms required by the mission. Yet, serious physical science is just a few centuries old, while we have pondered the mind-body problem for millennia. Why, then, are we still groping in the dark?

Reconsidering the parable of the blind men and the elephant, I realized that the situation was actually a little more complicated. Yes, there were scientists feeling various parts of its anatomy, but to take this parable further, we also need to consider the philosophers viewing the situation from the perspective of the mind. Being sighted, they can actually see their subject, but stand at a distance from which they cannot feel it. Looking in the direction of the groping scientists, they do not see an elephant at all. Instead, they see a kaleidoscopic rainbow. While scientists studying the brain talk in terms of mechanisms and structures, philosophers studying the mind speak of colours and drifting forms. Standing close to the philosophers, theologians also voice their view of the scene in terms that are alien to the physicalists. This dichotomy is the essence of the mind-body problem: how can such radically different viewpoints converge on the same entity existing in the same place at the same time, and what is the relationship between them?

To answer this question, we need to step out of the analogy for a moment and consider the methods at our disposal. We are capable of literally feeling the subject of the physical sciences: matter and energy. When these are beyond our sense organs – for instance, radiation outside the visible spectrum, the microscopic or the cosmic – we can build instruments with which we can broaden our perceptual range. Equally importantly, we can use our hands to manipulate the physical. Again, where our hands fail to suffice, we can build machines to extend our capabilities. These are the tools of empirical science that have accelerated our ability to understand and control the physical world we inhabit. The tools that allowed us to build and fly the Rosetta spacecraft to comet Churyumov-Gerasimenko.

While such tools can also be used successfully to study the workings of the physical brain, there are no scientific instruments with which we can see or feel the content of the mind: no device to measure the depth of sadness or the brightness of inspiration. We also lack the physical tools to build an idea or to cut down an illusion. While our personal experience of these phenomena is vivid, these factors prevent us from performing direct empirical science on the mind.

How is it possible that something as real and influential as the mind can evade the scientific method in this way? The simple answer is that such phenomena are not made of matter and energy and therefore cannot directly influence or be influenced by machines of matter and energy. Certainly, interaction is possible via the physical brain, but this is only an indirect effect mediated by the association between the two. A neural correlate is just the physical side of this relationship. As formulated in Chalmers' Hard Problem [1], even if we know everything about the neural processes involved, we are still faced with the question of why these are associated with the phenomenal experience. Determining the neural activity that accompanies the experience of the colour red does not constitute detection of the experience, and causing the experience by shining light of a particular wavelength onto the retina does not constitute an explanation for its existence.

Furthermore, this is only the tip of an immense iceberg. If all we had as sentient beings was the experience of the colour red we would lead impoverished lives. Even a bacterium has a richer perception of its surroundings. The challenge goes far beyond explaining the colour red. It extends to explaining the glorious curve of a rainbow, spread sparkling across a cloud-strewn sky and combined as an integral experience with the cool wind on your face, the sound of the first raindrops falling on dry earth and the smell of wettened dust; the feeling of spiritual awe it inspires; recalling the first line of Keats' poem *My heart leaps up when I behold / A rainbow in the sky*; drifting off to the classroom and the stooping English teacher, the smell of chalk on blackboard; to abruptly return to the here and now with the thought, appearing suddenly and without warning out of the subconscious recesses of your mind, that it would be a good idea to bring the washing in. Such rich and complex experiential phenomena cannot be explained on the basis of individual neural states, and the way in which these states combine to create the experience is even more elusive. You cannot open up the skull and see an array of coloured neurons forming a rainbow. The only way we can know it is there is if the person experiencing it (truthfully) tells us. Yet, for the person themselves, the rainbow is as real as real can be.

The resulting inability to perform empirical science on consciousness itself is a significant limitation for those studying the mind side of the equation, but this is not to say that they are powerless. They have at their disposal the reliable sharpness of logic as applied to the evidence of reported phenomenal consciousness with which significant and robust progress can be made.

The mind-body problem is the recognition of both sides of this relationship and the difficulty of reconciling our understanding of the two. This is in no way a problem for the mind and the body themselves. They are quite happy doing their thing, as they have done for millions of years. This clearly constitutes a stable and harmonious partnership that is undisturbed by our feverish attempts to pin them down in theory. It is our desire for understanding and control that stumbles on the apparent incompatibility of these two intimately connected aspects of reality.

While explaining the relationship between the brain and the conscious mind is in itself a major challenge, it is not the full scale of the problem. Shifting our focus from the biological to the technological, it was many years ago that Turing proposed a test of artificial intelligence on the basis of its ability to mislead us into thinking that it is human [2]. The question being, in what was then a hypothetical situation that a machine should pass the test, how we could prove that it was not a conscious, thinking entity. Now, 75 years on, the hypothetical has become real. We have digital systems which are able to converse with us in a human-like fashion. What proves them to be inhuman is not so much their failure to provide intelligible and appropriate answers as the scope and accuracy of their responses, which no individual human could match. In a functional sense at least, these systems are rapidly surpassing the abilities of our own minds. Furthermore, they do so not by following the explicit programmed instructions of software designers but by gathering, interpreting and generating information in a way that is comparable to the way in which we ourselves generate intelligent responses. The mechanisms they use – artificial neural networks – are broadly comparable to those used by our brains. It could now seem that the question is not whether but when these machines will become conscious. In this sense, the differences between the brain and the computer are diminishing, and the challenge of understanding them is converging.

To this expansion, we can add the fact that many aspects of brain function are non-conscious yet use the same neural mechanisms. From the physical perspective, all brain tissue looks much the same. There is also a fluidity between the two realms that challenges the exclusivity of consciousness. The solution must therefore also account for these parts of the human brain, and indeed the nervous systems of all other animals. Returning to information technologies, even if we conclude that they are faking consciousness, we are still confronted with the similarity between their functions and those of our non-conscious minds.

This proximity between the conscious and the non-conscious brings us to the question of whether the Hard Problem is limited to consciousness. Are there other phenomena that confront us with these same issues: whose nature cannot be derived directly from the physical states they are associated with? Which, like qualia, cannot be detected using physical instruments to prove their existence and measure their parameters? All such phenomena would need to be explained by our theory, and would lead to the question of what underlies this common characteristic, and what it tells us about the mind-body problem.

It turns out that even the simplest of information technologies falls into this category. If it seems odd to put a pocket calculator on a par with consciousness, I would like to present the evidence of the lowly binary value associated with a magnetic bit. To paraphrase Chalmers: "*Even when we have explained the performance of all the* ***electronic functions taking place in the computer*** *there may still remain a further unanswered question: Why is the performance of these functions accompanied by* ***binary values****?*" In this example, there actually is an easy answer to the 'why?' question: we have designed the computer in this way. However, this begs the more significant question of *how* a binary value is associated with a particular physical function or state: a question that reveals a surprising strangeness in even this most trivial unit of information. The simple fact is that the binary value, just like qualia, cannot be explained purely in terms of the physical state with which it is associated. Given only this physical state (without knowledge of the design of the computer it is a part of and preceding events), there is no way to derive the binary value, or indeed to determine whether there is a binary value associated with it at all. There is no sense organ or scientific instrument with which we can detect these '0's and '1's. Furthermore, in the workings of the computer, we see the same binary value being passed between physical states: one moment it may be stored in a magnetic state, the next it is being transported on an electrical current, only later to be passed on to a flash of light. Like qualia, then, binary values are also non-physical entities that are firmly but flexibly connected to the physical.

In spite of being non-physical, these values can have an observable physical effect, in this case on the behaviour of the computer. Indeed, it is only on the basis of their effects on the output of computations onto visible monitors and printouts that we can deduce their existence at all. This is in essence comparable to concluding the existence of a conscious state on the basis of the indirect evidence of behaviour exhibited by a person. As with the causative effects of consciousness and free will, this confronts us with the puzzle of a physical system being influenced by a non-physical factor: another observation that needs to be accounted for by our theory.

Only the most staunch panpsychist [3] would grant any degree of consciousness to the individual magnetic bit: phenomenal consciousness has specific characteristics that binary values clearly lack. Yet, they do seem to deserve a place in the same category of non-physical influential phenomena. Furthermore, binary values are only the starting point of function in the computer. It is at far higher levels of organization created through interaction between these fundamental components that computers exhibit the unnervingly humanlike responses of contemporary artificial intelligence. In this sense, the computer's binary values are comparable to the information associated with individual synapses in the brain which also need to be combined in large numbers to produce useful higher level functions, only some of which have the characteristics of consciousness.

The shared non-physical features of brains and computers have two direct consequences. The first is that a unifying theory is required that encompasses both: a theory concerning the specific type of information that underlies their function. The second is that having a collection of systems falling within this same explanatory framework may actually help us with this challenge of understanding them. Being the product of design, computers are a lot easier to understand than the messy evolved wetware of the brain and as such can serve as simplified models from which extrapolations can be made.

What, then, is required of a theory aiming to unite all of these phenomena, for which a physicalist explanation would seem to be incomplete? To start with, it must in some way combine the significant insights gained from each of the relevant existing philosophical and scientific disciplines. This is not to say that it must necessarily agree. Indeed, considering the opposing positions of some approaches, this would be impossible. It must, however, create a context within which all of these approaches fall and can be viewed from a broader perspective. The theory must also be unifiable with the general physical sciences, for which the volume of hard evidence is too great to tolerate any doubt. A further requirement is simplicity. The major steps forward in science generally involved the discovery of a relatively simple underlying theory that explained a seemingly diverse collection of complex special cases. For instance, evolutionary theory provided a unifying foundation for biology, genetics, palaeontology, comparative anatomy and biogeography. Similarly, the solution to the mind-body problem must encompass all of the non-physical phenomena mentioned above.

These requirements were the starting point for my own investigations. Consequently, I did not join an existing team to further the study of a particular part of the elephant's anatomy or fragment of the rainbow. This book will not present or advance cutting-edge thinking in these areas. Instead, I brought everything I had heard together to draw a conclusion that does not fit neatly into any of these individual camps.

It is up to you, the reader, to decide whether the reasoning and outcome of these investigations, as presented in this book, are valid or flawed. It is also up to you to determine whether they say something more fundamental about the mind-body problem or are merely a myopic view of one of the elephant's toenails.

Reader's guide

This book presents a novel solution to the unification of the physical and non-physical aspects of reality. The solution proposed – Emergent Information Theory – is a conclusion drawn from the combination of a large number of relevant scientific and philosophical claims, observations and theories. While these did not arise with the purpose of fitting neatly together, somehow we must find a way to integrate them into a greater picture without leaving too many gaps or having to shave off too many corners. There is, after all, only one reality. It is on this diversity of pillars that the theory rests, necessitating their inclusion both as support for and components of the theory itself.

The structure of this book is based on these considerations and offers you, the reader, alternative approaches. A sequential path through Part 1 presents a broad range of Evidence that leads to the Conclusion and also provides the components from which it is built. Part 2 starts with a general introduction to Emergent Information Theory, which aims and claims to unite all of these perspectives into an integrated explanatory framework. It then discusses in more detail how this relates to biological and technological information systems.

While this is a logical route to take, it means that it takes a while to reach this destination. Alternatively, you can start with the Conclusion in Part 2 and revert to the chapters of Part 1 when and where you require elucidation of the foundations on which it is built.

Moving on from either of these options, Part 3 presents a Discussion of a number of consequences of the theory, followed in the Epilogue by consideration of what will be needed to develop a mature science of emergent information.

Part 1

The evidence

Pieces of the puzzle

1.1 Information and the physical

1.1.1 Definitions of information

A chapter on definitions may not be the most engaging way to start a book. Unfortunately, in this case, it is unavoidable. Why? In the physical sciences words can be unambiguously associated with specific elements of reality. A 'planet' is a celestial body orbiting a star. 'Oxygen' is an atomic structure composed of eight protons, eight neutrons and eight electrons. This clarity, unfortunately, does not apply to the word 'information'.

Browsing through academic work on information soon reveals the reason for this situation: the phenomena being investigated are not composed of matter or energy. The words familiar to the physical sciences are absent from the vocabulary, which instead employs terms that are meaningless in a physical context. Consequently, these phenomena cannot be detected, defined, measured and distinguished in the way that physical entities such as oxygen and planets can be. And yet the entities and processes discussed are usually so firmly mathematically defined and logically robust that they seem just as reliable and real as anything physical.

The consequences of this state of affairs were succinctly described by Floridi when he wrote, not so very long ago, "*Philosophical work on the concept of (semantic) information is still at that lamentable stage when disagreement affects even the way in which the problems themselves are provisionally phrased and framed*" [4]. From his discussion of the various interpretations and frameworks that have been proposed, it is clear that the term 'information' is used in various contexts for a range of distinct phenomena [5]. Yet, it is generally used freely and with little consideration for this fact. Two factors would seem to play a role here. Practically, many of these disciplines are highly productive working with their own definition within their own theoretical framework, less troubled than Floridi by others using the word differently. More intuitively, information does not have the manifest strangeness of consciousness that underlies the ongoing debates around Chalmers' Hard Problem [1]. It seems a more innocuous term that is therefore employed more casually. However, the differences between these uses inevitably lead to the risk of apparent disagreement when in fact there is only a semantic difference. They may also lead to confusion when a term is used in a way that does not match with

DOI: 10.4324/9781003460541-2

a person's expected use and conceptualization of the word. For this reason, it is essential when discussing information to define exactly how the term is being used.

This book will use 'information' to refer very specifically to the phenomenon that underlies the functions of biological and technological information systems: a definition that requires us to elucidate the distinguishing features of an information system. At this stage, such a definition runs the risk of entering a Catch-22 situation. To say that it is a system that operates on the basis of this type of information is not particularly helpful. What is perhaps more helpful is to define what it is not. An information system differs from a physical system in that the relevant aspects of its input and output are not physical. It does not use raw materials to produce some physical product. This makes a heart and a pasta machine physical system, and a brain and an abacus information system. The purpose of this chapter is to consider this distinction in more detail and from different angles in order to secure a robust definition that can be reliably used in the discussions that follow.

1.1.2 Information and life

The use of the term information in this book is a conceptual neighbour to the pragmatic information described by Roederer, who states that "*Without 'observers' or 'users' such as life forms (or devices built or designed by intelligent beings), there is no information*" [6]. Both definitions only play a role in living organisms and (more recently) in tools built by intelligent living organisms. The reason for this special relationship between information and life is that it involves ascribing meaning to an external pattern or state (Bateson's 'difference that makes a difference' [7]).

It is this meaning that makes such information so valuable to living organisms [8]. The fundamental challenge faced by every living organism relates to the fact that it is extremely far from equilibrium. Creating and maintaining this situation is dependent on the continual – and specifically directed – expense of energy to resist the physical processes that would otherwise lead to decay and ultimately death. Both the acquisition and the effective use of this energy require sensitivity and responsiveness to the conditions surrounding the organism and to its own internal state. The generation of such responses is greatly aided by information processes. The physical buoyancy of a crab may cause it to come to rest on the sand as the tide goes out, but information processing is required to safely scuttle under a rock. In contrast, the moon does not need to process information to cause the tides that wash over the crab: it can simply go with the flow of the law of gravity.

The second reason for the connection between life and this type of information is that systems that work in this way are so immensely improbable that they will never arise spontaneously through physicochemical processes. They can only be created by the cumulative, progressive development supported by biological evolution; or subsequently through directed design processes performed by intelligent living organisms, such as those underlying our information technologies. The digital computer is an example of a designed system that uses bit states as representatives of binary values; the body's use of insulin to represent blood sugar levels is an example of a simple evolved system.

In the context of living organisms, the word 'information' is justifiably used most commonly in the context of the nervous system, which supports highly complex and specific coupling of stimulus and response. After the detection of relevant information by the sense organs, processing of this data in the sensory cortex leads to the creation of reconstructions of relevant aspects of the external world [9]. Such information then enters the internal parts of the brain, joining a great diversity of information processes working on the basis of various incoming and stored information to formulate an appropriate response. Finally, the brain needs to produce coordinated muscular activity, necessitating a conversion of the intention into instructions to initiate the required individual muscle contractions [10]. Throughout this chain of events, the responses to neural states are not based on the states themselves, but on the information associated with them.

This is not to say that all living processes are based on information. Many are purely biochemical or mechanical. Furthermore, some simple information processes could plausibly be functionally replaced by physical processes. However, there are limits to the complexity of adaptive and responsive functions that can be achieved through the evolution of physicochemical mechanisms alone.

In conclusion, only living organisms have the necessity, the motivation and the means to use this type of information. Under this definition, the Earth's biosphere is the only place in the known universe where such information exists, but here it has a truly essential role to play.

1.1.3 Information technologies

In this opening statement of his 1996 paper, Landauer refers to the specific type of information used in ancient and modern information technologies as follows: "*Information is not a disembodied abstract entity; it is always tied to a physical representation. It is represented by engravings on a stone tablet, ... a hole in a punched card, ... or some equivalent*" [11].

This is a rather narrow view of information, excluding as it does the far more ancient and ubiquitous information processes taking place in living organisms. However, the use of the terms 'tied' and 'represented' indicates that this is the type of information we are interested in. Furthermore, consideration of such information in these systems can be very useful since, having designed them, we know how they work. If we are careful to acknowledge the differences between information technologies and biological information processing, this may help us in our attempts to understand the latter.

Landauer's definition differs from Roederer's in that this information does not necessarily lead to some change in the system harbouring the information. The information is generally intended to be used by some separate reading-and processing mechanism, and exists regardless of whether this happens. While Roederer describes the observable effects that demonstrate the utilization of information, Landauer describes what information actually is.

Landauer's statement introduces the fundamental issue of representation. While he called this article 'The physical nature of information', his opening sentence actually claims the contrary. The use of the terms 'tied' and 'represented' indicate that information is distinct from the physical entities we use as a proxy for it. A more appropriate title would have been 'The physical relation with information'.

While these days the term 'information technology' is synonymous with the digital computer, as Landauer acknowledges the use of tools to supplement our mental abilities goes back deep into prehistory. As long ago as 35,000 years ago, humans were using tallies to register quantitative information [12]. In contrast with a tool with a physical function such as a knife or a bowl, the function of such tools is not based on their physical characteristics, but on the information associated with them. Sometime later, writing was developed as a way of storing linguistically formulated information and supplementing the ability to communicate information through speech. Here, the relationship between the physical carrier and information becomes more specific and also more arbitrary: any way of creating marking on any type of material can be used, and the symbols used are purely a matter of convention.

A more significant step was taken with the invention of technologies such as the abacus and mechanical calculating devices. These went beyond storing and transferring information to also processing it. Most recently, Turing's general purpose computer [2] unleased an explosion of information processing possibilities. Associated with this mechanization of information processing, we encounter Shannon's rigorous analysis of information loss during transmission [13]. All of these machines belong to the set of information technologies discussed in this book.

By definition, this type of information does not exist in the entity it describes. As observed by Korzybski [14], the map is not the territory. Instead, it is something created in another entity though interaction. When an object's temperature is measured and stored in computer memory, the information is attached to the memory device, not to the object whose temperature was measured. After all, the object itself has no need for this information, since it possesses the original physical property. The object is not influenced by the fact that another entity represents its temperature in this way, cannot cause this representation to be used in a particular way and is not changed when this happens.

1.1.4 Information in control

In both living organisms and information technologies, we have seen that information has an essential and causative role. In so far as such information is not a physical force or entity, this presents us with a dilemma concerning the causal closure of physical reality that was already cause for speculation by James Clerk Maxwell when he was laying the foundations of thermodynamics, and that remains a topic of discussion to this day [15]. This led to the thought experiment involving Maxwell's demon, a theoretical agent that employed only information to influence physical events and cause violation of the Second Law of Thermodynamics. In the words of Maxwell himself: "*let us suppose that ... a being, who can see the individual molecules, opens and closes this hole, so as to allow only the swifter molecules to pass from A to B .... He will thus, without expenditure of work, raise the temperature of B and lower that of A, in contradiction to the second law of thermodynamics*" [16]. This concept has recently been experimentally demonstrated [17], making information a very real and influential part of reality.

These theoretical considerations and experiments involve the type of information considered in this book: a measurement leads to a change of state, which is subsequently used as a representation of the measured state in determining the outcome of a physical action. The fact that the concept arose in the context of the causal closure of the laws of thermodynamics has, however, focussed attention on simple systems in which the apparent contradiction can be subjected to rigorous mathematical testing. There has been some discussion of the special role that such phenomena may have in living systems [18], but these too tend to focus on thermodynamics at the molecular level. It has not led to consideration of the causative effects of more complex information processes in either living organisms or technologies, and to an extent with good reason. Both brains and computers are energy hungry systems: it is not so that we see them defying thermodynamics by creating ordered physical structures without an accompanying expenditure of energy. What we do see, however, are systems whose functions appear to be determined by informational rather than physical factors. This introduces a different twist on Maxwell's musings that encompasses not just the Second Law of Thermodynamics. Is it possible that the laws of physics in their entirely are causally incomplete; that information processing systems introduce supplementary influences? It would seem at the very least that something is happening in such systems that is not entirely captured and explained by the laws that govern energy and matter.

1.1.5 Other definitions and uses

Beyond the use of information by organisms and information technologies, we encounter other uses of the word with subtly or fundamentally different meanings. The broad field of information theory [19] introduces the concept of the information entropy of a system, which relates to the amount of algorithmic information required to define a system [20]. This measurable parameter of a physical system, while relevant to its representation in an information system, is distinct from it. Since this value exists regardless of whether such a representation exists, this meaning of the word 'information' falls outside the definition used in this book.

Elsewhere in physics, the word information is used in very different ways. Quantum physics introduces a ubiquitous causative role for information through the involvement of observation in collapsing the wave function [21]. While there has been much discussion about whether or not this 'observation' entangles consciousness with quantum mechanics [22], the collapse of wave functions in the absence of interaction with living systems means that this, too, is a type of information that falls outside of the definition used here.

Moving into the domain of theoretical physics and mathematics, information is sometimes given an even more fundamental role. Following Galileo's proposition that "*this grand book—I mean the universe ... is written in the language of mathematics*" [23], it has even been postulated that information constitutes the true foundation of reality, of which the physical world is no more than an embodied representation [24]. Here, again the term is used in a very different way.

1.1.6 What isn't information?

A thought experiment may help clarify the significance of these different definitions: imagine a world without information. Doing so allows us to peel off a number of layers, depending on your definition. The first obvious casualty is perception. Without information about your surroundings created by your sensory systems, all conscious experience of the world would vanish. Indeed, without internal information, your brain would completely cease to function, as would the nervous systems of all other animals. Plants and animals also employ other mechanisms to behave responsively, for instance those involving hormones to transfer information. These, too, would cease to function. More fundamentally, without the information stored in their genomes, both animals and plants would be unable to produce the proteins that are essential to the function of their cells and life would grind to a halt. Though it would be the least of our worries, modern society would quickly derail as all information technologies abruptly failed. Evidently, then, this type of information is a crucial to our existence.

With the definition of information used in this book, the buck stops there. Whether or not an organism or device detects, stores and uses information about the state of a 'source' entity is immaterial to this entity or to its interactions with other entities. The tree can still fall in a forest and cause vibrations in the air: all that is missing is the conversion of these vibrations into perceived sound carrying the information that the tree has fallen. While life would be extinguished, having lost its ability to respond to factors that are essential for its survival, the physical universe trundles further on its way, oblivious to the loss it has suffered.

Using Wheeler's interpretation that "*all things physical are information-theoretic in origin*" [25], the outcome is radically different. Under the slogan '*it from bit*', removing information deletes the characteristics that define physical entities and determine how they interact. All forms of interaction would therefore vanish and the entire universe would freeze in a static, timeless state. Indeed, if we take information as fundamental to interaction and follow this down to the level of elementary particles, then matter itself would vaporise into a mist of quantum uncertainty as wave functions failed to collapse. Information, then, really is everything. Removing it leaves nothing.

These fundamentally and radically divergent scenarios demonstrate just how different these interpretations of the term 'information' are.

1.1.7 Disentangling information from matter

In Landauer's view of information technologies, and in property dualism, information is seen as a logical state or abstract property belonging to a physical state.

This acknowledges the fact that it is not a physical phenomenon, built of atoms or energy. It even concedes that it cannot be measured directly in the way that physical properties such as temperature or mass can be. However, information remains less than an entity in its own right: it is no more than a by-product or derivative of the physical. The question is whether such a limited, passive, dependent role is justified given its direct causative effect on the outcome of events taking place in computers and brains or whether, as Chalmers put it: "*It may just be...that there is a way of seeing information itself as fundamental*" [26].

The alternative proposed in this article is substance dualism. In this interpretation, the binary information associated with a magnetic state in a computer or neural activity in the brain is defined as a connected but separate non-physical entity in its own right.

This approach is different from and far broader than traditional substance dualism, which singles out consciousness or even the (human) soul as the exclusive addition to physical reality. Such mental substance, particularly in theistic worldviews, is often seen as entirely independent of the physical [27]. Based on this separation, the continuation of the soul in the absence of the body after death is deemed plausible.

Clearly, the binary value referred to above does not fit in such a philosophical context, being neither experiential nor spiritual and firmly dependent on its material substrate. And yet it would appear to also deserve to be included in the classification of non-physical substances. The question is how these two seemingly fundamentally different phenomena can be united in a single theoretical framework.

1.1.8 Information processes

The information associated with the computer's magnetic bits are not isolated, passive entities: their significance lies in the ways in which they can be combined and interact. This is systemically comparable to the way in which physical fundamental particles combine and interact in physical processes. The difference is that these informational processes are inevitably just as non-physical by nature as the entities involved, and in the same way. While associated with physical processes, it is not the physical process (for instance the opening of a transistor gate) that determines function. An entirely different physical mechanism (e.g. a pulse of light) could be used to the same effect. What is functionally relevant is the informational process, which cannot be detected or observed using physical instruments and yet produces observable effects (for instance the output of a calculation).

This situation led Abelson and Sussman to muse that "*A computational process is indeed much like a sorcerer's idea of a spirit. It cannot be seen or touched. It is not composed of matter at all. However it is very real*" [28]. As non-physical processes, such computational processes do not operate according to the physical laws of motion, thermodynamics and magnetism. However, this is not to say that they enjoy some kind of magical freedom: instead, they follow their own (logical) rules which are equally binding.

The same applies to information processing in biological systems. Here, too we see physical processes taking place, such as the combination of inputs to a neuron leading to an action potential, which perform no physical function but instead support a required informational process. Here, too, the process and that which it operates on cannot be seen or touched, and yet are still very real.

1.1.9 Phase space and the information dimension

The proposition that such information constitutes a real but non-physical phenomenon, rather than simply a property attached to a physical state, leads inevitably to the question of where this phenomenon exists. The interaction and combination observed between information entities necessitate differential proximity. Just as physical particles may interact when they are in contact but not when they are distant, so too must there be a locational explanation why some informational entities interact while others do not. When considering this 'informational space', there is again a risk of semantic confusion.

The term 'phase space' is used to refer to the conceptual space containing all possible configurations of a system: "*the canvas where we paint a system's dynamics*" James [29]. In a binary system, for instance, each element can be in one of two states, each of which is seen as a placing the system in a different location in the multidimensional space of possibilities. The larger the number of unique configurations, the larger the space [30]. Changes in the system then constitute trajectories through this space.

While phase space, like a map of a territory, provides information about a system, this concept is entirely different from that of the information dimension presented in this book. Phase space is the theoretical space encompassing the possible configurations of any system. The information dimension is the space containing the actual, current information associated with an information system in which they encounter each other and interact. Just as information is considered to be literally real but non-physical, a real but non-physical space is deemed necessary to house it.

1.1.10 Physical and informational dimensionality

A more ancient dimensional discussion concerns the location of the human soul. In the millennia before aviation, cosmology and geology, there was no necessary objection to placing heaven above the clouds and hell deep in the fiery bowels of the earth. Neither could be visited to disprove this narrative and theoretical objections were weak or lacking. Before the explosive growth of the physical sciences during the Enlightenment, it was not really even necessary to consider the distinction between the physical and the spiritual, or the body and the mind, as particularly significant. However, with the ever-sharpening demarcation of the physical, it became increasingly problematic to provide the soul with a home. Those philosophers and theologists who dared to face this issue came up with a diverse collection of positions [31], but one thing was evident in all of them: the soul could not be placed in the three spatial dimensions occupied by material substance.

The increasingly undeniable association of consciousness, and thus the soul, with the human brain didn't really help. Consider the following question: where are your thoughts and emotions? For these internal aspects of mind, the answer may today appear to be almost trivial: inside your skull, attached to the brain that generates them. If you close your eyes and try to localize your thoughts about this question they seem to be at least in the vicinity of your head. They are not, in any case, in the next room or on the surface of the moon. But under closer examination, this assumption starts to crumble. If you stub your toe, the pain seems to be in your toe even though it is clearly a product of brain activity, and your visual perception of the book you are now reading certainly does not seem to be located in the back of your brain, where your visual cortex is currently number-crunching data to produce it. Instead, it seems to be located in front of your body, in the hands that are holding it. Closing your eyes again, is it really so that you can localize your thoughts on this subject to some specific place in your frontal cortex where the neural activity involved in creating them is taking place? Or is it more some general, dark space in which they drift?

On the basis of such considerations "*strong localists ... maintain that the soul occupies a place that cannot at the same time be occupied by a material substance*" Heßbrüggen-Walter [31]. If this is the case then what is this place? Does it have something to do with the fact that in the brain's neural networks connect nodes at varying distances, thus breaking the usual association between physical proximity and functional relationship? It is certainly the case that the topology of these networks is entirely different from the three-dimensional space occupied by the brain [32].

The issue of locality is not unique to the (human) brain. It also applies to our information technologies. It may seem that, even if we accept the computer's binary values to be information entities, their association with physical states couples them firmly and comfortably with the physical dimensions. In this way, such information could be seen as no more than a non-physical layer coating the physical substrates which support them: a viewpoint closer to property dualism than substance dualism. However, closer examination reveals that it is not that simple. While the computer's memory may be structured in a more orderly fashion that the brain's neurons, proximity in the physical substrate still does not equate to proximity of associated information. In random access memory, neighbouring bits on the spiral tracks of a computer disk will frequently not carry neighbouring binary values. Conversely, the binary values involved in a particular informational function or entity may be spread widely across the disk. Rather like our thoughts, these composite phenomena cannot be pinned down to a particular location or neatly coupled to a structure in the three physical dimensions. This being the case, it would seem that we also need to provide them with an alternative space in which to exist.

The information dimension considered in this book is the space within which all of the non-physical information-based phenomena created by nervous systems and information technologies reside, interact and perform their essential functions. As such it must necessarily be considered just as real as that which it houses.

1.2 Systems theory

1.2.1 Hierarchical organization

Under the strict definition of information presented in the previous chapter, it can be considered as a very special case within the broader cosmic reality: a remarkable phenomenon associated only with living systems such as those inhabiting the thin film of a biosphere that covers planet Earth. In this context, we must expect it to adhere to the general principles applying to systems in general, even if within those principles it has its own specific characteristics.

In the most general sense, reality is fairly simple: it is a collection of interacting entities. The immense diversity of observed phenomena is a result of the different properties of these entities and the consequences of these properties for the way in which they interact.

Some of these interactions are fleeting: when two billiard balls collide, they momentarily change their speed and direction. The outcome of such a collision will depend on the mass and velocity of each of the objects, its elasticity and the angle of the collision. In this case, the interaction does not even alter the interacting entities; each simply goes off unchanged in its new individual direction.

Things can get more interesting when the entities combine through interaction. Sometimes, but not always. Some combinations are little more than upscaling. If two drops of water combine to form a larger drop, it is still just a drop of water. However, often these combinations lead to the creation of new, stable, larger entities that are different from their components. Quarks combine to form leptons, which combine to form atoms, which combine to form molecules, which combine to form materials, which combine to form planets, which combine to form solar systems, which combine to form galaxies, which combine to form the cosmos. This is the fundamental structure of reality: as Jagers op Akkerhuis puts it, "*The organization of nature is profoundly hierarchical, because from its beginning, interactions between simple elements have continuously created more complex systems, that themselves served as the basis for still more complex systems*" [33].

A special form of this hierarchical structure is seen in living systems. Biological molecules combine to form organelles, which combine to form cells, which combine to form tissues, which combine to form organs, which combine to form organisms. Above the level of the individual animal and plant this process

DOI: 10.4324/9781003460541-3

continues: organisms combine to form communities, which combine to form ecosystems, which combine ultimately to form the biosphere.

The biological levels of organization are extremely compact compared to those of physical systems. The full complexity can be seen in an ant weighing less than a gram: a remarkable product and demonstration of the power of biological evolution.

In both physical and biological systems, there is a necessary sequentiality to this process. Only when a lower level has been formed and stabilized can it provide a foundation on which the next level can be built. Atoms needed to exist before molecules could form; without the prior existence of cells, multicellular organisms could not have arisen. That being said, it is not a simple matter of running through this process until the entire universe is organized into neatly stacked layers, after which nothing else happens. The structures that form have various degrees of stability and resistance to change, allowing the abundant free energy to continually disturb the status quo at all levels. It is this that creates the dynamic world of tides and tornadoes; life and death that we see around us.

In designing and building machines, we exploit the same principle of hierarchical organization: nuts and bolts are combined to build engine components that are combined to build engines that are combined with various other functional components to build a car. A significant difference here is that the formation of structure is not spontaneous. The parts have no inherent tendency to come together in the required configuration, necessitating our external intervention to both create the system and prevent it from subsequently falling apart.

A common characteristic of all of these systems relates to the location of components. The interactions required to link components firmly enough to create a higher-level entity require them to be in each other's vicinity. Generally, this means that they must be in direct contact: entities that are distant from each other cannot combine in this way. Even in cases in which they do not actually touch, as in the planets forming the solar system, an appropriate location is a prerequisite for the necessary interactions between parts to take place.

A consequence of this stratification is that the viewpoint we chose when considering a particular phenomenon is of great importance. What is seen as a system when viewed from a lower level is generally considered an entity from the next level up and a component at the level above that. An atom, for instance, is clearly a system built of protons, neutrons and electrons but can also be approached as an entity with its own properties or as a building block for higher-level molecules. In other words, we use the term system when we recognize that a particular entity is built of a number of components, and entity when we prefer to ignore this fact and consider it as a unit unto itself that may constitute part of a higher level entity. This change in viewpoint does not, however, change the nature of that which we are observing. Except for at the most fundamental and cosmic levels, all components are also systems, and all systems are also components.

Given this ubiquity of stratified organization, we should expect information to follow this trend: that it does not simply exist and operate at one level but is organized into sequential layers. This introduces the question of whether and how the basal information entities described in the previous chapter are also hierarchically organized, and what unique properties arise at each level.

1.2.2 From the fundamental to the cosmic

The construction of wholes from parts is observable to some degree with the naked eye. We can see how leaves, stalks, roots and flowers combine to make a plant; how bricks, windows, doors and roof combine to make a house. However, it was not until the development of the necessary scientific instruments that all levels of the continuum from the fundamental to the cosmic could be appreciated. Only after the invention of the microscope [34] could biological organisms be observed at scales that allowed the development of cell theory in the 19th century [35]. On this basis, it became possible to reconstruct the hierarchical levels of organelle, cell, tissue, organ and organism that together explain the structure and function of multicellular plants and animals. Delving deeper with more advanced technologies eventually allowed the sequence to be drawn further down to the subatomic realm of fundamental physical particles and forces. Moving upwards, telescopes were necessary to discover the organization of planets into solar systems and solar systems into galaxies. Contemporary cosmology has extended this to the very largest structures in the universe such as galaxy clusters [36]. The scale of the whole with the respect to its smallest components is unimaginable: "*A galaxy is a million million million million times the size of an amoeba, and an amoeba is a giant compared with an electron*" Shapley [37].

Within the complete catalogue of every layer of reality that has now been thoroughly charted by the physical, chemical and biological sciences, one phenomenon is conspicuously absent. The type of information discussed in this book is undetectable at any of these levels, requiring us to reconsider the relationship between the two. From previous considerations, it would seem that this is not simply a matter of designing and building a clever instrument that is capable of detecting this element of reality, but that this is fundamentally impossible due to the non-physical nature of such information.

1.2.3 Degrees of emergence

A significant characteristic of this hierarchical organization is emergence, which can be defined as the existence of properties or phenomena at a particular level of organization that do not exist at lower levels [38]: the whole is more (or, at least, different) than the sum of the parts.

Looking out into the world, a spectrum of degrees of emergence can be observed. At the weak end, we see entities that are not really much more than the sum of their parts. If I stack bricks on top of each other, the resulting wall will be a brick-like object that is larger than an individual brick. If I fix the bricks together with mortar, they will even lose the emergent property of instability that results from the bricks being loosely connected as separate objects. What I now have is a wall with different dimensions than a brick, but that looks similar to and has very similar properties. Indeed, this is the intention. Such scaling increases size without introducing new characteristics. In nature, such 'stacking' is seen in crystallization processes. The 20 g Koh-i-Noor diamond has no different properties from a 10 mg diamond used in a cutting tool. Even its value is determined by little more than a linear equation. Scaling can also be seen in biological systems. When the weather turns damp and cool in the autumn, moss starts to grow on the rocks in the shady parts of my garden. This starts out with small isolated patches. After a while, in favourable conditions, their growth results in a complete blanket. This covering consists of more individual plants but is not different in nature from the patches that first arose. In terms of Van Gulik [39], these are all examples of 'specific value emergence'.

The next level of emergence sees new properties arise at a higher level of organization in a way that is predictable on the basis of the properties of the parts. This is the basis of all man-made machinery, in which a collection of components is intentionally brought together to create properties that are absent in any of the individual parts. A traditional light bulb has a filament, two electrodes, a glass container, an inert gas and a ceramic base. None of these components is any use on its own, but together they have the emergent capability of converting electricity into a continuous source of light. The simple design makes it easy to predict the function of the whole from the properties of the parts.

Design is not necessary for such emergence to arise. An example in nature is the rainbow. This is the result of millions of water droplets each refracting light and sending out an array of colours in different directions. Viewed from a particular location, this produces the emergent image of a crescent comprised of bands of colour that does not exist in any of the individual droplets. However, we can easily deduce that this will be the result of shining sunlight through a volume of air that contains water droplets. In biology, the properties of the musculoskeletal system show a comparable level of emergence. No single bone or muscle can walk, but they have mechanical properties that can be combined to create a system with this complex mechanical property. Such weak emergence does not lead to properties of a different nature.

The next level of emergence introduces the loss of extrapolative explanation described by Anderson when he wrote that "*The behaviour of large and complex aggregates of elementary particles...is not to be understood in terms of a simple extrapolation of the properties of a few particles*" [40]. Here, properties emerge that cannot be deduced by simply adding together those of the component parts. Take, for instance, the case of the atom. The properties of an atom do not exist in the protons, neutrons and electrons they are built from. More importantly, different compositions of the same protons, neutrons and electrons create different kinds of atoms with very different atomic properties. By studying atoms, we have learned much about the ways in which subatomic particles can be arranged and the properties that result from these arrangements. This even allowed Mendeleev to predict the properties of three types of atom in 1869 (gallium, scandium and germanium) which had at the time never been seen [41]. And yet, this is not to say that these properties are reducible in the way that the properties of a light bulb are reducible to its components. The reason for this is that the properties only emerge as a result of the interaction between components. Consequently, they can only exist when this interaction takes place (or is simulated or predicted in some other way) and not derived purely from the properties of the components in isolation.

These different degrees of emergence result from a number of parameters in the emergent system, one of the most basic being the number of contributing components. Large numbers are no guarantee for the generation of interesting emergent features. In the example of the diamond mentioned above, the addition of billions of extra atoms makes no difference at all to the emergent properties of a large or small diamond. However, in some cases, a minimum number of components is required for it to arise. For instance, a particular weather system such as a tornado may require a minimum volume of air in order to form. In other cases, a minimum number of types of component may be required to create the new characteristic, as in the case of the variety of cell types required to form a living multicellular organism.

Diversity of components also has another effect on emergence. Each of the components of diamond is an identical carbon atom, which reduces the number of different ways in which they can combine to form higher level structures. In collections that include different types of components these options blossom: the more different types are available the more alternative configurations exist. A clear demonstration of this is seen in the great diversity of macromolecules that are found in living cells that are constructed from only a limited number of atoms (largely carbon, hydrogen, oxygen and nitrogen). Another is the enormous range of species that can arise out of the same basic collection of cell types. The cells of a mouse, a moose and a mongoose are essentially identical, and yet the organisms show, in addition to many common features, also many distinct emergent properties.

Interaction between components is a very important – indeed, necessary – factor. If there is no interaction between components, then, by definition, there is no real reason to consider the collection of objects as an entity. The most basic form of interaction is physical contact – a fairly inevitable interaction between neighbouring objects. This is, for instance, sufficient to explain the hexagonal close packing of oranges in a box. Without external constraints, however, contact alone will not hold an entity together. This requires some kind of attractive interaction such as the electromagnetic forces that underlie the formation and stability of atoms and molecules. These forces also constitute elements of the system that contribute, along with the physical components, to its emergent properties.

Another significant factor determining the level of emergence is the amount of energy flowing through the collection. Without an external source of energy, components will remain static and interact less, which will generally lead to less interesting emergent phenomena. Some of the most interesting and dramatic emergent systems, such as tornadoes and other climate systems, are a direct result of large energy flows, and immediately cease to exist when the energy dries up. The availability of free energy is also an essential factor in the creation and maintenance of the complex non-equilibrium emergent structures seen in living systems.

The examples presented above concern the individual steps between parts and composite entities, but physical reality is organized in an extended hierarchy of levels of organization. While in some cases it may be possible to deduce emergent properties from the direct components of a system, this becomes increasingly difficult when we drop down a further level to that of the entities from which these components are built. The reason for this is simple: the properties at this level must first combine to create those of the components on which the system is based. The degrees of emergence at each level therefore multiply the difficulty in spanning the explanatory gap. To take a simple example, predicting the emergent property of a living cell from the atomic level is impossible without traversing the sequential stepping stones of the intervening levels of organization.

A consequence of this stratification is that everything that we encounter in our daily lives is far detached from the fundamental physical particles that ultimately underlie it all. We are, so to speak, floating many levels above this bedrock in a macroscopic realm containing entities and processes that are entirely alien and indeed meaningless when viewed from a subatomic perspective.

Applied to information systems, the question would seem to be not whether they exhibit emergence, but what degree and type of emergence this is. After all, the factors underlying emergence are clearly present: we see extremely large numbers of component parts that actively interact in a dynamic environment. On this basis, we should expect a significant degree of emergence to be exhibited, leading to non-reducibility of higher level properties to those of the basal entities from which they are ultimately constructed.

In this context, it is clear that this type of information is itself an emergent phenomenon. It arises out of physical processes taking place at a specific level of organization within the physical hierarchy: that of the brain as one of the cell-based organs in biological organisms and information technologies as one of the types of machines we build. Having not existed at underlying (sub)atomic or molecular levels, this justifies the consideration of this information as an emergent phenomenon associated with this level. There is no difference between the carbon atoms in a neuron or a skin cell, yet, in one case, they are part of a system in which information emerges, while in the other they are not. Nor is there a difference between the silicon atoms of sand and a silicon chip, yet while sand is no more than a relatively inert material, the silicon chip is part of a machine with dynamic information processing capabilities. What is odd is that in brains and computers, in contrast with systems with physical functions, there are no visible higher levels of organization. In the heart, for instance, we see valves and chambers above the level of the cell that are necessary for its pumping function. Similarly, in complex machines, we see structures at various levels of which the highest is directly associated with its purpose and function. Where, then, are these higher levels of organization in biological and technological information systems?

1.2.4 Origins of physical systems

In addition to mapping the structure of a system, a full understanding also requires us to elucidate its ontogenesis: how is it that the system came to be. This is not just necessary for completeness. Understanding origins can also provide answers to the question of why the system is at it is and functions in the way it does.

While we humans tend to approach function pragmatically through design and construction, the only systems whose existence can be explained in this way are those we create. Every other structure has no designer/builder and therefore must, by definition, have created itself. "*Throughout nature, decentralized components emerge into complex forms. It is through their interaction that components, governed by simple rules, self-assemble to create specific entities*" Bhalla, Bentley and Jacob [42].

Such physical systems arise spontaneously through self-assembly [43]: they are the direct result of the interactions between component parts according to the laws operating on them. This is not to say that understanding them is trivial. Since formative processes can be complex, and since it may also be necessary to consider processes taking place at under- and overlying levels, this can be seriously challenging. Furthermore, the products of such processes can be impressively complex and demonstrate intriguing dynamics, as in the case of the filigree snowflake [44] or Bénard convection cells [45]. However, their form is not determined by external design or influences, nor events that took place before the creation of the system itself. These two factors do apply to the other types of system, which are of particular importance to us: living organisms and designed systems.

1.2.5 Origins of living systems

On the topic of how living organisms come to exist, Aristotle was of the opinion that "*with animals, some ... grow spontaneously and not from kindred stock; and of these instances of spontaneous generation some come from putrefying earth or vegetable matter, as is the case with a number of insects*" [46]. Pasteur's elegant experiments [47] disproved this theory of spontaneous generation: we now know that there is no way in which a maggot could arise in a single creative act from rotting meat. Instead, a fly egg is needed which carries the heritable characteristics developed through millions of preceding generations: the iterative process of biological evolution by which, through multiple generations, systems of increasing complexity can arise [48]. While the systems themselves still self-assemble, the way in which they do so and the results achieved would be quite impossible starting from scratch. It is only through replication of this generative process combined with selection between multiple variations in each generation that systems can arise with the specific and remarkable characteristics of life.

The radical difference in generational processes and resulting system complexity that this facilitates justifies the use of a different term: rather than self-assembly, the construction of living systems is referred to as self-organization [49]. The fact that the purpose of this process is to produce functional high-level structures necessitates top-down causation. The counter-current filtering function of the kidney, for instance, requires specific types of cells to be anatomically correctly positioned. While facilitated and founded on intercellular interactions, the creation of the structure of the kidney is determined by the functional requirements of the organ as a whole. This principle applies not only to the creation of organs, but necessarily at each of the functional hierarchical levels of biological organization, all the way down to the molecular level [50]. It is this fact that underlies the difficulty we have

in predicting or controlling the systemic imbalances underlying diseases such as cancer, psychological disorders and sociopolitical disturbances [51]. As complex self-organizing systems, they cannot be corrected by redesign.

The reason why living systems require these different processes lies in the main feature that distinguishes them from the non-living [52]: the ability to create and maintain a far-from-equilibrium system by directed use of free energy to prevent the system from reverting to an equilibrium state [53]. Evolution is basically a process that in each generation selects those individuals with the greatest dynamic stability [54].

In living systems, there is one remarkable exception to the rule of self-organization in which the result is the product of design-based construction: the polypeptide sequences that form the basis for the cell's proteins. These do not form spontaneously but are sequentially chained together in accordance with coded genetics instructions [55]. However, both the genetic information and the mechanism that uses it are still the result of evolutionary optimization: there is no design for genome itself, nor for the construction process.

This latter point brings us to a common misconception concerning genetics. The observation of heredity (the similarity between parent and offspring), the fact that the genome is the only explicit information that is passed between generations and the correlation between genetic differences and phenotypic differences can together lead to the assumption that the genome contains a design for all structures in the multicellular organism. This is not the case: living organisms arise through self-organization, not through design-based construction. Developmental systems theory shows that many internal and external factors are involved in determining phenotype, including those at various levels of organization that influence gene expression [56]. Furthermore, comparative genetics demonstrates how genes are a necessary but not sufficient explanation for complexity in biological systems. For instance, particular gene-based pheromones are a prerequisite for social behaviour in ants but do not provide a design for this behaviour itself [57]. In explaining the origins of the brain's complex neural networks, we will need to consider these generic principles underlying the creation of biological complexity.

This is not to say that the genome is not an important factor in heredity and evolution. Through determining which proteins can be created within the cells of the organism, it can influence both development and function. The biochemistry of the brain, for instance, is an important factor. Genetic differences in neurotransmitters can influence excitability, and because different parts of the brain employ different neurotransmitters, these effects can be function-specific. Genetic differences in proteins involved in the formation of connections can also have a direct effect on, for instance, the brain's ability to form memories [58]. Certain psychiatric disorders can also be coupled to genetic factors [59]. These are, however, only contributions. They are not the exclusive determinants of brain structure and function.

1.2.6 Origins of technologies

This different class of ontogenesis is ubiquitous to the artefacts created by humans, including our immense diversity of machines [60]. Starting with an overall required function (driving down a road), we decide which parts we need (wheels, engine, electrics) and which components we need to build these parts (cogs, bolts, bits of plastic). "*The engineer, and more generally the designer, is concerned with how things ought to be in order to attain goals, and to function*" Simon [61]. In contrast to self-assembling and self-organizing systems, the system does not build itself: the components must be brought together in the required configuration. A further difference is that in the case of design and construction, function follows assembly. A half-built car cannot drive at half the speed: it cannot drive at all. A variation on this creative process lists the steps to be taken rather than the product itself, as in a recipe describing how to bake a cake. However, here too it is the end result that counts: a cake is only edible at the end of the baking process.

As in biology, there is a secondary aspect to machine design that is akin to evolution. The difference is that in this case, progress is not the result of natural selection between random variants, but directed selection between designs intended to improve function and solve problems with current versions [62].

The computers discussed later in this book clearly belong to this category of systems but, at the same time, form a subset with the very distinctive feature of being designed to perform informational, rather than physical functions. The question is whether this distinction is comparable to, say, the difference in function between a car and a cooker, or has more fundamental and significant consequences.

A further distinction between physical and living/designed systems concerns their position relative to thermodynamic equilibrium. Physical systems, being the product only of current interactions between their component parts, are always in a state of local thermodynamic equilibrium: as soon as something alters to disrupt this, they will smoothly move to a new equilibrium state. As temperature rises, the snowflake will melt; as temperature falls, the Bénard cells will dissipate. This is not the case with our designed machines. Even though they may be designed to be extremely robust, they will inevitably eventually fail without external intervention in the form of maintenance. In living systems, this factor is even stronger, with a constant expenditure of metabolic energy required to maintain their dynamic, far from equilibrium state. These factors would therefore also be expected to apply to living and designed information systems.

In the context of this book, the question we need to ask ourselves is how these considerations of origins relate to the brain and the mind. Does this involve no more than the normal formative processes of evolution-generated self-organizational processes, or is something more required? And how does the design and construction of information technologies differ from that of technologies with a physical function?

1.2.7 From form to function

The previous paragraph paints a static picture of reality: a description of its structures at various levels of organization at any particular point in time. Things become altogether more interesting when we consider the dynamics of systems: how interaction between their components leads to expressed functions, and sometimes to changes in the system itself.

The relationship between form and function allows us to place them on a scale ranging from strictly linear systems at the one end and complex and chaotic systems at the other. Strictly speaking, a linear system is defined as one in which the response to two inputs is a simple addition of those of the two inputs individually. Typically, such systems are also time-invariant: if we give the system the same input tomorrow, the response will be the same. These characteristics make linear systems relatively easy to design, model and predict: I say 'relatively' because engineering such systems involves a serious body of theory [63]. Programmed computers are classic examples of linear systems, designed as they are to reliably and repeatedly produce mathematically correct outputs to strictly demarcated inputs.

The relationship between form and function, input and output is fundamentally harder to determine in complex systems in which the cumulative effect of inputs is frequently not additive. Instead, they may exhibit threshold responses or amplification of small variations in input to major differences in output. Feedback loops and effects of one part of the system on another can lead to diverse and cascading effects. Other key characteristics of complex systems are hierarchical organization and emergence [64].

Perhaps more significantly, many such systems are adaptive: their history influences the way in which they will respond in the future, sometimes in a directed fashion that constitutes functional improvement towards an intended goal. This adaptivity may also exhibit itself in the form of robustness and resilience to external perturbations, either restoring the system to a desired state or granting it flexibility when confronted with variable inputs.

While many natural systems exhibit the characteristics of complexity, it will come as no surprise given the potential for adaptability that evolution exploits them to the full in living systems. Adaptability, flexibility and resilience are, after all, essential characteristic for survival. And of all of the biological organs, the brain shows the highest degree of dynamic adaptability. Even the simplest of neural networks can demonstrate learning and in highly encephalized animals such as mammals, and in particular humans, these abilities are extensive and essential aspects of their behaviour and survival. *"With its billions of interconnected neurons, whose interactions change from millisecond to millisecond, the human brain is an archetypal complex system"* Nicolelis [65]. To understand the brain, we will therefore clearly need to acknowledge its characteristics as such.

Such factors may also need to be considered in relation to information technologies. While many information functions are best served by the reliability of strict rule-based coupling of input and output, general intelligence requires the far more dynamic and flexible type of relationship that is characteristic of complex systems. From the earliest discussions of artificial intelligence (e.g. [66]), it was clear that linear programming would only take us so far. Since complex systems with these dynamic characteristics cannot be designed, it was necessary instead to create systems that develop their own functions using the adaptive evolutionary processes of machine learning [67].

1.2.8 Causation in emergent systems

While emergence is often considered as an upward constructive process, in which interactions at a particular level result in the events taking place at higher levels, this does not mean that causation only works in this direction. The discussion and debate on causality and (non)reductionism has a history that dates back to Aristotle's four types of causality (matter, form, agent and purpose) [68] and continues to this day [69].

What is eminently clear in the context of stratification is that every level of organization is governed by its own specific laws that are distinct from those of the underlying level and are, in this sense, emergent. To give a simple example, the chemical laws applying to the interactions between atomic species do not apply, and are indeed irrelevant, at the subatomic level. What is also undeniable is that what happens at a higher level cannot overrule laws applying to lower levels. However, it can supplement them. In other words, while a lower level acts entirely according to its own principles, the overall outcome can be determined by events at a higher level. As stated by Cambell, *"all processes at the lower levels of a hierarchy are restrained by and act in conformity to the laws of the higher levels"* [70].

To a degree this is a trivial statement. For instance, the stability of an entity is determined by interactions between its components, but this stability subsequently locks the entity's components into a particular role. A chlorine atom in a grain of salt's crystal lattice is not free to go off and interact with some other passing atom. Its exact location and behaviour is strictly determined by the structure it is a part of. Not only does the salt crystal have properties that sodium and chlorine atoms do not; its properties also exert top-down control over its component atoms. If the atom was instead part of a hydrogen chloride molecule, it would be equally firmly trapped as a component of a substance with the different emergent property of acidity. This would not change the nature of the chlorine atom: indeed, from the atomic point of view, nothing has really changed. However, what happens at a higher level does change the role that the atom plays in that which it is part of and, ultimately, the position and motion of the atom in space.

In stacked hierarchical systems, this top-down effect cumulates over multiple layers, resulting in an increasing causative separation. For instance, the role and effect of a salt molecule as an emulsifier in a chemical production process is different from its contribution to the maintenance of blood salinity in an animal. In both cases, the presence and quantity of salt is determined at a level that is entirely invisible and indeed irrelevant from the viewpoint of the chlorine atom. The atom is simply doing its thing at an atomic level, oblivious even of the fact that it is part of a higher level system, let alone the role it is fulfilling in this particular context.

The hydrocarbon chemistry exploited by living organisms is an extreme example of this distinction between causality at different levels of organization. The key characteristic of hydrocarbon chemistry is the possibility of creating an almost limitless number of macromolecules with different properties. This general purpose chemical toolkit facilitated the evolution of the biochemical processes and structures that are essential to the living cell. How this chemistry is exploited to this purpose is again determined at the systemic level. There is nothing special or different about the carbon in a haemoglobin molecule compared to one in a carbon dioxide molecule drifting through the air. Indeed, if we strictly limit our view to the atomic level, there is no way to even know that it is contributing to such remarkable phenomena at higher levels of organization.

Top-down control is essential for living organisms since this is the only way to maintain dynamic stability in such thermodynamically improbable and highly complex systems [71]. Cancer is an example of the disastrous consequences of component parts breaking free from such control mechanisms [72]. This strong emergence means that, while we may be able to explain the processes taking place at any particular level of organization on the basis of component properties, reducibility is minimal. It is, for instance, impossible to deduce the form of a beetle given only the collection of cells it is built from. Indeed, almost exactly the same collection of cell types and numbers in a different configuration could instead form an ant or a butterfly. Dropping down to macromolecular scales, while the genome certainly has a causative role at this level, the fact that the same genome can variously exist in a caterpillar or a butterfly clearly demonstrates the systemic control of outcome. The selective expression of various genes in different cell types is a classic example of such influences [73]: the proteinaceous components of haemoglobin, for instance, are produced in large numbers in red blood cells, but the gene is not used at all in other types of cell.

Given this ubiquity and significance of top-down influences in biological systems, we must ask ourselves not so much whether it also occurs in brains, but what form this takes and how it relates to the mind-body problem. Rather like the discovery of hydrocarbon chemistry as a generic solution to creating multifunctional molecules, evolution has in the brain found a generic solution for the creation of information functions. Here, too, we need to consider how the system ensures that the specific collection of functions it requires is selected out of the infinite number of possibilities. In the case of the cell's proteinaceous macromolecules, the options are at least limited to the set of configurations offered by the genome, a method of narrowing down the options that is not available to the brain when lying down the filigree network of connections between neurons that determines its function.

1.2.9 Understanding complex systems

This chapter has demonstrated that to fully understand the nature of emergent phenomena we need to combine a number of approaches. The first is structure: we can dissect the system to reveal its components. This is the easiest direction since it involves no more than the observation of entities, structures and characteristics. In this way, we can get an accurate picture of the static anatomy and properties of an entity, its parts and the parts of its parts but learn nothing about what it does.

The second approach is to consider how the entity functions. Observing its internal behaviour and how it responds and reacts to external influences will give us additional, and more significant, insights into its nature. In this way, we can bring the phenomena to life and see what it is doing in the here and now. We can also consider the relationship between the behaviour of its components and those it exhibits as an emergent system. In some weakly emergent examples, this may be fairly clear, but as complexity increases it can become difficult or impossible to determine.

Thirdly, to gain a full understanding, we need to understand its ontogeny: why the phenomenon exists in the first place. For this, we need to look back in time to find its origins: what events and processes cumulatively led to it coming into existence in the first place? Are these limited to the formative processes of the system itself, or was a preceding evolutionary process required? Having come to exist, what factors grant it the necessary stability to persist rather than falling apart?

We have also seen that considering the system only at its own level(s) of organization will fail to provide a complete understanding. The systems that we consider at any arbitrary level are necessarily dependent on components and processes in underlying layers. While the significance may rapidly fade through sequential levels, this only ultimately ends at the physically fundamental. It is also necessary to consider overlying layers: the systems that the entity is a part of. In some cases, the significance may be minor, but in others, the entity can only be understood in this greater context. In living systems, the animal or plant itself incorporates a number of organizational levels, from the molecular to the organismal, a factor that is also seen to a lesser degree in our designed technologies.

It is only by combining these lines of investigation and insight – structure, function, origins and hierarchical context – that we can fully appreciate and understand an emergent system. Consequently, when considering the information systems associated with brains and computers we will need to apply each of these approaches to gain a full understanding of their nature and existence. As Mazzocchi puts it: "*An epistemological rethink is needed to instigate a paradigm shift from the Newtonian model that has dominated science, to an appraisal of complexity that includes both holism and reductionism*" [51].

1.3 Biological information systems

1.3.1 Information storage and transfer

The use of information by living systems is not new: it goes back to the genetic information used in the first cells to build the specific proteins essential to their internal functions. Without this inherited information to tell cells which amino acid sequences to construct, life would not exist. As stated by Küppers, "*Systems of the degree of complexity of organisms, even at the molecular level, can arise and maintain themselves reproductively only by way of information-storing and information-producing mechanisms*" [74].

The genome uses a relatively simple system based on four coding elements (the nucleotides adenine, guanine, thymine and cytosine). Individually, these are insufficient to select between the 20 amino acids available to build proteins. Combining them in pairs would still only allow 4×4=16 different instructions to be given. Consequently, evolution came up with a coding system using groups of 3 (codons).

There is no necessary relationship between a particular codon and the information it carries. The codon AAA could just as well be used to select any of the 20 amino acids, as long as the rest of the system is configured to respond in this way. Already here, then, we see a system that works on the basis of the information associated with a physical state, rather than the physical state itself. Furthermore, there is no way of detecting the information associated with the codon AAA. While it is this information that determines which amino acid will be added to the sequence, it can only be deduced by observing how the system responds to the codon. This is, then, a clear example of the type of information considered in this book: a non-physical determinative factor associated with a physical state.

Multicellular organisms later came to depend on many other forms of this type of information. One example is the use of hormones as messenger molecules. These are produced in one part of the plant or animal as a response to a particular situation and carried through the vascular system to another part of the body where a response is required. Here, too, the physical properties of the hormone are not what counts, but the fact that the two systems have evolved to use it as a representative for a particular situation. In this way, the two systems can be functionally connected at a distance without having to build intervening physical mechanisms. For instance, when insulin is produced by the pancreas in response to rising blood

DOI: 10.4324/9781003460541-4

glucose levels, and the liver responds to the insulin by suppressing glucose release, the mechanism is based on the information carried by the insulin molecule, not on the insulin molecule itself. Just as with the codons in the genome, the relationship between physical carrier and information is entirely arbitrary: any macromolecule could be used to perform this function.

The concurrent evolution of excitable muscle, sensory and nerve cells in animals led to a significant increase in the biological use of information. As a mechanism for information transfer, the neuron has four major advantages over messenger molecules: speed, specificity, efficiency and broad applicability. Working on the basis of electrical currents means that responses can be much *faster* than solutions based on molecules being transported around the body. This allows the dynamic nature of muscular responses to be optimally exploited. The *specificity* is a result of the physical connection made between source and target: essential if muscles are to be selectively activated to generate a response. This contrasts with hormones, which pass through the bloodstream to all parts of the body. This specificity has the added advantage of a *lower metabolic cost*: a single impulse is sufficient, rather than having to produce (and later dispose of) large numbers of messenger molecules to raise general levels in the blood. Most significant, however, is that fact that this solution is *broadly applicable.* Given an appropriate sensory cell on the input side, the same type of nervous impulse can carry information about any relevant internal or external factor. Given appropriate muscles on the output side, it can also lead to any required response. This contrasts with hormones, with which evolution has to invent a new biochemical carrier molecule, production mechanism, detection mechanism and response mechanism for each new communication requirement.

In all of these examples, units of information associated with individual physical states are used in isolation: there is no dynamic interaction between them. As such, these systems could be justifiably explained on the basis of property dualism: while the information is non-physical, it can be considered as no more than an additional aspect of a physical state.

1.3.2 Information acquisition and communication

In order to be stored, transferred and used information first needs to be available. In the case of the genetic information discussed in the previous paragraph, this information is provided by the hereditary process but in general the organism needs to acquire this information itself. The most obvious and common way of doing so is to use sense organs to detect relevant factors in the internal or external environment.

With respect to the external environment, which is filled with opportunities and threats that are constantly changing, this method has its limitations. For instance, animals with stereoscopic forward-facing vision cannot see what is happening behind them and while you are focused on feeding yourself, your attention may well drift from avoiding becoming someone else's meal. There is consequently great advantage to be had in being able to supplement your own information with the sensory perceptions of others. Of course, this requires them to make this information available, for which various types of communication are used. Basic examples are already seen in plants, which produce volatile organic compounds to spread information about relevant environmental factors requiring a response [75]. Such mechanisms are directly comparable to the use of hormones to distribute information inside an organism and are also widely used for the coordination of behaviour in social insects [76]. In higher animals, pheromones are often used not so much to pass on information about the environment but in communication relating to reproductive behaviour, for instance in attracting mates [77]. The communication of environmental threats and opportunities in these species more commonly exploits sound, in this way benefitting from the advantages it offers in terms of speed and specificity. This has led to the evolution of a wide variety of auditory alarm calls in vertebrates and birds with which animals detecting a threat warn each other to mutual advantage [78]. "*In animal communication natural selection favors callers who vocalize to affect the behavior of listeners and listeners who acquire information from vocalizations, using this information to represent their environment*" Seyfarth and Cheney [79].

1.3.3 Information processing

Direct neuronal connections between input and output are still limited to the *transfer* of isolated units of information. This changes when neurons connect to each other in neural networks. Interactions between them then allow the combination of and interaction between the information they carry: information *processing*. On the input side, this allows the organism to respond to specific patterns and distinguish more subtle differences in its sensory environment. On the output side, it supports the generation of coordinated muscular responses and more complex behaviours. Between input and output, neural networks support various forms of information processing and storage such as learned skills and memories.

The interconnection of individual neurons to process information arose early in the evolutionary history of animals [80], possibly as far back as the Ediacaran period 600–700 million years ago [81]. As an evolutionary innovation it is of comparable significance to the origin of multicellular organisms, which similarly required the introduction of a new way of generating function from the combined activities of collections of cells [82]. However, in this case, function is not the result of the combination of the physical characteristics of cells, but of the information associated with them. As observed by Hopfield, "*computational properties of use to biological organisms ... emerge as collective properties of systems having a large number of simple equivalent components (or neurons)*" [83]. While not included in Maynard-Smith and Szathmáry's seminal work *The major transitions in evolution* [84], it would certainly appear to deserve a place at this level of significance [85].

As with multicellularity, this innovation will have started modestly, with the simplest of networks with limited capabilities. The relatively minor initial selective advantage then developed iteratively through the aeons into an immensely effective, powerful, diverse and complex survival tool. Today, it is exploited to varying degrees by species across the entire animal kingdom. Some animals, such as the much-studied flatworm *Caenorhabditis elegans* still have no more than a relatively small network with simple, static capabilities [86]. At the other end of the spectrum, we find the largest, most complex and most capable brains in vertebrates, including humans [87].

1.3.4 A new generic solution

In spite of the huge quantitative differences and some qualitative differences between the simple central nervous systems of a nematode worm and the human cerebral cortex, the same basic developmental mechanisms are involved in their formation. Indeed, once animals had embarked on this particular path, evolutionary constraints prevented a transition to anything fundamentally different [88]. The fact that the human brain is capable of writing sonnets while a flatworm's nervous system can do little more than help it to feed and avoid harm is not the result of anything fundamentally new being introduced, but a more extensive and advanced use of the same basic solution to information processing: "*fundamental similarities, in spatial and topological features as well as in developmental mechanisms for network formation, are retained across evolution*" Kaiser and Varier [89].

Having said this, we are not talking about simple scaling effects here, such as a larger muscle being able to generate a greater force than a smaller one. In the case of neural networks, the increase in scale leads to functions with a very different nature. Here, then, we see the clear signs of functional emergence in which the same components can be used as parts of systems with very different characteristics. In the brains of encephalized animals, all of the parameters that are necessary for emergence, as described in Section 1.2.3, are present in abundance. Their scale is immense, their components interact continually, and large quantities of free energy flow through the system. The significant difference with other forms of emergence in living organisms is that in neural networks it is not based on the combination of the physical properties of the parts, but the information associated with them. In this sense, brains also meet the fourth criterium for emergence: diversity of components. While the physical neural mechanisms employed may be generic, the information associated with them is highly diverse, depending as it does on the cause of the state, rather than the state itself.

1.3.5 Brain anatomy and support functions

While the function of the brain is informational, performing these functions presents a number of physical requirements. Like any biological organ, its cells require a blood supply to provide them with oxygen and nutrients [90]. Prominent in vertebrates is the unique physical protection that it enjoys, compared with other organs, in the form of the skull. Cooling is also an issue. "*The brain, as one of the metabolically most active organs, both at rest as well as during mental and physical activity, is vitally dependent on a continuous removal of metabolically produced excess of heat*" (Caputa [91]). All of these requirements are solved in the usual way by constructing structures and mechanisms with the required physical properties from cells with the necessary characteristics.

Alongside these physical requirements, the function of the brain is also dependent on having the right kinds of neurons in the right places. While the details of neuronal differentiation and migration in the developing brain are different from those of the cells of other organs [92], this is essentially a comparable process that can be based on the same general principles and methods as employed in morphological development of the other organs [93]. No fundamentally new mechanisms are required.

The resulting gross anatomy of the brain has been known for centuries, being well documented as far back as Vesalius' 1543 treatise *De Humani Corporis Fabrica Libri Septem* [94]. While researching the evolution of the central nervous system is problematic because these features do not survive fossilization, conclusions can be drawn from living relatives [95]. In addition, the fact that the vertebrate brain is protected by a bony skull allows conclusions to be drawn concerning the size and shape of the brain based on endocasts of fossil skulls [96]. A prominent example of this is the expansion of the frontal cortex in the evolution of modern humans, which is clearly visible in the increase in cranial volume and forehead height [97]. However, relating such changes to brain function is difficult. It is not even the case that there is a simple relationship between brain volume and intelligence [98]. The possibility of drawing conclusions on the evolutionary origins of brain functions on the basis of morphology is therefore extremely limited.

1.3.6 Where are the brain's functions?

While morphology alone may tell us little about brain function, measuring brain activity in vivo [99] has allowed much research to be done on the localization of specific functions in particular parts of the brain, although this does have limitations [100]. Techniques such as EEG (measuring electrical activity from the scalp) and even the more accurate electrocorticography (measuring such activity on the surface of the brain) have the disadvantage of only being able to detect activity over large numbers of neurons [101]. Rather than measuring electrical activity directly, fMRI measures the oxygen use associated with neural activity, but with a maximal temporal resolution of seconds and spatial resolution of hundreds of thousands of neurons [102]. Furthermore, as pointed out by Page, "*Even supposing that fMRI were able to tell us where a particular cognitive process was performed, that would likely tell us little of relevance about how it was performed*" [103].

Applying such techniques to high-level functions such as consciousness shows that they are not a function of a specific brain region but a product of activity across interconnected areas. Even visual experience involves activity in areas other than the obvious visual cortex [104]. One of the most famous examples of localization of function was the mapping of body parts to specific areas of the motor cortex [105], but this too has been shown to less clearly demarcated than often assumed [106].

In this, the informational functions of the brain differ from the physical functions of other organs, in which functions are clearly associated with specific anatomical features. For instance, while the ability to produce the sounds of speech is clearly related to changes in the vocal tract that can be followed in the fossil record, the required changes in the brain cannot [107]. Furthermore, even if we find out which brain region is associated with a particular function, this does not tell us how it works. This again is in contrast with other organs, in which function can be directly derived from cellular function and anatomical structure.

1.3.7 The connectome

The reason why brain function cannot be derived from its anatomy is that, in contrast with other organs, it is not determined by the physical interactions between neighbouring cells but by electrical signals passing through connections between neurons that may be some distance away: its connectome.

This network can be described at various scales. Macroscopically, white matter tracts containing massive numbers of axons connect various regions of the brain. Producing a comprehensive map of such connections was the primary objective of the Human Connectome Project launched in 2010 [108]. The fact that interaction in the brain is based on connectivity rather than anatomical location means that this approach gives us a better picture of the functional architecture of the brain, and how it differs from its physical architecture [109]. Graph theory can be used to define and describe these structures [110], showing them to have an entirely different topology than the physical brain. Indeed, the highly complex dimensionality of such structures does not conveniently fit in our familiar three Euclidian spatial dimensions at all.

This macroscopic connectome is really still only anatomical infrastructure: it is not the level at which specific functions are determined. For this, we need to move down to the cellular level. Microscopic investigation of the brain reveals that neurons come in a number of different types arranged in different architectures in different brain areas [111]. The evolution of these cell types can be explained on the basis of the usual selective processes [112]. However, even these different forms are only facilitatory to the ultimate purpose of the brain: to lay down specific synaptic connections between neurons. The scale of the connectome when viewed at this level is staggering. "*Inside ... a cubic millimeter of neocortex, fifty to hundred thousand neurons use 4 km of axonal cable to form three to fifteen hundred million synapses with each other*" (da Costa [113]). The human brain contains around 100 billion neurons, each of which may make synaptic connection to thousands of other neurons. This makes large brains certainly the most complex structures on our planet and quite possibly in the universe [114].

The task of mapping such enormous connectivity networks in real nervous systems is immensely challenging. Only with the development of the Focussed Ion Electron Microscopy [115] did it become possible to image brain tissue with sufficient resolution to trace individual synaptic connections. While the complete mapping of the 302 neurons of the neural network of the flatworm *Caenorhabditis elegans* was completed in 1986 [86], it has been estimated that mapping the 250 million synaptic partners of the brain of the fruit fly *Drosophila* by hand could take 40 years [116]. While automation of this process could in principle significantly speed this process, imagine for a moment applying this method to the human brain. The technique involves slicing the brain into thin slivers for electron microscopy and therefore, self-evidently, cannot be applied to the living brain. Since the brain is a dynamic network in which connections are continually strengthened, weakened, made and broken, such a synapse-level snapshot would only present the connectome as it was at the moment of death. More importantly, this structural description would not include the fact that not all synapses have the same effect. At the biochemical level, the discovery of acetylcholine as a mediator of this communication between neurons [117] heralded the discovery of a suite of neurotransmitters variously used by different types of neuron in different parts of the brain, and with different effects. One of the most significant differences is the opposing effects of excitatory and inhibitory synapses. Such factors are clearly essential, in addition to the mapping of the connections between neurons, to understanding the function of the network.

1.3.8 How does it work?

Even with a complete description of its physical structure and mechanisms, we still have no explanation for the functions of the brain. As pointed out by Kay, "*It is important to distinguish between functional models and mechanistic models of neural information processing*" [118]. The reason for the dissociation between mechanism and function is that the same physical mechanisms – the passage of electrical impulses from one neuron to the next at synaptic junctions [119] – underlie all of its very diverse functions. Consequently, this generic underlying mechanism cannot in itself account for the differences between them.

Such dissociation would not be possible in organs with physical functions, which necessarily use different kinds of cells and mechanisms with distinct physical characteristics that combine to create the required function. Since it is the associated information, and not the physical mechanism, that forms the basis of brain function, it does not require this diversity of mechanism.

Conversely, even when neural networks exhibit the same input-output relationships, the mechanisms used to process information may be different. Self-organizational processes can generate the same results using different combinations of connections and weights. For instance, investigation of the brain area processing sensory input from a mouse whisker shows that even such a simple function in the vertebrate brain is based on different synaptic connectivity patterns in different individuals [120]. Consequently, even if the relationship between physical mechanism and informational function were to be mapped for one mouse, this would not tell us how the next mouse performs the same function.

An additional difficulty in deriving brain function from mechanism relates to the very limited function of its basic elements. The information associated with a single synapse is in itself functionally insignificant. Similarly, single synaptic discharges are functionally useless. The transition to useful functions is not just a matter of scaling up, as it is in many physical organs. A single muscle cell is also useless, but only because it is too weak. Combining millions does not lead to anything new: simply to the required increase in tractive force. This is not the case in neural networks where instead immense numbers need to be combined in order to build the hierarchical levels of organization, each with its own emergent properties, necessary to culminate eventually in meaningful information and useful information processes. The immense scale and dynamic nature of the connectome offer more than ample material and ideal conditions for such emergent levels to arise and operate. However, we have seen that this emergence is not based on the combination of the physical effects of neuronal mechanisms, but on the integration of the non-detectable informational phenomena associated with them. Higher level function is consequently not based on observable higher level physical mechanisms.

To an extent this is a trivial observation: it is eminently clear that the brain's cells do not combine their physical characteristics to generate organ-level functions in the way that, for instance, the cells of the kidney or heart do. However, the consequences of this distinction are significant, leading to an almost complete intractability. If it is not even possible to detect and measure the informational aspect of individual neuronal states and events, higher level functions arising through the combination of these basic units will be still more inaccessible.

1.3.9 How to wire a neural network

The formation of a functional connectome lies at the centre of any theory of the brain. The first step is to get cells with the right characteristics in the right places. For this, we have nothing fundamentally new or different to the general evolutionary and developmental processes involved in the creation of organs. The creation of the connectome then starts with the growth of axons along the required paths to find their synaptic partners, a process involving various chemotactic and mechanical cues [121]. Experiments in *Drosophila* have shown that the physical position of neurons is not even the defining factor in this process: even if neurons which need to connect are moved, they still manage to find each other [122].

At this level of organization, natural selection can operate as a means of sorting effective from ineffective architectural options for the various areas of the brain, creating its morphology and selecting other features such as neuron type and, most directly, the genes required for the production of neurotransmitters. However, simply getting the neurons in the right places does not result in anything useful. With the positioning of neurons and the laying down of axon pathways, we still only have a basic architecture in which the real work can commence: the making, strengthening, weakening and breaking of connections in such a way that the specific circuits are created that are required to ultimately support its informational functions.

As we saw in the previous paragraph, the same function may employ different connectivity patterns in different individuals. This means that they cannot be inherited in the usual fashion: their formation is not a matter of repeating the formative processes that led to the same function in your parents. Instead, they are created uniquely by each individual: "*The entire system resembles a patchwork of subnetworks assembled by a complicated history of tinkering, rather than an optimized system that results from some clean unified design*" (Varela [123]). Nor is this just a matter of fine tuning some initial setup laid down in the womb. The total number of synaptic connections in humans and other vertebrates grows considerably in early life and then falls back to a stable total number in adulthood through the selective pruning of up to half of these connections [124]. Even at the macroscopic level of connectivity between brain regions, significant changes occur in the course of childhood, adulthood and senescence [125]. In this sense, your current brain is consequently very different from the one you were born with.

To this we can add the fact that, in contrast with an animal's physical functions, many informational functions are not static. While the prenatal development of the brain's connectome ensures that a newborn infant possesses the behavioural capabilities required to keep it alive at this stage in its development [126] later in life it will need to display different cognitive abilities and skills. This contrasts with other organs, which generally perform the same functions throughout the animal's life.

What is particularly remarkable is that the brain remains functional throughout all of these changes. This is no trivial matter. After all, in a neural network with a million potential and a thousand actual connections, the vast majority of connection patterns will do nothing useful. With the network in a continual state of change, strong directed control is required to prevent order from decaying into chaos not just on these longer time scales, but also under short-term dynamic alterations in connectivity [127].

One of the more well-known and extensively researched forms of synaptic plasticity is the Hebbian strengthening of connections on concurrent activity commonly and neatly described as 'cells that fire together, wire together' [128]. More recent studies have demonstrated that the dynamics of the synaptic plasticity involve more factors [129]. The formation of functional networks in the brain is in this sense a complex and diverse self-organizational process taking place after the creation of the required architectural system. The question is how these processes lead to the great diversity of informational functions observed.

A significant part of the answer is to be found in the effect of embodiment: the intimate link between the brain and the body it is a part of through proprioception; and between the brain and the outside world through the body's sense organs and musculoskeletal system. There is a self-evident and necessary connection between the brain's perceptual functions, the available sense organs and the content of the outside world it relates to. Nagel's musings on what it would be like to be a bat [130] are one demonstration of this. Without the information provided by sonar sense organs, a brain will not develop the capability of constructing a sonar image of its surroundings; given such input to an appropriate cortical architecture, a bat will inevitably develop such circuits. Much research has been done on the effect of sensory input on the developing visual cortex [131, 132]. Experimental evidence of these effects is seen in the abnormal development of the visual cortex of kittens reared from birth in an artificial environment composed exclusively of vertical or horizonal stripes [133].

On the output side of the brain, the musculoskeletal morphology of the animal will determine which locomotory and behavioural functions cannot, can and must be supported by the brain. For instance, an animal without wings will not develop circuits to support flight, while a bird necessarily will. These effects of embodiment will also, for instance, lead to significant differences between the neurology of an octopus compared with a vertebrate [134].

The fact that the body's physical, sensory and motor systems grow and develop together supports a high degree of functional integration. As we saw in the above example of the mouse whisker, this is not to say that all brains of a particular species or lineage will build the same circuits to achieve the same function. Quite the contrary, the self-organizational processes involved will always result in a unique end result in each individual. However, the end result will be in all cases necessarily comparable. This is, then, a form of convergent evolution rather than fixed heredity.

Another factor is the effect of feedback applied to variable, repeated instances seen in the development of physical skills through training. Such processes lead to observable changes in circuit connectivity in the motor cortex [135]. Significant changes in connectivity have even been observed at the macroscopic level in individuals who have learned to play a sport [136].

While these various external and internal physical factors clearly exert an influence on the self-organization of the brain's neural networks, this effect is different from other self-organizational processes in a very significant way. The product of this effect is not a physical structure with physical properties, but a multi-level informational system that only delivers the required emergent functions at the highest levels of organization. Indeed, a significant feature of dynamic neural networks is that, in contrast with self-organizing systems with a required emergent physical function, there is no physically imposed preference for one connection over another. Effectively, the connectome has at this level an almost perfectly flat thermodynamic landscape, opening it up to other influences determining the patterns of synaptic connectivity. This is exactly what we would expect of a system that has evolved to be governed by non-physical influences. The remaining question is how such influences are exerted.

We have seen that in such complex systems, lower level components need to be determined on the basis of high-level requirements through top-down control. Yet, in this case, the relevant high-level structures and functions are informational, not physical. The observable physical changes in connectivity realized by, for instance, Hebbian learning are associated only with the very lowest level of information entities and processes from which these functions are built. An explanation for the formation of function in the brain will therefore need to provide a way of bridging the gap between high-level informational and low-level physical events.

1.3.10 Nature and nurture

These considerations of the origins of function bring us to the longstanding debate on heritable and acquired behaviours: nature and nurture. We have seen that, at the level of the neural circuit, all functions of the brain are the product of self-organizational processes. It is eminently clear that this level of organization in the brain is not genetically determined. In a purely quantitative sense, it would be impossible. Even if the entire genome were dedicated to wiring the brain, it would contain insufficient information by many orders of magnitude to determine the connection patterns of even a tiny part of the brain. Qualitatively, while chemotropic effects may explain the direction of axon growth, there is no mechanism by which gene-coded proteins could determine which connections are or are not laid down between specific neurons. Systemically, we have seen that in biological neural networks, functional circuits are not predetermined but form in each individual as unique solutions to required functions. This is regardless of whether it concerns functions that are comparable in parent and offspring (nature) or those learned or developed by a new generation (nurture).

We have also seen that embodiment leads to inevitable similarities in brain functions between individuals of a particular species. Here replication between generations is a consequence of convergence of developmental processes, not transferral of the specific neural circuits used by a parent to its offspring. The fact that all bats have sonar senses is not a result of the function itself being directly heritable, but of the effect of being in a bat's body on the developing brain. In addition to such directive influences on general capabilities, learning by experience also has an influence on common behaviours even small-brained animals. It has, for instance, been demonstrated that spiders adapt their initial web-spinning behaviours on the basis of individual experiences [137].

In humans, the cultural environment is a significant factor in the replication of behaviours from parent to offspring. Similarities in brain functions of subsequent generations that could be considered as inherited may well be a result of imitation and cultural forming [138], rather than parent-offspring transferral. Such social conformity will in general stabilize society through the normalization: a restriction to the degree in which its members can develop different exhibited behaviours [139].

These factors serve to illustrate the fact that inheritance and genetics are not synonymous. We saw earlier that biological systems in general are the result of self-organization rather than design, with the genome only providing instructions for the production of proteins that are essential components of this process. In addition to the genome, a host of epigenetic factors are influential in determining the ultimate physiology of an animal [140]. We have also seen that in the brain, an additional level of self-organization follows the correct positioning of cells: the determination of the specific connections between them. The distinction between these various causes is therefore important when considering, for instance, the behavioural similarities observed in experiments in which identical twins are brought up in different environments [141].

These arguments are not to say that genetics has no role to play. As in other organs, the specific proteins coded for by the genome are influential components. Different versions of these proteins, derived from different genetic alleles, can have significant consequences. Examples are seen in the effects of genetic variations on mental diseases [142] and intelligence [143]. However, "*recognising the existence of genetic influences will not dilute the power and potency of social influence, parenting, or the environment, but add nuance to understanding their effects on our behaviour, our experiences, and our personalities*" Barlow [144]. Such effects can extend no further than general characteristics and tendencies; they do not determine the specific functions performed by the brain. Similarly, the architectural structures employed by different brain regions may provide necessary conditions for the development of their specific functions but are not sufficient explanation for these functions themselves.

A consequence of the unique origins of brain function is the fact that, in addition to heritable characteristics, an individual can develop novel functions that are absent in their parents. This ability is taken to an extreme in humans. While it is impossible for an individual to grow wings, it is quite possible to learn to fly an aeroplane even though your parents lack this skill. Indeed, the success, progress and adaptability of humans as a species are not based on an increase in heritable brain functions, but the expansion of the capacity to develop novel functions. While this may seem trivial, it is a direct consequence of the fundamentally different relationship between physiology and function in the brain compared with other organs. While the introduction of new physical functions requires the evolution of new structures and mechanisms, the brain is a general purpose device that can develop new functions using the same structures and mechanisms. It is surely the most impressive achievement of evolution that it created an organ with such functional flexibility. Ironically, in doing so, evolution also necessarily released control over these functions, transferring this to non-physical self-organizational processes taking place within each individual.

1.3.11 Imitation, language and the communal brain

In the specific case of modern human brains, the cultural aspect is of paramount importance. Indeed, it has been proposed that imitation is the single factor that distinguishes modern humans from other species [145]. What is clear is that specific adaptive processes within the connectivity networks of the human brain, involving mirror neurons, allow humans to replicate observed behaviours in others. While imitation is also observed in other species [146], its extent in humans is unique. Imitation is not realized through replication of specific neural circuits, since there is no way for one brain to know which circuits another brain utilizes, nor to replicate connectivity patterns using such a design. Instead, the overall functional result is presented as a target for the dynamic self-organizational processes taking place. The relevant brain areas will then adapt their own pre-existing connectivity patterns in such a way that the behaviour can be replicated.

The influence of culture on human brain functions can be seen as a form of extended embodiment: in addition to the individual's body, the social environment within which the individual is embedded provides both boundaries and possibilities for the development of brain function [147]. Here, we see a recursive effect. The cultural context of an individual is itself an emergent phenomenon created by the current and historical interactions between individuals but subsequently becomes a determinative factor in the capabilities, behaviours and mindsets of its members [148].

A specific and highly significant example of human imitation is the use of language [149], a complex brain function involving multiple brain regions [150]. While the architecture of the human brain is primed for language acquisition [151], the actual language learned is determined by the individual's social environment. A significant feature of language is that, in contrast with other imitated behaviours, it does not have a physical function. Instead, it leads to the creation of a common coding system that supports the transfer of information between brains. At the population level, this supports the dissemination and evolution of ideas that is the topic of memetics [152]. The advent of writing, the printing press and more recently digital communication technologies removed the necessity of physical proximity for such interactions between individuals, thus increasing the scale and geographical spread of active communication networks from the village to the global human population.

The extensive exchange of information between brains that is facilitated by language underlies our capacity for cultural and technological innovation. Social networks constitute integrated informational systems existing at the group level; 'collective brains' with abilities that far exceed those of any individual [153]. "*Just as thoughts are an emergent property of neurons firing in our neural networks, innovations arise as an emergent consequence of our species' psychology applied within our societies and social networks*" (Muthukrishna and Henrich [153]). This is partly due to the combination of the specific individual cognitive skills and memories of many individuals. Another significant feature is the longevity of these systems. The collective brain outlives any individual or generation: indeed, it has existed since the birth of civilization and will continue to exist until its end.

Historically, isolated populations of humans each had their own collective brain. As these populations expanded and interacted more, this separation broke down. Skills were transferred and individuals moved between populations, taking with them their own cultural inheritance. The introduction of global communication technologies – starting with physical mail, followed by telegraph and telephone, and most recently the various forms of communication facilitated by the internet – removed the dependency on physical location for interaction between individuals. This is not, however, to say that there is now a single global communal brain. The fact that individuals may interact within diverse groups on the basis of familial, professional, religious or other interests creates an overlapping landscape of such systems, some fleeting, some ephemeral, some existing for thousands of years. Those with a lasting nature continually develop and adapt on the basis of the novel contributions made by individuals, but at the same time strongly influence their members functionally, intellectually but also morally. Religions are classic examples of higher-level systems which, after an initial period of active development, then became relatively fixed in imposed ritual, world view and behavioural standards.

1.4 Philosophy and religion

1.4.1 Philosophy of the mind

Millennia before neuroscience gave us insight into the working of the brain, philosophers were pondering the nature of the mind. In fact, the roots of philosophy must date back to the moment that humans become able to pose explicit questions: the birth of symbolic language itself. As with all evolutionary innovations, the significance of this turning point will have been what it added to existing possibilities. That was not in asking and answering pragmatic questions such as 'How do I make fire?' or 'Which berries should I eat?'. To have survived up to that point it is clear that humans were capable of solving such challenges without language. Instead, symbolic language was unique in allowing the formulation of abstract questions such as 'Who am I?', 'Where did I come from?' and 'Why is the world the way it is?' It is not just that without language our predecessors were unable to discuss metaphysical theories. Language also supports the internal structuring of our thoughts, allowing us to construct such questions and answer them in the form of hypotheses and theories. Even before the advent of writing, which gives us direct historical access to such musings, oral history indicates that early humans were doing the same.

Historically speaking, philosophy was a generic approach to understanding reality. It was the Enlightenment, exemplified by the publication of Newton's *Principia* in 1687, that created a distinction between philosophy and the empirical sciences. Philosophy as a discipline and method quickly lost territory as science proved to be more effective and reliable in explaining and controlling the physical world. This progression included the physical brain which we now know to be directly associated with the phenomena of consciousness and mind. Yet, this does not mean that the topic of the philosophy of mind was promptly superseded by a science of mind for one very simple reason: the thoughts and sensations that are so clearly revealed to us through our own conscious experience are in all other ways intangible and thus inaccessible to the traditional methods of empirical science.

In the limited space available here, it is not possible to do justice to the millennia of serious philosophical work that has been done considering the mind. At best, I can pick out a few elements that are of particular relevance to the task at hand. These start back in the 17th and 18th centuries with a number of opposing

DOI: 10.4324/9781003460541-5

and mutually exclusive solutions proposed to solve the puzzle of the connection and distinction between the body and the mind. On the one hand, Rene Descartes postulated substance dualism: that the mind and body are separate entities, composed of different substances, and connected through the pineal gland [154]. This contrasted with Spinoza's neutral monism [155], which saw both mind and body as manifestations of an underlying deterministic reality which he called god (in a non-Abrahamic sense) or nature. This can be seen as a precursor to the materialism that has since dominated in which this underlying reality is physics, from which all else is proposed to be derived. Thomas Hobbes made this more explicit, with a literal interpretation of materialism [156]. At the other extreme, we see idealism, as proposed by George Berkeley [157], in which the material world has no existence independent of the mind.

Each of these approaches has its own weakness. Cartesian dualism stumbles over the connection between the pineal gland and the mind. Spinoza's monism fails to provide a firm account of the proposed underlying reality. Idealism necessitates an unscientific 'mind of god' to explain the continuity of physical existence in the absence of human observation. Materialism, for all its proven power in taming the material world, entirely lacks the necessary acknowledgement and explanation of the very core of our existence: the fact that "*Minds are non-material entities: entities with properties not possessed by any material object*" (Heil [158]).

In spite of the immense progress made in other fields of intellectual endeavour, three hundred years on there is still no consensus on the mind-body problem. At the one extreme, we still have proponents of idealism [159]; at the other staunch materialists [160] who see a ghost in the machine that will evaporate as our understanding of the brain grows. Research on the neurological side seeks to solve the puzzle in this way by investigating the neural correlates of consciousness: the observable physical events that are associated with a particular subjective experience [161]. There is, however, a justifiable objection that such approaches evade rather than solving Chalmers' Hard Problem: that even if we understand every last detail of the workings of the physical, we will still lack an explanation for the non-material phenomena that are its very purpose. Indeed, such experiments inevitably lead to speculation on why it is that some neural activities lead to consciousness while others do not [162]. As a consequence of the failure of science to provide an exclusive and satisfactory answer to this question, the philosophy of mind remains an active area of human intellectual endeavour alongside neuroscience with, to this day, a broad range of different approaches and standpoints [158].

In recent decades, a number of theoretical approaches have been developed to explain the existence of consciousness based on the discoveries of neuroscience. These focus on the specific and quantifiable requirements of a physical system in order to be conscious. One example is Integrated Information Theory (IIT) which relates characteristics of consciousness (axioms) with physical characteristics (postulates), allowing calculation of a system's integrated information, which is then equated to the degree of consciousness [163]. Another contender, global workspace theory [164] proposes that consciousness requires and is the product of integration of brain functions: a necessity in a large brain capable of concurrently performing multiple tasks. A very different approach, based on the observation that both consciousness and quantum mechanics share the characteristics of non-locality, irreducibility and indeterminacy attempts to link the two [165]. This has led to attempts to rehabilitate free will by coupling it with quantum indeterminacy, although the justification for a resurgence in libertarianism on this basis is hotly debated [166].

Other branches of philosophy take consciousness as a given and instead set their sights on a critical appraisal of the world outside of our experience. After all, as Eddington observed, "*no one can deny that mind is the first and most direct thing in our experience, and all else is remote inference*" [167]. Such considerations vary from mild forms, starting with Kant, that merely comment on the inherent unreliability of our sensory perceptions in informing us about this external reality, to more extreme claims that it is consciousness that creates it. Kastrop makes this position particularly explicit: "*We, as well as all other living organisms, are but dissociated alters of cosmic consciousness, surrounded by its thoughts. The inanimate world we see around us is the extrinsic appearance of these thoughts*" [167a]. A different interpretation of the primacy of information over the physical is seen in Bostrom's speculations on the probability that we and our world, including even our conscious minds, are a simulation in the computer of an advanced civilization, rather than an independent reality in its own right [168]. That such radically different interpretations still exist of what must be, ultimately, a single reality is remarkable to say the least. To make matters worse, they do not even consider the full scope of the challenge.

These approaches focus on consciousness because, as a demonstrably real and yet non-physical phenomenon, it presents the most explicit challenge to radical materialism. However, the existence and significance of the subconscious have also long been acknowledged [169]. Indeed, much or even most of the activity in the brain is not conscious, including functions that equal or even exceed those that are associated with consciousness in terms of complexity. The distribution of brain areas associated with consciousness demonstrates that there is not some special part of the brain which functions in a fundamentally different way to generate consciousness; nor is such a distinction identifiable in the physical architecture of the brain. At a cellular level, the same processes underlie both conscious and non-conscious functions.

The non-conscious functions of the brain are just as physically undetectable as their conscious counterparts. Indeed, explaining them could be considered a harder problem since we do not even have the possibility of subjectively perceiving them and reporting our observations. While their existence is evident from their effects, they remain entirely in the dark to both objective and subjective observation. In this sense, explaining the non-conscious mind may turn out to be an even greater challenge, certainly not something that can be brushed off as an easy computational problem. However, difficult it may be to solve the riddle of consciousness, any theory that fails to also explain the brain's non-conscious functions must consequently be considered incomplete.

1.4.2 Philosophy beyond the mind

The philosophical consideration of consciousness does not stop at the level of the individual. Even before the internet provided a global communication platform, Teilhard de Chardin speculated as follows on the consequences of the similarity between the interactions between a brain's neurons and those between individuals: "*between the human brain, with its milliards of interconnected nerve cells, and the apparatus of social thought, with its millions of individuals thinking collectively, there is an evident kinship*" [170]. This leads him to propose the existence of an 'envelope of thinking substance' above the physical incarnation of human society, which he called the noosphere.

Many other proposals have been made concerning the communal non-physical aspects of human society. Carl Jung presented the concept of a 'collective unconscious', a realm of universal conceptual patterns connecting all humans and providing a foundation for their thoughts, feelings and behaviours [171]. Earlier, Hegel had already discussed the idea of an 'absolute spirit', a form of consciousness that transcends the individual mind and towards which humanity is progressing [172]. Ken Wilber has attempted to unite a wide range of philosophical perspectives into an integrated theory of individual and communal consciousness [173].

In this area, the philosophers are on their own: there are no scientists investigating the physical correlates of communal consciousness. This is doubtless partly due to the absence of any explicit objection on the part of this consciousness, if it exists, to being considered non-existent. It is, after all, the demands voiced by humans to acknowledge and explain their conscious experiences that fuel and support research into the neural correlates of consciousness at an individual level. A second factor is that the material substrates associated with such phenomena – groups of communicating individuals – are less easily demarcated and experimented on than coherent structures in the brain.

This having been said, it would seem likely or even inevitable that interactions between conscious minds lead to the creation of some type of higher-level phenomena. Indirect evidence can be seen in observable group behaviours such as mass hysteria [174]. The question is, however, whether we should expect such phenomena to be an extrapolation of what we experience as consciousness as individuals. In general, in hierarchically organized complex systems, the characteristics of a particular level are something entirely different, not just more of those seen at their underlying level. For instance, liquid water is not a higher level of molecularity than the molecules it is composed of but a material with its own, non-molecular characteristics. There is consequently reason to presume that the informational phenomena associated with communities have their own unique emergent characteristics, which will differ by nature from the instances of individual consciousness from which they are built. Furthermore, there is also a possibility that some of these higher level phenomena are constructed from non-conscious components. Mass hysteria, for instance, would appear to arise out of and influence such processes at the individual level.

An additional factor is the conclusion drawn on the basis of research into the neural correlates of individual consciousness that one essential requirement is scale: immense numbers of multiply connected neurons constantly interacting with a frequency in the millisecond range. Even in today's globally connected world, interactions between individuals fail to meet these quantitative requirements by orders of magnitude. Another difference is the type of interaction. In the case of neurons, this is a simple and meaningless electrical impulse; between individuals, it generally takes the form of content-rich and meaningful verbal communication. These differences would seem to indicate that Teilhard de Chardin's 'kinship' is too superficial to support an assumption of higher levels of consciousness.

A robust theory of mind should also shed light on this deeply significant aspect of human existence, ideally providing an explanatory framework on the basis of extrapolation from the individual level.

1.4.3 Religion and the soul

Up to now, we have discussed the mind from the perspective of philosophy and science, both of which have the purpose of rational and critical evaluation of alternative explanations. While philosophy cannot rely on the empirical methods of science, it is subject to its own strict rules of logic and reasoning as ways of developing and testing theories, arguing their validity and discarding those which are found lacking. However, long before the cultural development and formalization of such protocols, early humans also required answers to the existential questions they faced. Prehistoric art shows clear indications of religious ritual and belief in the supernatural long before the first written records provide explicit evidence. Even then, humans were formulating answers to existential questions and recording them in this way. "*The immense heritage of prehistoric art describes myths and beliefs, which were the intellectual patrimony of human society*" (Anati [175]). While interpretation carries the risk of anthropomorphism, other animals also exhibit behaviours that, in humans, are characteristic of religiosity [176].

In the absence of rigorous methodologies, these early solutions to life's deeper questions could only be based on observation, perception, inspiration, intuition and imagination. While many individuals will have come up with their own ideas and ideologies through the course of history – and continue to do so to this day – a small number gained a following that grew, evolved and consolidated to become the world's religions and mythologies [177].

Today, belief in the supernatural and authority-based religion can be seen as an obsolete and irrational view of reality and the human condition that is in conflict with scientific realism. A clear example is the ongoing battle between biblical creationism and evolutionary theory [178]. However, even this example shows the relationship between science and religion to be more complex [179]. Ultimately, the historic roots of religion are based on the same need for understanding and were, when they were conceived, among the best answers available.

The problem with religion compared with philosophy and science is that, being belief-based and culturally embedded, established concepts and theories tend to be maintained even when demonstrably better explanations have been found. It is here that the creationism vs evolution debate becomes problematic: the overwhelming evidence for evolution and lack of evidence for creationism means that the only rational conclusion is to reject the latter. This is the case for all of the archaic ideas about the physical world which have now been superseded by robust scientific theories, and yet are still defended by the more orthodox versions of religions. Taking centuries-old scriptures literally when they defy direct evidence is not, in general, a good way of convincing anybody with a healthy degree of scepticism.

Another issue with religions as an explanatory framework is their great diversity. The fact that each claims ultimate truth, while being unable to justify this claim on the basis of anything more than belief, provides reason to discard them all. After all, if each of them is contradicted by all others then surely none of them can be true. Their continued existence can seem to rely entirely on social indoctrination within closed communities.

However, when considering the mind-body problem, the same criticism could be levelled at the scientific and philosophical communities. Here, too, belonging to a particular (academic) group requires adoption of its particular theories. While these may be based on more rigorous thinking than religious beliefs and pass logical and mathematical testing, the fact that the immaterial mind cannot be directly detected means that their predictions cannot be tested in order to disprove or support them. The ensuing lack of consensus within the scientific and philosophical communities can justifiably be compared to the diversity of religious beliefs. Until such time as science and philosophy come to a consensus, there is no united front with which religious beliefs can be challenged.

To this issue, we can add a number of key advantages held by religion. Firstly, it provides explicit and unambiguous answers to the existential, moral and behavioural questions faced by individuals in their personal and social lives. The solutions proposed by the philosophical and scientific communities tend to involve obscure terminology, complicated logical arguments or complex mathematical formulae. This makes them difficult to follow for all but those conversant with the specific academic discipline, limiting their adoption within the general population. Furthermore, rather than providing clear guidance, they only indirectly relate to such everyday issues. Religions remain, in this respect, a more accessible, attractive and applicable option. Consequently, even in the modern technological world, the majority of the population still subscribes to a religious belief [180].

To gain general acceptance, a scientific or philosophical competitor will first need to be comprehensible to a lay person, and this is something that may also justifiably be expected. While performing scientific research requires discipline-specific skills and knowledge, the foundations of physical science can be explained to a child. This should also be true for the explanation of the foundations of mental functions and spiritual experiences [181]. The mechanisms by which religious belief systems persist in the face of contradictory evidence are interesting in themselves and of importance if we are to overcome such irrational but persistent mindsets and spread the theory of mind beyond the ivory towers of academia [182, 183].

Some religious ideas and habits can be explained away on the basis of superstition and demonstrably incorrect reasoning, but others are not so easily discarded. While this does not mean that they should necessarily be taken as literally correct, they should at least be accepted as valuably insightful. As such they are at least deserving of acknowledgement, serious consideration and possibly even the adoption of valuable elements.

An example of such a contribution is the fairly ubiquitous consideration of the human soul as a real, spiritual entity that is independent of and in essence more important than the physical world. In many religions, this is even taken so far as to propose that the soul can persist after the death of the physical body. This dualistic worldview became formalized in Greek philosophy [184] and persists to this day in the intuitive assumptions on the nature of the mind that are prevalent in the general population, both religious and secular [185]. This demand for acknowledgement of the mind as a non-physical phenomenon bears a direct relation with Chalmers' academically formulated Hard Problem. The experiences that pervade our daily lives present themselves as convincing evidence that there is something that justifiably begs an explanation that cannot be provided by the physical sciences. As long as science refuses to step outside the bastions of materialism, it will be unable to provide a satisfactory alternative with which to challenge these aspects of religious belief.

In addition to their interpretations of the nature of the sentient human individual, religions generally propose the existence of various types of deities as conscious agents with greater influence and power than the individual [186]. A large part of this agency – for instance as causes of natural phenomena – has been replaced in recent centuries by scientific explanation of physical processes. However, there remains a valid question concerning the possible existence and nature of higher levels of spiritual existence.

This leads inevitably to consideration of the relationship between such deities and the communal mind discussed earlier. The axiom of most religions that their god is the creator of all things excludes such a relationship. After all, such an entity would need to predate all that it creates, including humanity, not arise from it. However, some lines of New Age spiritual and religious thought do entertain such possibilities. Examples include Ernest Holmes' seminal work 'The Science of Mind' [187] and Eckhart Tolle's more recent concept of 'Presence' as a form of universal intelligence [188].

Following the discussion of such higher level spiritual entities, we encounter the question of where they are. The physical heavens and subterranean fire as dwelling places for god and the devil are no longer tenable since we have launched rockets into space and come to understand the geophysics of our planet. Indeed, our current understanding of the physical universe shows it to be, in its entirely, an unsuitable dwelling place. If we are to seriously consider such non-physical entities as being literally real, we therefore also need to provide them with an alternative place to exist.

The challenge for philosophy and science is either to come up with a single, convincing rational explanation for these higher levels of spiritual existence, or to provide definitive proof that they cannot exist. Only then can we justify any request to leave the deities behind us as a mindset that has served us well in the past but is no longer required.

Similarly, only when a clear and convincing explanation can be provided for human nature, the meaning of our existence, good and evil, and free will can we expect people to relinquish the religious beliefs that are currently their only available option.

1.5 Technological information systems

1.5.1 How information technologies are different

There is a fundamental difference between the technologies we design and build to perform physical functions on the one hand and those we design for informational functions on the other. In the latter, both the entities and the processes that produce these functions work on the basis of informational, rather than physical, properties and laws. This distinction leads to specific requirements for the physical materials and mechanisms used in the construction of these technologies.

Almost all physical interactions lead to some change in the states of the entities involved, thus imbuing information about the prior state of each entity in the other: the type of representational information required. This is not, however, to say that all such information can be used as a basis for designing and building an information technology. So what makes the interaction between pen and paper, and the other substrates used in information technologies, so effective?

One requirement is an exclusive relationship between the two states, which is often not the case. Take, for instance, the kinetic energy in the form of wind that is generated when the heat of the sun interacts with the atmosphere. The speed and direction of the wind carries information about the sun's heat, but this is mixed up with many other factors. While it may theoretically be possible to untangle these various influences, it would be extremely difficult and is therefore unlikely that animal senses would evolve, or machines would be designed, to use the wind as a representative of the sun's heat.

Even when an exclusive relationship does exist, the information may not be practically useful. The velocity of a stationary billiard ball after being struck by another ball will be determined purely by the velocity of the ball that struck it and the angle of the impact, but designing a technology that exploited this information would be anything but convenient. An additional factor is longevity. Writing a message in the sand will mean that the information is erased by the next high tide. When designing our information technologies, we therefore selected or created materials that were specifically suited to the task. "*Compared with earlier media, such as clay tablets and wood strips, paper dramatically facilitated reading and writing and improved information density*" (Goda and Kitsuregawa [189]). Later additions to the list of physical media included punch cards, vinyl records the Braille system before things went digital with magnetic media.

DOI: 10.4324/9781003460541-6

The existence of conveniently embedded information following an interaction is a start, but for it to be of any use it must be possible to also extract it. Until this happens, a written page is no more than paper with ink on it. While most people would recognize it as representing information, only those with the ability to read the alphabet and language used will be able to extract the information it contains. Doing so is not a matter of perceiving physical materials but of recognizing the intention behind the making of these marks, which exists in the form of associated information that is not directly detectable.

Having extracted the information, a process or system is required that uses it in some way. While physical processes are governed by the physical laws that determine the way physical entities interact, information processes are governed by laws that apply to information, the most important in our information technologies being Boolean logic. An example of a physical process is the transfer of kinetic energy between billiard balls according to Newton's laws of motion. An example of an information process is the NOT operation in which the absence of a component has an active causal effect, something that is not possible in a physical process.

The application of non-physical laws to information does not mean that information processes are detached from physical reality. As Landauer states [11], they are tightly connected to specific physical processes. The distinction is that the outcome of these processes is determined by the associated information rather than by physical properties.

This distinction can be illustrated by the different uses of a transistor, an electronic device that selectively allows current to pass between its collector and emitter depending on the current applied to its base. This physical mechanism can be employed to construct circuits whose input and output perform a logical function such as AND or OR. When used in a different circuit, the same electronic component can perform the physical function of amplifying a signal. In the former case, the transistor base current is used to represent information that a particular state is or is not present; in the latter the same current is used as a physical signal to be amplified.

Such an effect can also be seen in the use of some mechanical components. A cog wheel in the gearbox of your car is used for the physical effect of altering the transmission ratio between the rotational speed of the engine and the wheels of the car; in a mechanical calculator, a cog wheel may be used to cumulate a numerical value. It is, then, not the mechanism itself but the way it is used that determines whether it has a physical or informational function, whereby only some of the mechanisms used in physical machines are suitable for information technologies.

1.5.2 Physical support systems

It is understandable that textbooks on computer hardware (e.g. [190]) focus on the components of the computer that are directly related to their informational function: the processor, the memory, the means of transferring information between components and, with a bit of luck, something about the 'peripherals' by which interaction with the human operator is facilitated. However, without electricity, a frame to bolt the components to, a box to keep them safe and ventilation to keep them cool, the computer could not operate. "*Technologies of system packaging, thermal management and power supply are considered essential in server design and development*" (Wei [191]).

The components performing these physical functions are designed and built just like any other machine, in accordance with the applicable physical laws. A computer casing is built with the required robustness and lightless: physical properties. A power supply is designed to provide a source of electricity with the required stability, voltage and current: all measurable physical characteristics.

Such supportive functions are also seen, albeit to a lesser degree, in other information technologies. The frame of an abacus provides physical stability for the beads which perform its informational functions; the binding of a book holds together its pages in the order required to allow them to be read in the correct sequential order.

While clearly an essential aspect of these technologies, these components are not the topic of this book and will therefore not be considered further: their mention here is simply to explain this exclusion.

1.5.3 Information storage and transfer

In addition to supporting direct appropriate responses, evolution has granted animals two further informational capabilities with great survival value: memory and communication. The former allows, for instance, a squirrel to find its buried nuts; the latter helps social animals to alert their herd members to an approaching predator. In humans, these abilities were taken to a next level by the social evolution of symbolic language [192]. Not only did our large brains allow us to store more of our own gathered information; in this way, we could also learn from others.

However, even these extended capabilities had their limits and, having already exploited tools to supplement and extend our physical capabilities, early humans were soon doing the same with information. This is already apparent in narrative hunting scenes in prehistoric art [193], which clearly had a communicative rather than a physical function. The earliest information storage functions are seen in tally systems, such as marks on bones, in which a number of marks correspond with a number to be recorded. One of the most famous of such historical artefacts is the Ishango Bone, found near a fishing village on the shores of Lake Edward in Congo and dating from 9000 to 6500 BC. While this has been proposed to have been used as a mathematical tool [194], its actual function remains contentious [195]. The use of physical tools such as knives and needles can be easily derived from their physical properties but we can only guess how the Ishango Bone was used. This is a consequence of the fact that it is not the observable marks that underlie its function, but the way in which these were used to represent information. The same marking could have a different meaning depending on its position in a sequence and the numerical base used.

This dissociation between the physical representation and information content took a step further with the independent invention of writing in various cultures around the world [196]. The conversion of the sounds of a spoken language to letters is quite arbitrary: there is no direct relation between the sound of a spoken 'a' and the written letter 'a'. Without knowledge of this association, it is impossible to read a text; without knowledge of the language, it is not possible to know what it means – or indeed if any information is stored at all. A long-standing demonstration of this dependency is seen in the Voynich Manuscript, a 240-page book dating from the 15th century that to this day has resisted all attempts to extract the information that it may – or may not – contain [197]. This has led some to conclude that it is a hoax, not actually containing meaningful information at all, but since it is impossible to prove this absence, efforts to decode it continue.

Functionally, writing was significant in removing the limitation of temporal and physical proximity to syntactic communication between individuals. After centuries during which this was limited to handwritten manuscripts, the printing press was a significant step forward in allowing mass production. This can be compared to the industrialization of physical production, which similarly reduced the price per unit and thus the availability to the masses. The book, however, distributed information rather than physical products within human populations. Today, such this does not even require a physical medium, with texts published on the Internet immediately available the world over.

While texts are in the first instance no more than linear sequences of letters, this is not to say that this is sufficient to explain their function. Indeed, a string of letters considered only at this level is meaningless. Texts demonstrate their own form of hierarchical organization with emergent properties: letters combine into words which have meanings that cannot exist in the individual letter; words combine into sentences with a type of information content that cannot exist in an individual word. This is not a physical form of emergence: it is not the case that the letters o, i and l combine to form the word oil in the way that the atoms carbon, hydrogen and oxygen combine to form physical oil. This is because the word is the product of combining the information associated with physical representations, and not the physical representations themselves.

This hierarchical informational organization is key to the production of meaningful texts. Since the words are subservient to the overall message, and the letters are subservient to the words, the creation of texts is based on top-down causation. It is this which determines where on the pages of this book a particular word occurs, and which letters have been printed to create the word.

While writing allowed syntactic information to be stored for later consumption, other technologies extended the possibilities for communicating in real time. Telephones extend the range of the spoken word between two people and radio introduced the possibility of broadcasting to the masses. Television later supplemented this with visual communication. Mobile radios and telephones took these options out of people's homes to follow them wherever they were. In all of these examples, a physical medium is used not for its own properties, but for the information it carries.

1.5.4 Mechanical information processing

In the technologies described in the previous paragraph, the information is only stored and transferred, not altered or processed. While the possible use of the Ishango bone for mathematical calculations remains contentious, the abacus is an early example of a tool with a clear and explicit information processing function [198]. The invention and the use of mechanical calculating machines in the 17th century introduced comparable but more advanced capabilities [199]. Using these tools involved pressing keys and turning handles to generate the answer. "*The history of mechanical computing machinery in its essence is the story of the numeral wheel, and the devices which rotate it to register digital and tens-carry values*" (Chase [199]). While the same kinds of gear-and-lever-based mechanisms were used as in machines with physical functions, such devices differed in having informational functions and producing informational outputs.

The reason why these early information processing machines were exclusively fixed-function numerical calculators was because calculation is the easiest information process to mechanize. Jaquard's loom, invented in 1801, is retrospectively considered as a first step on the road that led to a more general purpose programmable computer [200]. The loom used punch cards as a design for the automated weaving of patterns in cloth. While its function was based on representational information associated with the cards, its output was a physical material rather than processed information. In this sense, it was not an information processing device.

Punch cards entered the service of information processing late in the 19th century to solve the very pragmatic problem of the US census of 1890. The 1880 census, done by hand using a tally system, had taken seven years to complete. On the basis of the estimated increase in population (to over 62 million), the 1890 census was expected to take more than ten years – by which time the next census would already have been started. The results would therefore have been outdated before they were known, so an alternative was desperately needed. The solution thought up by a Census Department employee, Herman Hollerith, was to use an electromechanical device to automatically read cards on which the positions of punched holes represented specific data [201]. In this way, the result of the 1890 census (62,622,250 people) was released in just six weeks.

Hollerith's machine didn't just speed up the tally of this total. The storage of diverse data on punch cards also allowed in-depth analysis. The machine included an automatic electrical tabulating machine with counters that accumulated the results. Using various switches, operators could instruct the machine to examine each card to see whether its associated information included certain characteristics, such as profession, marital status or number of children. When a card was detected that met the specified criteria, an electrically controlled sorting mechanism moved it into a separate container. This made it feasible to generate information such as the number of engineers living in a particular state that owned their own house and were married with two children. In doing so, it allowed large amounts of raw data to be processed to extract trends and statistical information.

The diversity of information stored on the punch cards clearly demonstrates the distinction between the information stored and its physical substrate. Exactly the same physical token (a hole or lack thereof) could be associated with information as diverse as address, age or profession, depending on how the machine was used. The information stored could therefore no longer be directly derived from the physical substrate, as in the case of writing, instead requiring knowledge of which position had been allocated to which information.

This dissociation meant that Hollerith's machine was not limited to the census information it was originally designed for. It could be used for any large quantity of information that could be stored on punch cards, heralding the start of automated data processing. After completing the census Hollerith formed the Tabulating Machine Company (later to become International Business Machines, or IBM) to exploit the commercial value of his invention.

1.5.5 Electronic information processing

The next significant step forward was the invention of the programmable computer. The first person to design such a machine was Charles Babbage in the early 19th century, but he never managed to build what would have been a massive mechanical device for a lack of interest and funding [202]. Another key development, in the mid-19th century, was George Boole's combination of mathematics and logic to formulate Boolean algebra [203]. However, it took two 20th-century innovations to really get the ball rolling. One was Alan Turing's vision "*Let us imagine the operations performed by the computer to be split up into 'simple operations' which are so elementary that it is not easy to imagine them divided* further" [204] and his theoretical design of a universal computing machine comprised of a head that can read and write symbols on a tape and move left and right; a state register in which the current state of the machine is stored; and an action table that tells the machine what to do when it encounters a particular symbol and is in a particular state.

The final requirement was technological. Building such a computer Babbage-style out of mechanical cogs and levers was never going to be a practical solution, and it was only when the necessary electronic components were invented that the computer age could really start. The original electronic computers, developed with the additional motivation of winning the Second World War, used thermionic valves [205]. These computers were still enormous, used large amounts of electricity and were also not particularly reliable. It was the invention of the semiconductor integrated circuit in the 60s that provided the physical mechanism needed to launch the information age.

While Turing cleverly proved that his theoretical machine could perform any calculation, and while theoretically any information processing task can be expressed mathematically, directly programming a Turing machine using his 'simple operations' (what is now called 'machine code') is extremely difficult. Even something as simple as an arithmetic multiplication requires a deep understanding of the nature of the computer's physical operations and how they relate to elementary information functions. For computers to fulfil their potential, an alternative way of translating required functions into these basic operations was needed.

The term 'translation' already alludes to the solution found. Computer languages were developed that bridged the gap between the low-level instructions required by the computer and the higher-level functions that were meaningful to programmer. As with spoken languages, these languages consisted not only of 'words' but also a grammar (or syntax) determining what it means when selections of words are brought together in a particular sequence.

In this way, the programmer can instruct the computer 'IF x>5 PRINT x' without having to know which underlying sequences of machine code operations are being performed. This higher level of organization carries the tell-tale signs of emergence: it has properties that cannot exist at the underlying level. Furthermore, the many different ways of combining a limited number of low-level components allow a great diversity of high-level functions to be created. Nor is this hierarchical organization limited to two levels. Above the level of the instruction, we have subroutines with functions that cannot exist in a single instruction; above the level of the subroutine, we have modules and programmes with properties that could not exist in a subroutine.

As in the linear strings of letters forming texts, the linear nature of the tape in Turing's machine (or of storage addresses in modern computers) is therefore misleading. While physically the computer may read and write bits in sequential order, its informational function cannot be explained by simply stringing binary values together. Furthermore, the emergence seen is not the product of physical combination magnetic fields or electrical currents, but of the information associated with them. Finally, as with texts, the positions of magnetic bits with a particular orientation in the sequence need to be determined by the higher level informational structure or process they are a part of.

The original microcomputers were operated with a keyboard to enter alphanumeric characters and a monochrome monitor to display output as a fixed grid of letters and numbers: the material on which a computer applies its functions, and which it produces as output. This alphanumeric information, while still relatively simple, is an emergent phenomenon existing at a level above the fundamental binary basis associate with the computer's bits. In the punch cards used in earlier information technologies, a single hole was associated with a discrete and complete item of information, such as a profession or age. The computer's binary information, in contrast, is quite meaningless. While a single bit may be unambiguously associated with the numerical value 0 or 1, even the information associated with two bits is dependent on the convention used: reading binary 10 from left to right gives the value 2, while reading from right to left gives 1. The relationship in the case of textual information is still more arbitrary: there is no necessary or direct relationship between the letter A and the binary sequence 01000001 used to represent it in the ASCII coding system.

Further developments such as the introduction of graphic user interfaces and cursor-driven software allowed computers to deal with very different types of information. In addition to text processing and numerical calculation, it became possible to process images, music and film – indeed, any kind of information that can be digitized. Coupled with these changes was the introduction of new peripheral apparatus connected to the computer itself. On the output side, we got colour printers and digital music players. On the input side, we got image scanners, digital cameras and recording devices. Each of these devices involves a conversion between binary data and information about the physical world using coding systems comparable to the ASCII code used for letters and numbers. For instance, the RGB system digitally represents more than 16 million distinct colours using two hexadecimal bytes for each of the primary colours red, green and blue.

It is this broad capacity to represent information that underlies the immense power of the general purpose programmable computer. While solving different physical problems requires the design and construction of different machines, Turing proved theoretically that all information problems can be solved using a single machine. This is because the same physical states and mechanisms can support different information processes working on different types of information. This also allows computers to easily combine information concerning different physical factors. For instance, temperature, humidity and wind speed measurements can easily be processed to determine a wind chill factor. A mechanical device with this capability may be feasible but would be massively more complex and difficult to design and build and could then only perform this single function.

As for all designed technological solutions, the structure and function of a computer program is easily comprehended. This is not to say that their users understand them, nor even that any individual involved in their construction may understand the entire system, but ultimately, the structure and function of every part is designed and known by somebody. The processes of design and construction that created the systems are also entirely transparent, holding no mysteries or secrets. And yet the relationship between the physical substrate and the designed solution is even more arbitrary than in Hollerith's tabulating machine. Given only a particular sequence of physical bit states, there is no way to determine which information or function it is associated with, or indeed whether it is associated with anything meaningful at all. This is because the functions performed are informational, rather than physical, and therefore non-detectable. The output of these processes also consists of non-physical information, necessitating its conversion into a detectable form: commonly by converting it to print or projecting it on a monitor.

1.5.6 Causation in information systems

The practical considerations discussed in the previous paragraph resulted in the development of stacked hierarchical layers of organization in the programming of digital computers. The functions for which they are designed and built are only to be found at the highest level. Like in machines with physical functions, each component is subservient to this ultimate purpose. This forms a nested sequence, with each component also composed of subservient subcomponents, on the basis of which Ellis and Drossel have concluded that "d*igital computers are modular* *hierarchical structures in both physical and logical terms. Because they are structured, higher levels can constrain and control lower level dynamics*" [206].

This subservience is illustrated by the interchangeability of components: the ultimate function can be realized using any arbitrary choice of processor architecture and computer language. Even the structure of the software is not determinative: there are many alternative ways of constructing a program to perform the same function.

If we consider the question of what determines the state of a particular bit or a particular electronic action to take place in a processor, the ultimate answer lies in the human who has designed the program to perform a particular function. In an operational sense, however, once this design has been implemented, the computer functions as an independent system. The states of its many physical components are then determined by the program that it is running in combination with the data on which this is operating. While these systems are not strongly emergent in the sense of self-organizing complex systems, it is still the case that downward causation takes place on the basis of the emergent properties of higher levels of organization.

1.5.7 Expert systems

Most of the computer software we use in our daily lives does nothing more than perform operations on input directly provided by the user, be that storing sequences of letters we provide to create a document or performing a calculation that we have provided the instructions for. This situation is very different in expert systems [207] in which the computer uses stored, formalized human knowledge on a particular topic to perform specific task that would normally require human intelligence. This approach has a number of advantages. To start with, by applying formalized rules rather than the rather opaque and unpredictable way in which humans operate, they can provide more consistent results. Secondly, it is possible to combine the expertise of multiple human experts to allow a greater body of expertise to be applied than any individual human could provide. Pragmatically, such systems can be replicated more quickly than human experts and can also be employed in dangerous environments where human experts would be reluctant to go.

A classic example of an expert system is the chess-playing computer, in which the rules and strategies of the game have been stored and can be applied to play the game against a human contender. While early versions did not even match the performance of a novice human, IBM's Deep Blue supercomputer made headlines in 1987 by beating world champion Garry Kasparov [208]. Deep Blue achieved this victory in a relatively traditional way, by searching through a set of alternatives. It was largely brute force computing power that allowed it to win where other chess-playing programs had failed. It did not develop its own strategies, nor learn from experience in the way that a human masters the game of chess.

The fact that a computer could play and win a game of chess is a demonstration of the fact that many of the games we play as humans are informational rather than physical. While chess may usually be played using moving physical pieces on a physical board, it is not the physical properties of these pieces that determine their behaviour but the logical rules of the game. It is learning, mastering and applying these logical rules that allow us, or the computer, to play the game regardless of its physical manifestation.

1.5.8 Machine learning

It is unsurprising that programmable computers can easily outperform brains in many predetermined information tasks, for instance the reliably storage of information or the performance of numerical calculations. In this, they are comparable to the tools we build to solve the limitations of our bodies to perform physical tasks. Expert systems extend these capabilities to more complex functions. The usefulness of such solutions is based on the fact that, if correctly programmed, they will reliably produce the same correct answer to the same question. One disadvantage of this approach is that the programmer must invent and explicitly code each individual function. The amount of work this involves increases with more complex tasks and can become impossible in situations in which the input and required output are not known in advance. More significantly, such fixed relationships between input and output fail to benefit from the advantages to be gained by learning: the form of iterative improvement employed by humans and other animals to develop their skills.

Artificial intelligence (AI) is an attempt to solve these limitations. "*The main focus of AI research is in teaching computers to think for themselves and improvise solutions to common problems*" (Clark [209]). The designer then only needs to create a machine with these adaptive capabilities. Releasing control of the input-output relation in this way also allows AI systems to continually adapt their responses in the light of experience. Earlier successful applications of machine learning were seen in fields ranging from medical diagnosis [210] to various applications in industry [211] and robotic control systems [212]. Other examples in entertainment include the generation of realistic behaviour of characters in gaming environments [213] and film making [214].

While it could seem that AI is the inevitable next step forward for information technologies, this is not necessarily the case. In many or even most situations, we are still best served by traditional computer programs, designed to reliably produce a predefined response to e specific input. In situations in which the challenge is partly rule-based and partly adaptive, the most effective solution may be to build a hybrid system in which one part is a conventionally designed computer program and the other based on machine learning [215].

A wide range of methods and mechanisms are used to facilitate machine learning [182]. Alongside the mainstream silicon-based technologies, recent years have seen an increased interest in approaches that can be grouped together under the term 'unconventional computing' [183]. These vary from molecular computing (which harnesses chemical reactions, molecular switches or DNA molecules to carry out specific computational tasks) to the use of hydraulics [184]. Such methods further emphasize the distinction between the physical substrate and its informational function: the diversity of material substrates that can be used to create information systems is in sharp contrast with the limited options when building physical tools, for which the substrate self-evidently needs to have specific physical characteristics that relate to its function. You cannot, for instance, make an effective hammer out of water or power a hydraulic system using steel. The calculation $2 + 2 = 4$ can be performed by any number of physical mechanisms.

A characteristic of these examples is that they are designed and built to learn how to perform a specific task. Moving on from such single-function systems, the next level of ambition is Artificial General Intelligence (AGI): a system with a broader developmental capacity that allows it to respond appropriately in a wide range of informational contexts [216] and in this way more closely resemble human intelligence. The consideration of such systems inevitably leads to speculation as to whether or when such systems would come to match and surpass the abilities of the human brain. In the early days, such musings were purely theoretical. Back in 1950, Alan Turing proposed an Imitation Game as a test for machine intelligence [2]. In this thought experiment an interrogator must distinguish between a human and a computer purely on the basis of answers to questions posed. If the interrogator fails, then the computer has won and must be considered intelligent in the human sense of the word.

Recent developments with Large Language Models (LLMs) such as the highly popular ChatGPT satisfy many of these requirements [217]. Through convincing text generation combined with access to a wide and varied source of general knowledge such systems appear capable of passing the Turing Test. Indeed, this has led to consternation concerning the risk of students using such tools to generate assays which they would be unable to write themselves, but which would not be recognized as such [218]. Indeed, ChatGPT's main weakness in passing the Turing test is probably its honesty in confessing to be a non-human AI language model. Versions that have been programmed to lie on this point, claiming to be sentient and to have emotions, are unnervingly convincing. A second issue is that such systems are actually too intelligent: no individual human would ever be able to answer such a broad diversity of questions. A test on a list of Mastermind general knowledge questions, in which ChatGPT not only provides the correct answer but also additional context, demonstrates that in this sense, they have already surpassed humans in terms of generating the output we associate with general intelligence.

The apparent intelligence of LLMs is, however, illusory. In contrast to expert systems, these systems harbour no contextual information. All they do is produce strings of words on the basis of probabilistic models trained by analysing texts produced by humans. In this sense, they constitute a variation on the theme of Searle's Chinese Room [219] in which he considers a situation in which a person successfully produces Chinese responses to Chinese questions on the basis of instructions concerning how to respond to particular symbols, without any understanding of the Chinese language [220]. The success of these solutions is, however, testimony to the power of machine learning: their entire functionality is not based on hard programming but on rules developed by the system itself through the parsing of huge volumes of existing text.

1.5.9 The mysterious ways of artificial neural networks

The fact that most AI research focuses on artificial neural networks (ANNs) and more recently larger scale deep neural networks (DNNs) is no coincidence. Such systems are relatively easy to simulate in a digital computer and, perhaps more importantly, the effectiveness of biological neural networks demonstrates the potential of such systems. In both cases, inputs are converted to outputs by passing through a connectivity network in which the specific connections between nodes are determined by self-organizational adaptation based on feedback effects from prior passages [221]. These similarities mean that ANNs can also serve as models to gain insight into their more complex and less tractable biological counterparts.

Considerable progress has been made in investigating how such networks, consisting of an input layer of nodes connected to an output layer through one or several intermediate layers, can process information. From the early days, theoretical analysis has been done of the potential logical functions of (artificial) neural networks [222] and these continue to be developed [223]. Another line of research concerns how networks can best be analysed and described [224].

Much of the work done in this area is utilitarian, investigating how particular types of neural networks can be applied to the solution of specific information-based problem. Their potential has long been recognized in fields as diverse as clinical medicine [225], stock trading [226], image recognition [227], autonomous vehicles [228] and robotic control systems [229]. In each of these areas, neural networks have been successfully deployed, replacing conventional computing in situations requiring adaptability and an ability to deal with incomplete and noisy real-world data. They are also often useful when dealing with dynamic complex systems and non-linear relationships in which an explicit algorithmic description may be difficult to find. In situations where the problem requires the characteristics of both rule-based and adaptive processing, neural networks can be combined with traditional programs in hybrid systems [230].

The adaptability of these systems sets them even further apart from machines with physical functions than the programmable computer. In the latter, as in physical machines, function is a result of design and construction, albeit with non-physical components. ANNs do not create function by implementing a predefined design, but simply through cumulative trial and error. It may seem trivial to observe that a random pile of nuts, bolts and other components cannot spontaneously or with some encouragement change into a washing machine, and that a washing machine will not improve through many washing cycles, perhaps even coming up with entirely new ways of cleaning clothes or even branching out into washing cars. Yet, this is exactly what we see in neural networks. Starting with a randomized network, they iteratively alter the relative positions and strengths of connections in order to create a functional system that improves its performance with experience. From the same starting point, given a different task, they can develop entirely different functions.

A significant aspect of neural networks of any complexity is their fundamental intractability. "*Given that DNNs [Deep Neural Networks] are epistemically opaque it is, in many instances, impossible to know the high-level, logical rules that govern how the network relates inputs to outputs*" (Duede [231]). While it is possible to deduce the informational function of a small group of nodes, this becomes increasingly difficult as numbers increase. By the time we get to the numbers of nodes and architectural complexity of DNNs lead we encounter what is effectively a black box. The way in which a particular input leads to a particular output cannot be derived from the vast numbers of connections and weightings [232]. Indeed, different networks trained to do the same task and producing comparable outputs do so in different ways [233]. In these respects, they are comparable to the unique connectivity patterns that are created in the brain to perform a particular function.

One cause of this dilemma lies in the fact that the way in which neural networks generate output from input is not algorithmic in the way that a computer program is. A neural network that learns to add numbers does not do so by combining Turing's basic logical operations to build a formal algorithmic solution to addition. Instead, it develops pathways that progressively come closer to achieving the desired input-output relationship, whereby a risk of error always remains. It is for this reason that tasks that can be explicitly described in an algorithmic sense can better be entrusted to conventional computer programs.

More fundamentally, we have seen in programmed systems that it is only possible to derive non-physical informational effect from measurable physical states on the basis of the predefined coding systems and languages used in their design and construction. Since function in neural networks is the product of training rather than design, and of the combination of connection weightings rather than syntactic logical operations, it is not possible to reverse engineer the associated information processes by decoding. Consequently, we have no way of determining what is actually going on 'inside' these neural networks.

This intractability is an issue in relation to demands that the algorithms underlying AI systems should be transparent. However useful they may be, unless we understand how they reach their conclusions, it seems risky to trust them [234]. And yet understanding them in the way we can understand a designed machine or computer program is not possible. Some insight into their operation can be gained by observing intermediate stages in the process [235]. However, this does not constitute a deciphering of the operation of the network. While it is possible to train a neural network against generating undesirable output or to place filters on acceptable output, this is not the same as understanding how the connection weights cause the transformations between the layers of the neural network and produce a particular output in the basis of a given input. As the scale and complexity of these systems increases, so too will their intractability.

1.5.10 How to build a neural network

While it has been demonstrated that neural networks are Turing complete [236], designing a fixed-weighted neural network to perform a particular function in the way that deterministic computer programs are written would be extremely difficult. Building a system with the degree of complexity of even the simplest of applications would be implausible but would also be pointless since this is not the kind of task that we require of neural networks.

Instead, research on ANNs focuses on meta-design: how they can be built to optimize their ability to develop and improve their own functions through self-organization. "*The design of ANNs happens more at the abstract, architectural level instead of at the fine-grained detailed level. This is because of the self-organizing property of the ANN's at the fine-grained levels*" (Mantri and Thomas [237]). This task is not simply a matter of constructing a random network and letting it do its thing: the ability to develop useful functions necessitates specific mechanisms and parameters. In this area, much has happened since the initial considerations of the workings of neural networks in the 1940s [222]. The development of back-propagation methods in the 80s [238] was an essential step towards building neural networks that could be effectively trained by adjusting connection weights on the basis of the difference between the actual and the desired output. Convolutional neural networks [239] subsequently facilitated diverse applications related to image recognition, while recurrent neural networks [240] are particularly good at speech recognition and dealing with other forms of information that flows through time. More recent developments include deep belief networks [241] and advances in natural language processing [242]. In each of these examples, specific features lead to neural networks that are well suited to solving a particular type of problem.

Building an effective neural network is consequently no trivial business: it goes beyond selecting an appropriate network architecture. Many variables such as the number of layers and nodes, activation functions, loss functions and optimization algorithms need to be chosen and fine-tuned. The diversity of options, the complexity of contemporary platforms and the demanding theory behind parametrization mean that the effective construction and use of neural networks today require considerable expertise. Indeed, it is comparable to the design of physical machines in terms of the options available and the skills involved. With, of course, the very significant difference that, since these machines perform informational rather than physical functions, the theoretical and practical foundations are entirely different. These are not based on physical laws, properties and mechanisms but on more abstract mathematical and logical features.

Unsurprisingly, the fact that such work is complex and time-consuming led to the question of whether computer systems could help out. This resulted in the design of neural architecture search (NAS) systems [243] which are themselves capable of designing neural networks, or at least assisting in their development. Some of these systems use evolutionary algorithms [244] making them systemically comparable to the processes underlying the ontogeny of biological neural networks: a variation-and-selection process is used to find neural networks with the desired learning abilities.

The use of evolutionary processes to create self-organizing systems further increases the distance between the human designer and the end result. Not only is the functionality not designed; even the system developing the functionality is not designed. The only direct human influence is in designing and creating the evolutionary process to create a system capable of developing a solution to a particular problem. Ultimately, it is still the human who determines the problem to be solved and the success of the solution, but the details of the problem-solving process are two steps removed from any direct determinative influence.

Here, again, it is interesting to contrast physical and informational technologies. We have already seen that the physical equivalent of a neural network (a system capable of developing physical functions by altering its own configuration) is implausible. The ability of a NAS system to iteratively improve the ability of a neural network to configure itself takes this to the next level. While a physical computer is used to run such systems, this should not mislead us into thinking that such systems are 'just' physical machines. The computer is no more than the physical substrate that is used to build an informational environment in which this sequence of creative processes can take place.

1.5.11 How to train a neural network

Having built an ANN with an appropriate architecture and parameters, we still have nothing of any use: this is only the starting point for the self-organizational processes which lead to the formation of applicable functions. The most common methods used as a basis for these processes are supervised learning, reinforcement learning and unsupervised learning. In supervised learning, the network is provided with a set of inputs and outputs as training data, and its connections are iteratively altered on the basis of its ability to replicate these 'correct' relationships [245]. Eventually, such a neural network can become reliable in classifying input data and become increasingly so with additional experience.

Reinforcement learning involves a similar type of feedback effect on connectivities but is not based on predefined input-output data sets. Instead, outputs based purely on trial and error are judged with resulting rewards or penalties.

A more open-ended approach is seen in unsupervised learning, in which the neural network is presented with data with no a priori desired output and given the task of uncovering patterns and regularities. It does so by examining the input data's statistical properties and exploring relationships within the data provided. This approach can be useful in for feature extraction in large volumes of unstructured data and in searching for anomalies in the data.

While the data involved in traditional AI often relates to real-world phenomena such as medical images or recorded behaviour of individuals, the systems themselves remain isolated from this world. Rather than collecting real-time information, they retrospectively analyse gathered information to draw conclusions on what has been, operating entirely in the realm of abstract data. Their output is not some direct interaction with their subject matter, but information presented to their human operator.

In contrast, robotics introduces a necessity to perform real-time functions in the physical world. Here, we encounter the distinction between the physical world in which such systems need to operate, and the informational world in which the processes governing their behaviour take place. Bridging the gap between the two requires an accurate and up-to-date reconstruction of relevant aspects of the physical world and the robotic agent within it. The robot therefore needs sense organs and methods of processing the information generated by them.

For the many applications of AI in industrial production processes [246], this is relatively easy. Since a factory can be designed as a reliably structured environment, the robot can be provided with maps, removing the necessity for it to learn this information. One challenge in which the adaptability of machine learning, in combination with the speed at which such systems operate, can be of value is in the recognition of deviations from the intended situation, for instance in identifying and rejecting production defects [247].

The story is different for autonomous agents operating in the complex, unstructured and unpredictable outside world [248]. Here, we encounter Moravec's Paradox [249]: the observation that while computers easily surpass the human brain in the logical and mathematical capabilities we hold in the highest regard when thinking about intelligence, they struggle to match the sensory and motor abilities of an insect brain when it comes to autonomously negotiating an unpredictable, messy physical environment. The recognition that autonomous agents require a very different type of sensorimotor intelligence than can be provided by fixed programming led to the introduction of a new paradigm which is strongly dependent on embodiment [250]. Only by directly coupling sensory input and motor output to the developing neural network can the system develop and operate as an integrated physical-informational entity.

One application which has received much attention in recent years is that of scene and object recognition in autonomous vehicles [251], which can clearly not operate safely without such capabilities. Military applications present similar demanding requirements [252]. Such applications generally employ specific types of reinforcement learning [253], and the changeability of their environment means that they never reach an optimal end-point. Instead, while basic capabilities may stabilize, in applying them they need to continually adapt their connectivities to the specific characteristics of novel situations they encounter.

The quantitative determination of the connectivity patterns of large-scale networks is a challenge in itself, requiring advanced forms of connectivity analysis [254]. Where this is possible, it reveals a fundamental lack of reproducibility [255] resulting from the self-organizational processes that underlie the development of function in such systems. Exactly the same naïve neural network, trained on identical data, may achieve different results depending on the specific path taken in its development. Equally significantly, even if the final states of the two instances generate apparently identical results, the stochastic nature of the process will mean that their fine-grained connectivity patterns will differ.

While at a basic level the ANNs used in these systems can be defined on the basis of individual connections between nodes, this is not the level of organization at which they function. The specific weights of their connections have no value individually, only as contributions to the large-scale processes they are a part of. The self-organizational nature of the training process selects combinations of weights which together achieve the desired results. In other words, these weights are ultimately determined by higher-level factors: "*Information embedded at higher organizational levels is the most important locus of causal control of the system*" (Newsome [256]).

Strictly speaking, it is not even the weights themselves that are of importance but the informational effects associated with these weights. In itself, this should not come as a surprise: we have seen that the same applies to designed computer programs where it is not the bit state that is of importance, but the binary value associated with it. The only difference is that in neural networks the weights are not based on external design but on internal self-organization, and also that they are not associated with such simple standardized information. A weight may represent a different information depending, of course, on what caused it to have its particular value.

1.5.12 Networks and integrated digital systems

The previous paragraphs discussed the digital computer as an isolated device. In the case of its predecessors – mechanical calculators – this was functionally inevitable: they could not easily be functionally combined. However, the use of electrical currents in digital computers opened the possibility of exchanging information by connecting them using conductive cables. Today, this is so ubiquitous that it is easy to forget the early days in which computers were placed on desks or in rooms with only a power cable to feed them with the necessary electricity. What then started out as closed networks of computers within buildings or organizations quickly expanded to the current global internet, in which computers the world over can communicate and cooperate. More recently, the inconvenience of being tied down with a physical cable was removed by the trend towards wireless communication methods such as WiFi and 3/4/5G.

The benefits of connecting computers that perform the same functions are limited. Where networking becomes really powerful is when the participating nodes are given specific roles, for which they can be optimized: "*Networks provide or create a mechanism whereby programs and resources residing in computers attached to the network may communicate and exchange information*" (Wecker [257]). In this way, metasystems can be created in which the whole is more than the sum of the parts. Today's computing devices are generally part of such larger functional infrastructures: communities of computers, each with its own part to play. There are client-server systems, mobile apps operating together with backend cloud services, network infrastructures involving routers, firewalls and switches.

A comparison can be made with a factory in which a complex product such as a car is manufactured. Here too, various machines with different functions are required to create the end product. The significant difference is that all of the machines in a factory production line need to be in the same building for the (physical) output of one to serve as the input for the next. With the possibility of information being transported at light-speed through connectivity networks, this limitation does not apply to composite information systems, whose components may be distributed anywhere around the world.

The result of these developments is that the computer with which the individual interacts is often no more than an interface that gives access to the capabilities of a much larger integrated digital system comprised of large numbers of nodes working in unison. The complexity of these systems requires that they are divided into component parts, and that the parts are organized in distinct layers, with the design and construction of each requiring specific technical expertise. We have long since passed the stage where any individual human is capable of harbouring all of the skills required to create such systems.

Part 2

Conclusion

The origins and growth of the information dimension

2.1 Emergent Information Theory

An introduction

As we have seen in the first part of this book, the solution to the mind-body problem needs to encompass more than the in-your-face challenge presented by consciousness. It must include the entire diversity of biological and technological systems that have in common the fact that their function is based on information, rather than physical characteristics. We have also seen that the physical and the informational are tightly connected in such systems, requiring us to consider them as integrated systems. This broader scope provides us with many pieces that may contribute to solution of the puzzle, each with its own part to play. The question is how these can be brought together to create a coherent whole.

Emergent Information Theory (EIT) provides an explanatory framework that could do just that by combining the type of information defined in Chapter 1.1 with the discussion of emergent systems in Chapter 1.2 to formulate what is, essentially, a simple proposition: that the specific type of non-physical information produced by these systems is hierarchically structured to form stacked levels of organization, each of which exhibits its own emergent properties [258]. The second part of this book will show how this interpretation can be applied to the nature and workings of the biological systems discussed in Chapter 1.3 and the technologies considered in Chapter 1.4.

To appreciate the theory and how it differs from other approaches, we first need to take a closer look at the information generated by physical interactions. Returning to the example of two billiard balls colliding, we have seen that the new trajectory of each of the balls carries information about the velocity, mass and direction of the other ball before the collision. This applies not only on the billiard table but to every interaction between objects and particles at all levels of organization from the subatomic to the cosmic. The gravitational orbit of a planet also carries information about the mass and position of its parent star. Any characteristic or property of an object that exerts an influence through interaction will lead to the creation of such information associated with the affected entity; different types of interaction will lead to the creation of different types of information.

Significantly, each element of information created in this way is indivisible: it is not built of component parts. This is in contrast with the entities the information relates to and those with which it is associated, which are generally constructed out of multiple layers of physical organization. The mass of a billiard ball is the

DOI: 10.4324/9781003460541-8

sum of countless billions of molecules, which are composed of atoms, which are composed of subatomic particles. The information about its mass that is attached to the ball that it struck, on the other hand, is elemental, non-divisible. Information of this type can therefore be seen as a fundamental entity, and as such deserving of a name. In accordance with the nomenclature of fundamental entities in physical reality, it would seem appropriate to name it an 'information quark' or, more compactly, a *quirk*.

The remarkable thing about this information is that it is not physically detectable. There is no sense organ or device with which you can identify or measure it. It is just not a technical difficulty, it is in principle impossible for the simple reason that it is not composed of matter or energy, and therefore cannot interact with a physical detection mechanism. The only way we can know what information is present is by deducing it from knowledge of preceding events.

In all normal situations, in which physical processes take place based only on the immediately applicable laws of physics, quirks are no more than passive bystanders. A billiard ball sent on a new path may carry information about previous encounters, but this has no role to play in future events. If it goes on to hit a third ball, what happens will be determined entirely by its current velocity and direction. The information it carries about the ball that contributed to its current state has no effect. Nor do these quirks have any way of interacting, combining or collaborating: they remain totally isolated entities.

While the whole of physical reality is 'coated' with a colourful layer of this specific type of non-physical information, its existence can justifiably be seen as a trivial by-product. Being non-physical these quirks may not be able to reside in physical space, but as isolated entities, they do not require their own dimensionality. Instead, they can comfortably reside in a one-particle-deep layer spread over the three Euclidean dimensions. There is consequently little reason to consider this type of information as anything more than an abstract curiosity: an understandable response is 'So what?'.

This all changes in living organisms. Slowly at first. Initial uses of quirks still only exploit them as individual entities: nothing more than messengers. As such they gain influence, but can still be viewed as no more than derived properties. It is in the neural networks of animal brains that we are obliged to acknowledge their true nature. It is here that quirks start to interact and combine as entities in their own right according to their own laws. Since quirks are non-physical, so too are these laws and the phenomena built from them. As in physical systems, such constructions are generally more than the sum of the parts. Just as quarks combine to form atoms with properties that are not present in their component quarks, so too do quirks combine to form entities with properties that do not exist at the quirk level. This is the 'emergence' in EIT which requires the acknowledgement of quirks as entities in their own right, and as the fundamental components of a non-physical dimension to reality. In small numbers, this effect is limited, but the billions of quirks produced by neural activity in brain are sufficient to support not just one but several levels of hierarchical organization.

It is this that makes EIT an explicitly substance dualistic theory. Considering such information as a mere property of physical states fails to suffice in the face of this independent generation of an entire realm of non-physical entities and dynamic processes. On the other hand, it distinguishes itself from traditional forms of dualism, which typically only claim a special status for consciousness, in including the full scope of all information-based phenomena.

Consciousness thus becomes just one example of an extended class of phenomena that do not belong to the physical realm. Until relatively recently this class was limited to the close-knit family associated with the brains and nervous systems of animals. Only in the last century or so did they gain company in the form of the information technologies we have designed and built to supplement the functions of our brains in a way that is comparable to that in which our physical technologies extend the capabilities of our physical bodies. As with physical technologies, this does not entail replication of structures and mechanisms. When building tractors we do not reverse engineer the bones and muscles of the horses that previously pulled the plough. Instead, we design a machine that is even more effective at producing the required traction. With this being a physical function, both tractors and horses are ultimately built from physical quarks. Similarly, when we replaced human calculators with mechanical calculators we did so not by replicating brain mechanisms, but by designing machines which were even better at performing the required numerical operations. While employing different methods, they both perform informational functions that are the result of the combination of quirks.

Together, brains and computers generate immense numbers of quirks, and anything that exists must exist somewhere. In addition to the logical argument that a non-physical substance cannot occupy a physical space, both brains and computers demonstrate strongly non-Euclidean functional topologies that are radically different from the physical substrate with which they are associated. These are far more complex than can be compressed into a simple layer spread over the three spatial dimensions. Instead, we see a distinct information dimension that exists alongside the physical, while remaining attached to it. Since our sensibilities are finely attuned to the three physical dimensions occupied by our bodies is it as difficult to envisage such a dimension as it is a fourth or fifth physical dimension. Yet, this dimension will necessarily be just as real as the substance it houses.

EIT thus shows that a view of reality that is limited to that which is composed of physical matter and energy and exists in the physical dimensions is fundamentally incomplete. By explaining what it is that exists alongside physical reality, where it exists and how the two are connected it extends the boundaries of a law-based, integrated reality beyond the physical dimensions, through the interface of brains and computers and into the information dimension created by them.

2.2 Biological information systems

2.2.1 How evolution opened the door

Biological evolution has a remarkable ability to exploit any aspect of reality that can contribute to the survival and success of individual organisms. Quirks proved to be one of its most remarkable and useful resources.

To understand why, we need to consider the greatest challenge for living organisms: that of maintaining their far from equilibrium state in the face of external perturbances and internal deviations. If, like the billiard balls, living systems were to allow their components to respond only according to the physical laws immediately applying to them, they would slide inexorably towards thermodynamic equilibrium and the organism would die. Preventing this requires adaptive and homoeostatic responses to changing external and internal circumstances. In other words, biological processes need to be governed by external factors: Bateson's 'difference that makes a difference' [7]. This is made possible by the evolution of systems whose behaviour is determined not by the properties of their components but by information associated with these components relating to external differences. Here, then, quirks became significant and active participants.

Evolutionary processes are gradual and incremental, and its exploitation of quirks is no exception. The most ancient examples, which are so simple that they can easily be missed, are seen in single-celled organisms. When a sensor molecule on the surface of a bacterium detects a nutrient its configuration is changed by the interaction. The subsequent response to this change is mediated by the altered state of the receptor, but needs to be based on the nutrient concentration. In contrast with colliding billiard balls, the difference that makes the difference is not the state of the receptor itself but the condition that caused this state. The system uses the receptor state to represent this factor by responding not to the state itself, but to the quirk associated with that state. The mechanism can use any arbitrary molecule or state as long as the response process recognizes it as representing the external situation. This is, then, a system that has evolved to work on the basis of the quirk associated with a state rather than the state itself, as illustrated in Figure 1.

An important feature of such systems relates to the existence of entities. The physical components exist regardless of whether or not there is a stimulus.

DOI: 10.4324/9781003460541-9

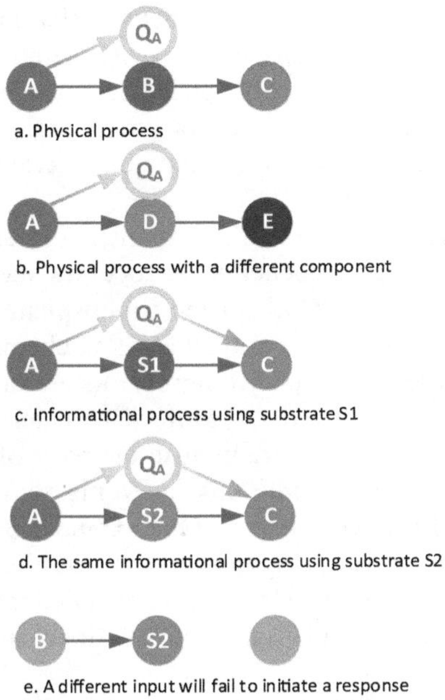

Figure 1 (a) In a physical process, when an entity B interacts with another entity C, the outcome is entirely based on the state of B. The previous interaction between A and B leads to the creation of quirk Q_A carrying information about A, but this has no influence. (b) Changing one of the components therefore alters the outcome. (c) In an informational process, while mediated by the physical state of sensor S, outcome C is determined by the information (Q_A) carried by S concerning A. (d) The determinacy of the quirk is demonstrated by the fact that the receptor can be replaced without changing the outcome. (e) Conversely, a different external influence B will not lead to the creation of Q_A and therefore fail to generate a response.

The quirks, in contrast, only exist when they are created by a particular interaction, such as that between A and S2 (but not B and S2) in Figure 1. The existence of the physical substrate therefore does not necessarily indicate the existence of an associated quirk. Conversely, quirks are entirely dependent on their physical substrate. There is no way for them to exist except as a by-product of a physical interaction.

While such situations are seen in all types of organisms, this is not to say that all biological processes operate in this way. For many the direct billiard-ball type of response suffices. Take, for instance, the growth of a plant shoot. If this encounters an obstruction, then its progress will be redirected by physical interaction between the object and the plant. Growing in the direction of the sun, on the other hand, could not be realized using such physical mechanisms between the sun (billions of miles away) and the plant. Yet, it is clear that what ultimately determines the outcome is the position of the sun relative to the growing tip. Achieving this response therefore requires a sensor mechanism to operate as an intermediary between an external factor and a response system.

This specific example starts with photosensitive cells spread over the surface of the shoot responding to light intensity by releasing the hormone auxin, the differential concentration of which causes cells on the darker side of the stem to elongate more than those on the lighter side. It is not the physical properties of the auxin molecule that the system responds to, but the quirks associated with it that carry information about the sun's position.

Such distinctions are also seen in the organism's internal processes. On the one hand, we have purely physicochemical processes such as the production of the cell's primary energy source, adenosine triphosphate. While this is a fairly complex process, it involves no more than a set of chemical reactions that will inherently take place when the required ingredients are brought together. On the other hand, we have hormonal control systems. Characteristic of these systems is that the condition and the response are in different parts of the organism, making direct physical interaction impossible. Instead, a messenger molecule is used to bridge the distance and connect the two. One example is insulin, which is produced by cells in the pancreas in response to detected blood sugar levels and has its effect in the liver and fat tissue. Hormones are called messenger molecules for good reason: it is not the molecule that is of functional importance but the message (quirk) that it carries.

These systems are highly selective. We have seen that every physical interaction produces quirks, but only a marginal fraction of these quirks is relevant to the organism. What evolution has necessarily done is to frugally create systems that are sensitive to the very limited number of differences that actually make a difference, while ignoring the vast majority that do not. This has resulted in systems exploiting a range of quirks concerning factors that are available, relevant, and for which a sensor mechanism could be constructed. In this way, through the course of evolution living organisms have become ever more capable of using captured information about internal and external factors to generate responses that further their survival.

Significantly, this characteristic cannot arise spontaneously in physical systems. An evolutionary (or design) process is required to create systems in which component states are taken not on face value but to represent some other state. It is for this reason that they are only seen in biological organisms and technologies designed by them.

At this point a 'So what?' response is still understandable. It is quite possible to provide a complete functional explanation for these systems without so much as a mention of the role of information. Indeed, it could be argued that evolution has done little more than create a physical process that can be, but need not be, viewed in this way. At the same time, it is clear that something different is going on. After all, as can be seen in the above examples, it is easy to distinguish between processes that employ representative information in this way and those that operate purely on the basis of physical interaction. When a component can be replaced with another component with different physical properties without altering the function of the system, then it belongs to the category of informational systems.

2.2.2 Neuronal interaction: from specific to generic

Evolution would not be evolution if it did not build on its previous successes. For all of their value, systems employing messenger molecules have a significant limitation. Since each messenger can carry only one type of quirk and specific mechanisms are required to convert each stimulus to a required response, an entirely new physical system needs to be evolved for each information-based process. Evolution's solution to this inconvenience was the neuron: the electrically excitable cell.

The start and endpoints of neuron-based response mechanisms are still specific. Light-sensitive cells respond exclusively to light of a particular frequency while touch sensors react only to mechanical pressure. In this sense, they are comparable to the sensory cells described in the previous paragraph. The difference is that both respond in the same way: not by releasing a specific chemical messenger but by releasing the same neurotransmitters at their synapses to transfer their quirks to the response mechanism.

On the system's output, side most neurons stimulate muscles with a particular function in the musculoskeletal system. Some influence other specific bodily functions. For instance, neurons in the pineal gland regulate the secretion of melatonin, a hormone involved in the sleep-wake cycle and circadian rhythms. So here, too, we see specific physical responses based on different information. The distinction is that in all of these cases, the quirks are carried by the same types of neurotransmitters released by upstream neurons.

The fact that these systems do not employ exclusive messaging molecules means that another method was needed to ensure that each input results in the required output. The solution evolution found was to lay down insulated connections (axons) between input and output neurons. Since neurons only have an effect on other neurons with which they have synaptic connections, this allows quirks to be specifically channelled and contained within a particular response system. The axons of neurons carrying very different quirks can even run alongside each other without cross-talk interfering with the responses they mediate. This is also far more efficient: rather than broadcasting quirks over the entire body by spreading hormones though the circulatory system, a directed message can be delivered to a specific target cell.

The use of the same mechanism to couple stimulus and response allows the two to be connected using generic interneurons. These all work in the same way, responding to neurotransmitters released from upstream neurons by generating action potentials from their synapses to pass this response on to downstream neurons. This makes interneurons information agnostic: they can pass on any quirk and thus support the coupling of any sensory input to any response (Figure 2).

These systems distinguish themselves in another important way. The fact that a neuron's axons can be centimetres long – extreme distances at a cellular level – affects the relationship between the functional location of quirks and the physical location of the cells they are associated with. Intercellular interactions usually require direct physical or chemical contact between neighbouring cells. With information transfer by axon, on the other hand, a direct informational relationship

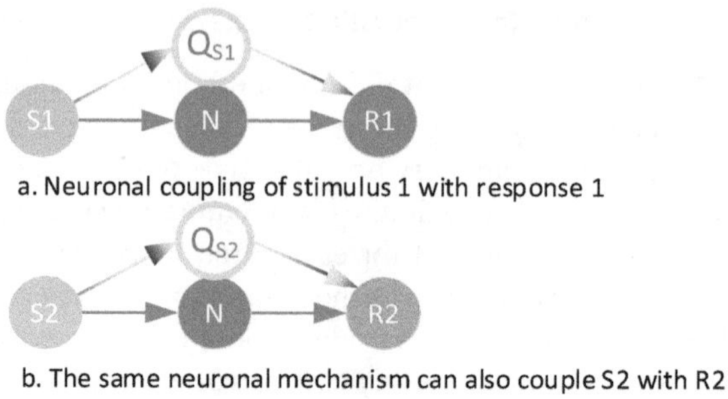

Figure 2 As generic carriers of information-based quirks, the same neuronal mechanism can be used to couple different stimuli and responses.

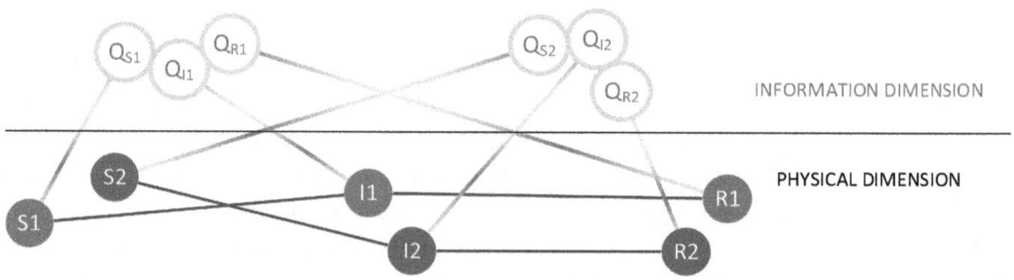

Figure 3 The functional location of quirks does not correspond to the physical locations of the neurons they are associated with. Those associated with neighbouring sensory neurons S1 and S2 are distant, while those associated with distant sensory neuron S1 and response neuron R1 are proximal.

can be created between cells that are separated by considerable distances. Functionally speaking, the physical distance between the neurons becomes irrelevant. Viewed from the perspective of their associated quirks, axons cause distant cells to become neighbours. Conversely, the quirks associated with neighbouring neurons will lack functional proximity if their associated neurons are not connected. In this way, compact informational systems can be created that are physically distributed over the entire organism (Figure 3).

An additional advantage of neurons is that the use of electrical impulses rather than diffusion through body fluids increases the speed with which quirks can be transported around the body. The classic example is seen in reflexes, in which sensory and motor neurons are directly connected to generate near-immediate responses.

In these examples, the linear transmission between neurons means that there is still a one-to-one relationship between physical states and their associated quirks, allowing a complete explanation to be given purely from the physical perspective. Consideration of the system from an informational perspective can still be considered superfluous even though it is the information, and not the physical state, that is the causative factor.

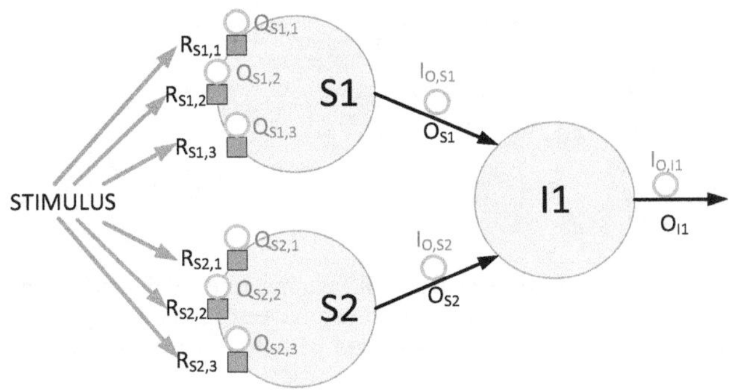

Figure 4 The combination of inputs to sensory cells via an interneuron viewed from a physical perspective.

2.2.3 Neuronal networks: from connection to (de)construction

Up to this point, evolution had succeeded in creating a more efficient, faster, generic way for the organism to exploit quirks to generate a diversity of specific stimulus-response mechanisms at a distance. Such systems still cannot produce integrated responses to combined sensory information. However, the directed transmission of quirks between neurons through synaptic connection had the potential to remove this limitation. It opened the possibility of one-to-many and many-to-one connections between neurons to form networks in which quirks can combine and interact. In this way, evolution introduced cross-talk and broke the isolation of the quirk.

The combination of quirks this permits does not necessarily result in anything radically new: it can be no more than a solution to the scaling problem faced by larger organisms in which individual sensory molecules or cells are replaced by multicellular sensory organs. Even to maintain the same functionality, the responses of all of these cells needed to be combined. The simplest, two-cell version of this is schematically illustrated in Figure 4. Viewed as a physical system, we see two sensory cells (S), each with a number of receptor molecules (R) which interact with a particular external stimulus. The change of state caused by this interaction generates an outgoing action potential (O). The action potentials of both sensory cells impinge on an interneuron (I) which, if and only if it receives input from both sensory cells, responds with its own output action potential indicating consensus on the existence of the stimulus.

This situation looks rather different when viewed from an informational perspective (Figure 5). There we see that the most basic, indivisible information entities (quirks) associated with changed receptor states are combined additively to form the information that the stimulus is sufficient to cause an action potential in a sensory cell. Subsequently, this information is combined to create the next level: the Boolean AND information that both inputs have been detected. This information is associated with the output of the interneuron.

While there is clearly more going on in this system than in those discussed in the previous paragraph, the result is still a one-to-one relationship between a

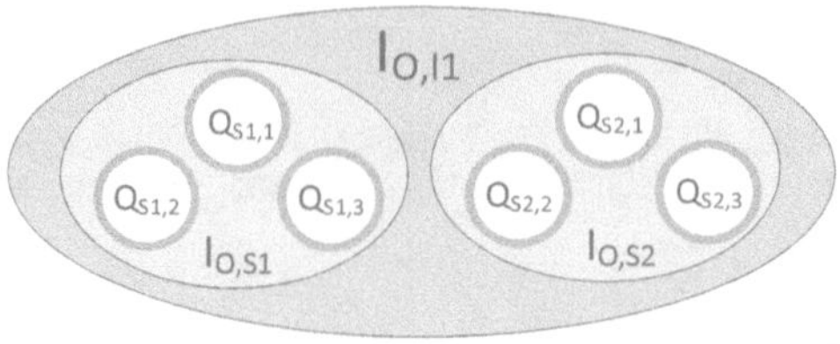

Figure 5 The same situation viewed from the perspective of the information dimension. Two levels of additive combination can be seen: from the quirks associated with receptors to the information associated with the cell, and from this to the information associated with the network.

stimulus and a response. As such the necessity to consider this as anything more than a sequence of physical events remains limited. Having said this, the difference between the two viewpoints has increased considerably. Comparison of Figures 4 and 5 demonstrates a further separation between physical and informational locality. The receptor molecules are located on the surface of the sensory cell, which may be some distance from the axon carrying the output of the interneuron. Their quirks, in contrast, are not at a distance from the information associated with this output. Indeed, they are a part of it. The AND information is constructed from them through two levels of combination. In order for this to be the case, they must be in the same place, indicating that this place cannot correspond to the physical location of the neuronal states they are associated with. Given a choice between these different viewpoints, the fact that these systems have an informational rather than a physical function makes it more appropriate to choose the latter.

The information produced by this three-cell network would be still of limited value to an organism. It provides little more than consensus on a threshold input intensity. Even the simplest of visual systems, such as those seen in jellyfish, go further by comparing information from several light-sensitive organs to determine the external light gradient, thus allowing the jellyfish to swim towards or away from the dark. This is functionally comparable to the hormone-based ability of a plant shoot to grow towards the sun, but now mediated by a neural network. On the one hand, then, it may seem that evolution has not made much progress, simply producing the same result using a different mechanism. However, this very fact has a deeper significance by demonstrating an important feature of biological information systems. The fact that they evolve to perform informational rather than physical functions means that the mechanisms used are unimportant. A completely different type of physical system (hormonal or neural) can be used, as long as this allows the associated quirks to do what is required of them. This is fundamentally different from the situation in organs with physical functions, in which the creation of function requires mechanisms with appropriate physical properties. For instance, even though the two organs are relatively similar in performing circulatory functions, it is not possible for the heart to pump air or the lungs to pump blood. The differences in physical properties between liquid blood and gaseous air necessitate specific and distinct physical mechanisms.

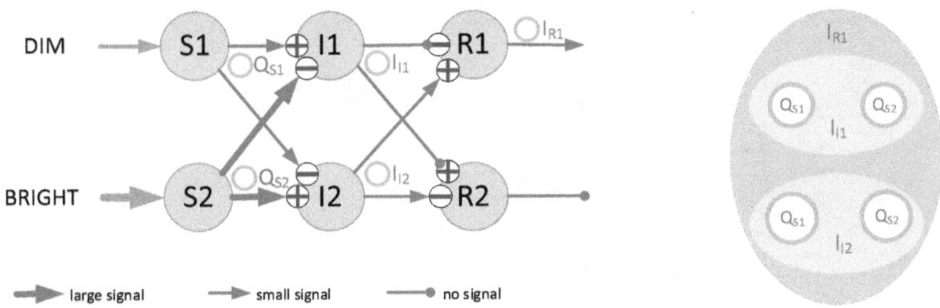

Figure 6 A simple circuit comparing two inputs, in this case light intensities, viewed from a physical (left) and informational (right) perspective.

The example of comparison of light intensities in the plant shoot and the jellyfish already takes a step beyond the additive combination of inputs. Figure 6 shows a simple neural circuit with this capability, based on a combination of excitatory and inhibitory connections. Viewed from a physical perspective, we see the bright light on S2 resulting in a strong excitatory effect on I2 and a strong inhibitory effect on I1; the weaker input to S1 leads to weaker effects. As a consequence, I2 is stimulated to generate an output while I1 is suppressed. If instead S1 received the brighter input, the situation would be reversed. If both received the same intensity, the excitatory and inhibitory effects would be equal, and neither I1 nor I2 would generate output. The fact that I2 is stimulated and I1 is not causes R1 to be stimulated is and only if S1 received a stronger input than S1.

Here, we see a new facet of the distinction between the informational and physical perspectives. The output of S1 carries the information Q_{S1} that it has received a weak input; Q_{S2} that S2 has received a strong input. While the effects of these inputs to I1 and I2 are different, the fact that they carry the same quirks (Q_{S1} and Q_{S2}) means that I1 and I2 carry the same information, in spite of being in different states. This information is, however, still ambiguous. It is only when I_{I1} and I_{I2} combine in a subsequent response system (R1) that the information about the external difference between the light falling on S2 and S1 is confirmed (I_{R1}), allowing the animal to respond with confidence that this is indeed the case. What is notable here is that the lack of output from I1 also contributes to this process by contributing information (I_{I1}). In physical systems, something that doesn't happen can never have an effect, in information systems an absence can also have a causative influence.

While the function of this system can still be explained on the basis of electrical currents passing through a circuit, it is clear that, compared to the simple additive functions illustrated in Figures 4 and 5, physical and informational structure and function have grown even further apart.

This simple example demonstrates the necessity for a minimum number of components to generate a particular effect. If the outputs (or lack thereof) of I1 and I2 were to be used in isolation, they could lead to incorrect conclusions and therefore responses. The lack of output from I1 could, for instance, also be due to S1 and S2 receiving the same light intensities whereby neither is stimulated.

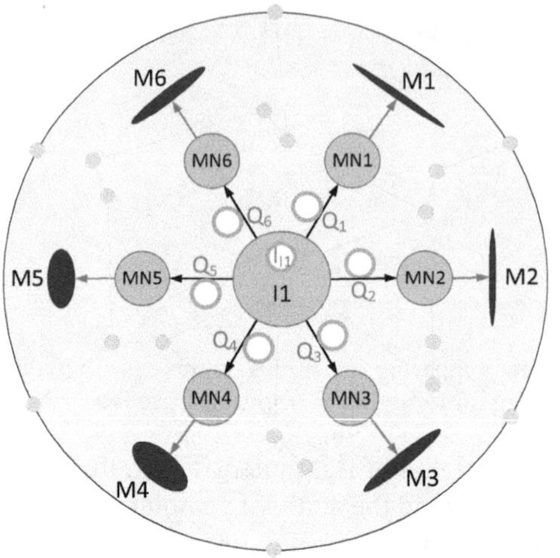

Figure 7 Decomposition of a required physical response into coordinated actions of various muscles: a simplified version of a jellyfish changing direction. The intention (I_{I1}) arising from the processing of sensory input (grey) generates differentiated instructions (Q_x) to various motor neurons (MNx) to contract or relax muscles (Mx).

The generation of unambiguous, accurate and reliable information therefore requires networks of a complexity that is proportional with the sensory detail required.

Such information about external differences that make a difference to the organism is just one prerequisite for more subtle and specific responses that better support the animal's survival and success. It would be worthless without the ability to produce specific, complex responses. Even without neurons organisms are capable of a limited range of graded and differentiated responses. As we saw in plant phototropism, cells elongating at different rates depending on the information they receive about relative light intensity can allow the plant to grow towards the light. In response to a nutrient gradient, a bacterium can move forward, backward or tumble by using this information to determine whether to rotate its flagella clockwise, anticlockwise or in mixed directions. Here, simple distinctions lead to simple responses.

The use of neural networks to generate behaviour in multicellular animals starts with comparably simple functions. Returning to the example of directional swimming in the jellyfish, the light gradient perceived on the sensory side needs to be converted into differentiated responses of radial muscles. To this end, the result of the decision-making process is broken down into individual instructions for muscle fibres to either contract or not (Figure 7). At the output interface between the informational and the physical we are, then, back to indivisible quirks associated with individual states. Here, however, causation is reversed. While on the sensory side an external physical effect leads to the creation of an associated quirk, here a quirk leads to the creation of an associated physical response.

Again, while the function of this system can be completely explained on the basis of the physical events taking place, the reason for these events cannot be found here. It is the information associated with the state of I1, and not the state of I1 itself, that determines the differential actions of the muscles. After all, there is nothing about the physical state itself that relates to the jellyfish turning left rather than right. The information associated with this state, on the other hand, provides a clear explanation for why the network is wired the way it is.

2.2.4 Information combination and emergence

A general characteristic of the evolutionary transition to multicellularity was the allocation of intracellular functions to organs. While in microbes a biological function is performed by a molecular process, in multicellular organisms the same function requires the construction of an organ with a specific physiology composed of many cells of different types. The function does not exist in any of the individual cells, but is an emergent feature of the organ as a whole. A heart muscle cell cannot pump blood, nor even can a heart valve. It is only when all of the parts of the heart are brought together in a specific way that the organism has a way of creating vascular circulation. Viewed exclusively from the cellular level, this circulation is a meaningless concept: it is only when a set of components with the required physical properties are brought together in a specific way that it even exists as a phenomenon.

Such complex structures with strongly emergent functional properties are only seen in biological organisms. This is because they can only come to exist as a product of evolutionary processes operating over deep time periods. This is neither coincidental nor trivial: without this degree of functional emergence organisms could not exist at all.

We have seen that the transition to multicellularity had a comparable effect on the organism's sensory and motor capabilities. Responses based on the quirks associated with states of individual sensor molecules in microbes were necessarily replaced by sense organs in multicellular organisms. This upscaling does not necessarily lead to emergent phenomena. Simple additive combination only results in more of the same. However, we also saw that such combination of quirks can lead to the creation of types of information that cannot exist at the underlying level.

In the example of the jellyfish, there is already something brewing in the quirk layer that covers the physical dimensions. Evolution has taken a significant step in building a system whose behaviour is based not on single quirks associated with individual states, but on derived information compiled from many such quirks. In this way, the jellyfish is able to reconstruct a highly relevant feature of its physical environment – which direction is upwards, towards the surface and the sun – allowing it to respond in a way that furthers its survival and success.

Taking a further step forward, evolution added more light receptors, arranging them in the two-dimensional arrays seen in the retina, and vastly increased the number of interneurons to create a visual cortex. Such numbers serve to increase the necessity for consolidation but also, more significantly, the potential for information processing. Here, specific network topologies go beyond the recognition of gradients to support the reconstruction of a diversity of visible features in the outside world such as edges, textures and motion. These are also information phenomena built from the quirks associated with individual receptor states, but on a far larger scale and higher levels of organization.

To make a comparison between informational quirks and physical quarks, the systems described in the previous paragraph are comparable to the creation of atoms. While a hydrogen atom has emergent properties that are not present in the three quarks it is built from, the distinction is not great and it is relatively easy to derive the latter from the former. Taking a step further, the relationship between the properties of a water molecule and the 30 quarks it is composed of is less direct, partly because of the increased numbers, but also because of the required intermediary atomic level of organization. Its properties are not the result of the combination of those of quarks, but of those of atoms composed of quarks. The next step upwards, to bulk properties of liquid water such as surface tension and fluid dynamics, takes us into a realm that is entirely alien to the quarks from which they are ultimately composed.

As the scale of neural networks increased from tens to billions of neurons and even more synaptic connections, so too did the numbers of quirks and combinatorial possibilities. Managing and exploiting these huge numbers inevitably required the sequential creation of a number of levels of organization, each with its own emergent properties that form the basis for the next level. With the distinction, of course, that with quirks being non-physical, non-detectable entities, the same applies to the entities built from them. Consequently, even when it is possible to identify the quirks associated with a particular physical state, this will tell us little about the emergent phenomena they are a part of. As in physical systems, the properties at the highest levels that constitute the purpose of the system will be entirely alien to those of the fundamental quirks from which the entire construct is built.

One example of such combinatorial emergence relates to the integration of different types of sensory input. This permits the construction of a multisensory reconstruction of the animal's surroundings in which visual, auditory, olfactory and tactile features are united. The full experience of the flickering flames, the smell of the smoke, the crackle of the burning wood and the heat of a bonfire is something that neither of the senses could produce in isolation. The advantage of such sensory integration to the organism of such a capability is self-evident. This enriched reconstruction allows it to accurately negotiate its physical surroundings, recognizing opportunities and threats. Through the course of evolution this function has consequently become one of the most effective and essential informational functions of living organisms.

Even here, the staunch physicalist could claim that brain's informational functions are no more than an abstract, passive derivative of physical processes. However, given the fact that the physical substrate can be substituted as long as it supports the same informational processes, a reversal of this primacy is appropriate. The fact that the nature, structure and characteristics of these phenomena can be explained on the basis of the combination of component parts over several levels of organization also shows them to be more than fleeting figurative figments of the imagination. Instead, they present themselves as a collection of ordered, rule-based entities and processes that are in many ways systemically comparable to those seen in the physical dimensions. In this sense they are equally deserving of the term 'real'. The non-detectability of these phenomena should not be seen as proof of their non-existence as real phenomena, but evidence that everything that is real is not physical.

On the output side of the brain, the evolutionary expansion of the scale of neural networks supported the creation of far more complex behavioural responses. For instance, motility in an insect involves the coordination of each of its six limbs. Even the simple action of moving forwards requires timed instructions to numerous muscles in each limb. Turning towards or away from a particular element of the animal's surroundings involves an adaptation of this basic mechanical function. Many animals also employ various gaits to move at different speeds, such as the horses walk, trot, canter and gallop, each involving different cycles of muscular activity. Beyond locomotion, these developments led to the possibility of the entire range of observed essential, specific and purposeful behaviours from the spinning of a spider's web to the sexually parasitic mating behaviour of a male angler fish.

All of these behaviours are ultimately based on quirks giving instructions to muscles fibres through the neural impulses they are associated with. At this most fundamental level, there is a one-to-one relationship between informational and physical events. However, each is subservient to the larger scale phenomena it is a part of, and whose emergent characteristics are what matters to the organism. Both the individual quirk and the individual muscle contraction are only of any value in this broader context.

As schematically demonstrated in Figure 8, this means that functional emergence is seen on both the informational and the physical side, but that the two are only coupled at the lowest level at which quirks determine the smallest scale of muscular responses. While the informational intention (I_2) relates to the integrated response produced (R_2), their nature and the way in which they are constructed from these fundamental elements are entirely different. On the physical side, it is physical interaction between muscle contractions that leads to first-level functional components and subsequently to the final result. On the informational side, it is informational interactions between the quirks that lead to the construction of higher level informational functions.

The transition between the high-level informational intention to turn right and the high-level physical action consequently necessitates informational decomposition that results in physical recomposition.

The ability to generate complex responsive behaviours is anything but a marginal phenomenon. It necessarily evolved alongside the anatomical changes required to execute them. There is no point in having limbs unless you have the ability to produce coordinated instructions on the basis of which they can be used to produce motion that is in the interest of the organism. Again, to consider this aspect the organism as unreal is to negate its essential and integral evolutionary significance.

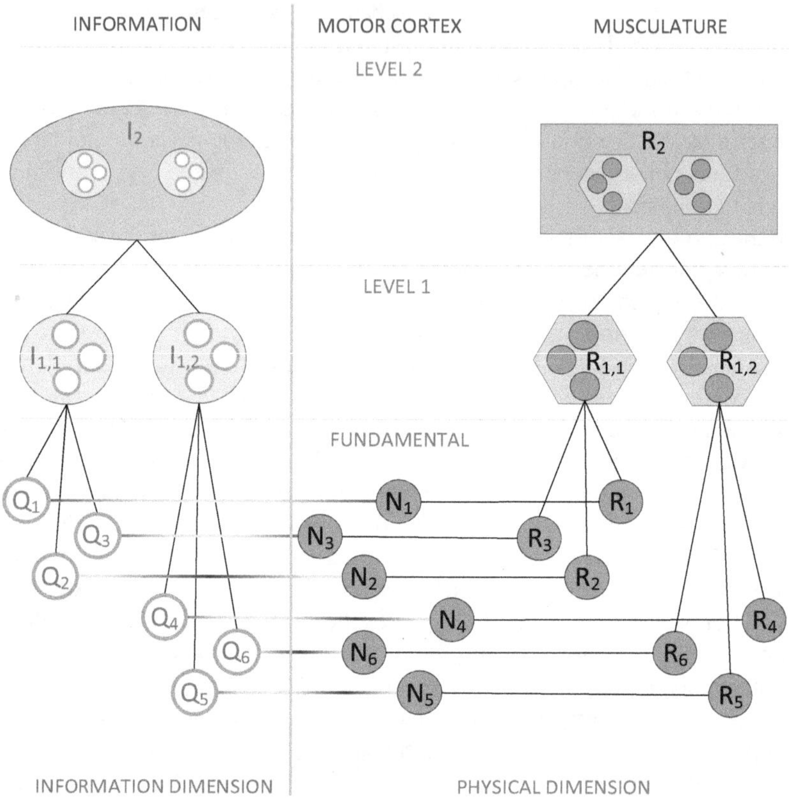

Figure 8 A symbolic representation of the emergent levels of organization on the informational and physical side of responses orchestrated by the motor cortex. At the fundamental level, quirks (Q) associated with neural impulses (N) are connected to micromuscular contractions (R). On both sides, fundamentals are organized in sequential levels of organization to reach phenomena that are meaningful to the organism.

2.2.5 Information storage: memory

The ability to construct emergent informational entities and processes from the fundamental quirks associated with neural states is not only useful for the real-time generation of responses to current inputs. The quirks and structures created need not be used immediately: they can also be stored for later use in the form of memory.

The fact that memory is so central to our day-to-day functions can lead us to underestimate what a remarkable phenomenon it is in allowing previous events to influence current actions. This is also something that is not possible in physical systems, where that which happens can only be a product of current interactions. It is trivial to point out that a billiard ball cannot suddenly be jolted into motion by a ball that rolled across the table the day before, but learning to play billiards effectively facilitates such effects. Remembering previous shots allows the player to repeat those that were successful and avoid past mistakes. This is possible because recalling a memory of the original experience is realized by reconstructing it using the same combinations of quirks, which have been stored but latent in the intervening period. Here, again, it is relevant that 'the map is not the territory'. Reconstructing the original physical event is not possible; reconstructing its representation in the information dimension is.

Memory provides further evidence for the distinction between external events and our sensory perception of them. While a memory may not be as vivid as the original experience and is not hard-wired to the timing and content of sensory input, it is of the same nature. It is based on the same information and experienced, albeit to a lesser degree, in the same way. In addition to using individual memories in this way, a further advantage is that they can be combined to detect trends and extract general principles. The observable causative effect of memory on behaviour is further strong evidence for the acknowledgement of informational phenomena as real. While the direct coupling of sensory input to motor output could plausibly be brushed of as a sequence of physical events, this explanation cannot be used to explain away the effects of prior events.

The advantage of this capability over and above the immediate response to incoming impulses is self-evident, allowing animals to avoid threats and seek opportunities on the basis of previous experiences. There is, however, a cost involved. Since the storage of a memory requires a permanent allocation of the neural states associated with their component quirks, memory capacity is dependent on brain size. Those animals that cannot afford or house a large brain will therefore necessarily have limited memories. Here, we also see a distinction between short- and long-term memory, whereby the former only temporarily requires and reserves such capacity.

The memory capacity of large brained vertebrates such as humans is extensive and is supplemented by the possibility of extension in the other direction: into the future. By constructing predictions about what has not yet happened, it is possible to preemptively prepare for what is to come, and to plan interventions that will change some future situation. This is again something that is not possible on the basis of direct physical interactions in the here and now.

2.2.6 Dimensionality of the brain's information content

Through acknowledging and explaining the existence of quirks and quirk-based entities and processes as non-physical, EIT grants them the required literal existence. Accepting them as such does, of course, necessitate expansion of the boundaries of that which is real beyond the physical to include the entire range of informational content created by living organisms through the operation of their nervous systems. It also requires a place for these phenomena to exist.

We have seen that the brain's quirks are directly connected to physical neuronal states, but that this does not mean that they share the same functional location or dimensionality. When considering this difference, we can take one of two approaches. The first takes the point of view of its physical substrate, the brain.

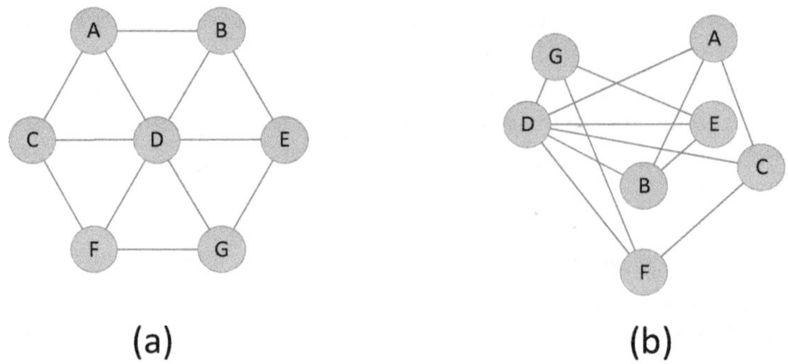

Figure 9 Nodes in hexagonal close packing (a) and a random network (b) in which this same form is present but geometric location no longer corresponds with the two dimensions in which the nodes are located.

This already makes it clear that the brain is radically different from other organs, whose functions invariably ensue from interactions arising from physical contact between neighbouring cells. Instead, the use of axons of variable lengths allows cells almost anywhere in the brain to connect, interact and thus together contribute to a particular function as effective neighbours. On the other hand, neighbouring cells that are not interconnected will have no functional relationship. Even viewed from a physical perspective, then, the brain does not operate in three neat orthogonal dimensions, but in the highly convoluted topology of a small world network.

Figure 9 demonstrates this for the simple example of seven nodes at equal distance – the recognizable regular configuration of two-dimensional hexagonal close packing. In a network, as long as the connections remain the same, physical distance becomes irrelevant and the nodes can be located anywhere in physical space. On this basis, the randomized network in Figure 9b contains exactly the same form in spite of the fact that node G, which is bottom right in the first case, has moved to top left. Even in this most basic of examples, we see that the physical location of a node is quite irrelevant.

In this specific case, the hidden form is two-dimensional, making it possible to rearrange the nodes in such a way that the hexagonal form is restored. The network can in this way be 'flattened' to two dimensions. However, this is no necessity or even tendency for such networks. In general, the topologies of such networks, being effectively unrestrained, will be far more complex. In Figure 10a, the nodes are in exactly the same location as in Figure 9b but the connections have been altered. As a result, it is no longer possible to represent the form of the network in two dimensions with connections of equal length, as demonstrated in Figure 10b. Instead, it has a more complex dimensionality that is typical of this type of network.

It is plausible that this simple example could be plotted in three dimensions. Since we are used to living in a three-dimensional world, envisaging some of the nodes coming out of or sinking into the page to make the connections equal lengths is relatively easy. Then Figure 10b can almost be seen as a three-dimensional cube. However, this is only the start. Figure 11a shows a projection of a regular

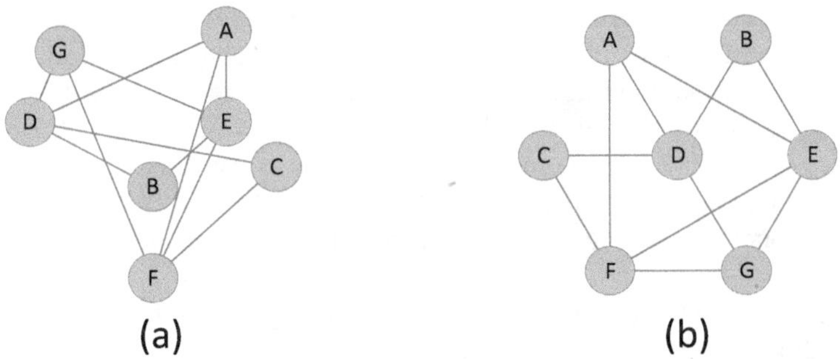

Figure 10 (a) Altering the connections between the nodes of Figure 9 (b) results in a form which can no longer be 'flattened' into two dimensions in such a way that all connections have the same length (b).

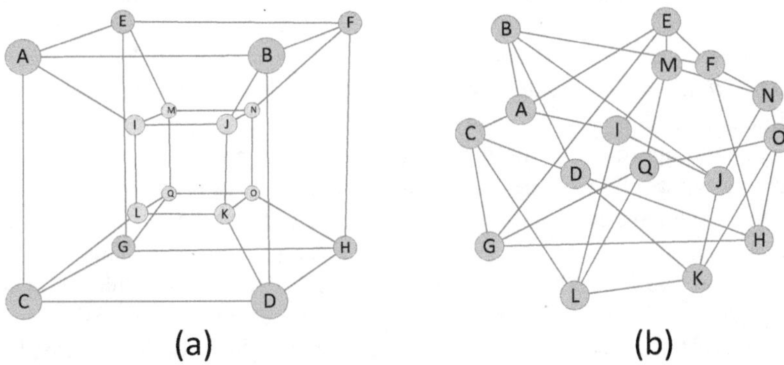

Figure 11 A 4-dimensional cube as it appears projected onto two dimensions (a) and in a randomized network (b).

four-dimensional cube, or tesseract, onto the two flat dimensions of the page. In this geometrical form, all of the connections are actually the same length, making the cube in the middle just as big as the outside cube. The reason it looks smaller is because it is further away in the fourth dimension. All that is required to create this structure in a network is to join 16 nodes with 32 connections. Figure 11b shows the result of randomising the position of the nodes without changing the connections. The tesseract is just as present, but it is now impossible to see any geometrical regularity. The flat two-dimensional network as printed on this page has no trouble containing this four-dimensional form, nor would it have any problem supporting regular or irregular structures of any other dimensionality. Similarly, the three-dimensional networks of the brain can support the existence of any number of high-dimensional spaces and forms far more exotic than the tesseract. All that is required is an appropriate degree of connectivity.

The example of higher dimensional cubes illustrates two geometrical features of such networks. The first is the effect of the number of connections per node. In a 2-D square, each corner is connected to two perpendicular edges; in a 3-D cube with three; and in a 4-D tesseract with 4. In these, regular geometric forms, then, more connections lead to more dimensions. The second is that the volume of these forms can be greater than that of the network in which they exist. A 2-D square with sides of length 2 has an area of 4; a 3-D cube of the same size has a volume of 8; a 4-D cube has a volume of 16 and a 5-D cube 32. In other words, by increasing dimensionality, networks can create geometrical volumes far greater than their own size.

It is specifically the use of connections of varying length that permits this situation. Ordinarily, there are geometrical limits to the number of entities that can be in contact with each other. In the case of hexagonally close-packed spherical objects, it is six in two dimensions and 12 in 3 dimensions. These are typical of the numbers of cells that can be in contact and interact in cellular tissues. The same applies to grid-based networks in which only neighbouring nodes are connected. This is radically different from the thousands of connections that many neurons make in the brain. Furthermore, being organic rather than designed the brain does not limit itself to such neat and regular topologies as that of the *n*-dimensional cube. Different parts of the brain may also have very different network topologies and dimensionalities.

The second approach to the dimensionality of the brain's information content is from the perspective of the informational entities and processes generated by it. Of these, we have seen that some parts are regrettably inaccessible but others (our conscious experiences) are at least subjectively observable. This begins with qualia such as the proverbial redness of the rose. A rose may reflect light with a wavelength of 700 nm but the redness of a rose is not a property of the rose, it is a construct of the brain. The rose continues to exist when you look away, but the redness disappears as the light stops triggering retinal cells to send red quirks into the visual cortex. The reflected light also causes more than just redness to be created. Additional features such as the nested curl of its petals and the shadows cast combine to form a three-dimensional reconstruction that, like the redness, cannot be detected in the brain because it is an emergent informational phenomenon.

Neural networks destroy any correlation between physical and informational location. It is not so that the visual reconstruction of the rose resides in some equivalent space in the visual cortex. While the primary visual cortex does have a direct spatial mapping with the retina, as we move deeper into the brain the relationship between neural location and location of the information about the visual field that it is associated with breaks down entirely. It is not so that a neuron associated with information about an object in the bottom left of the visual field will be found in the bottom left of the visual cortex. We can therefore conclude that, in spite of the reconstruction being three-dimensional in order to accurately represent that which it is modelling, this bears no relation to the three dimensions of the visual cortex. Instead, it is a portion of the multidimensional space created by the brain that has been created in such a way as to have this property.

Apart from this sensory reconstruction, our conscious experiences contain a diversity of additional content: from emotions to thoughts, memories to plans, ideas to theories. While some of these may be related to aspects of our sensory reconstruction – for instance the fear of seeing a spider – they do not have the same dimensionality. Our sensory reconstruction of the roof of a house is larger and higher than its front door, but such qualities are meaningless when applied to the non-sensory content of our information dimensions. While we may talk about higher morals or base instincts, huge generosity or narrow mindedness, these terms are used in a purely figurative sense. It is not so that a distance can be measured between the morals and the instincts, or that generosity can be too big to fit in a box.

These informational thoughts and emotions appear to be 'inside' us, often in a rather visceral sense when they have an effect on our bodies. We can feel the chill of fear throughout our bodies, be gutted by bad news and have our hearts broken; but this is clearly through the perception of our body's response, rather than the actual location of the causative emotion. Less emotive phenomena such as the thoughts elicited by reading this book create the impression of being 'in our heads', but then not in the literal sense. While we now have a fairly good idea of which parts of the brain are involved in which functions, it is not so that you stop reading for a moment to consider this statement, you experience these thoughts as existing at a particular place inside your skull. The inevitable conclusion is that none of these phenomena, while eminently real and of the most primary importance to us, can be located in physical space.

All of these complex informational phenomena arise at high levels of organization and are composed of large numbers of the quirks associated with the states and activities of multiple neurons. This composition means that these neurons must be connected, and as such will be proximal in the network topography of the connectome. Within this dimensionality, then, these phenomena have a defined locality, even though this bears no relation to the physical dimensions of the brain. While some of the physical states involved may be micrometres apart, others may be on opposite sides of the brain. Similarly, a phenomenon composed of millions of quirks will, in the information dimension, be larger than one composed of thousands, but these scale differences do not equate directly to the volume occupied in the brain. Phenomena of the same size can be distributed over large areas or concentrated in a specific place.

This dislocation between physical and network dimensionalities makes it even more difficult to observe the informational phenomena associated with the brain's function. Not only are they non-detectable; the locations of the physical states on which they are based do not even correspond with the locations of their associated information. Together these factors explain why it is not possible to see the structures and processes underlying the brain's functions by cracking open a skull and looking at it in the way that it is possible with, for instance, the functions of the kidney.

In conclusion, it is in the brain's network-based dimensionality that the quirks associated with physical states exist, interact and combine to generate the higher level informational functions of the brain. The multidimensional topology of these neural networks creates an information dimension that is massively larger by volume than the brain itself, creating space enough to accommodate all of the conscious and non-conscious content of the mind.

2.2.7 Structural causation and control

The preceding paragraphs show that the function of nervous systems is not determined by the physical properties of their component cells but by the connectivity patterns between them. What is also clear is that these patterns do not serve to produce a physical function but to create, transfer and combine quirks in such a way that the high-level emergent informational entities and processes are created that are required by the organism to produce appropriate responses to sensory input. These networks are consequently not random. If they were, they would produce nothing more than noise. The question that follows is how the specific connectivity patterns required are formed.

For the simplest of neural networks, such as the 302 neurons of the roundworm *Caenorhabditis elegans*, the neurons and connections are put together in the same way in all individuals. The construction of such neural networks is in this sense comparable to that of other organs. That axons need to be led through specific paths to connect to their target neurons is unique to neural networks but can be mediated through the type of chemotactic mechanisms that are generally used to appropriately position migrating cells. The fact that the product of these processes is informational rather than physical is then of lesser significance to the formative process. The end result is an organism whose fixed, quirk-based information functions and physical functions combine to support a limited number of useful responses.

These methods have their limits, and as neural networks grew by orders of magnitude, a different mechanism was required to connect their neurons. The solution was found in various forms of synaptic plasticity: the activity-based creation, strengthening, weakening and breaking of connections. This results in the alteration of connectivity patterns and thus the ways in which quirks are created and combined to form functional emergent informational entities and processes.

This new method had a significant spin-off advantage: it led to dynamic networks that allow informational functions to be developed and changed within the lifetime of an individual. This possibility is in itself remarkable and unique to the organism's informational functions. Other organs perform the same function throughout the animal's lifetime: a heart does not, for instance, suddenly develop the ability to digest food. Doing so would require alteration in the numbers, types and locations of cells with specific physical properties to create a new functional physiology: no mean feat. The functional flexibility of the brain is made possible by the fact that its cells do not perform a physical function, but the generic informational function of supporting the creation and interaction of quirks. Consequently, the brain can change its function freely without moving a single neuron by simply altering its connectivity patterns.

This unusual method of creating and changing function has significant consequences for the maintenance of function. Many cells have significantly shorter lifetimes than the organism they are a part of. Skin cells, for instance, live only for about a month. This is no problem for the function of the skin, which can easily be maintained by continual cell division producing replacement cells of the same type in the same place. The fact that brain function is based on connectivity rather than the location and physical properties of its cells means that this is not so simple for the brain. This is not because replacing the neuron would be an issue: we have, after all, seen that the neuron is a highly generic functional unit. The problem is that the new neuron would need exactly the same connections as its predecessor with nearby and distant partners, and that these connections are determined by an activity history that the new neuron lacks. As a result of this issue, neurons are among the longest lived of all cells, many surviving the full lifetime of the organism.

The crucial question is how synaptic plasticity leads to networks with the required informational properties. If this were to be a random process, it would not have this effect. There is clearly no design-and-construction involved, which leaves self-organization as the only alternative. We have seen that the self-organization of biological structure is determined by the required top-level systemic functions. However, in contrast with other organs, in the brain this systemic level is not physical but informational. There are no emergent physical structures with an interest in or dependency on which neurons are connected and which are not. In other words, it is necessary that high-level non-physical processes determine the physical structure of the network.

For this to be possible, evolution first had to weaken the influence of the otherwise dominant physical laws. This is exactly what the brain does in the connectome. Starting with an initially unconnected foetal network, there is no physical reason why any particular connection should form, strengthen, weaken or die off. In this sense, it is a completely flat thermodynamic landscape that is consequently open and susceptible to other influences.

One of the physical mechanisms used to alter connectivities is the Hebbian 'cells that fire together, wire together': a low-level mechanism that is itself functionally informational rather than physical. After all, there is no physical reason why it would be a good idea to use this method of altering connectivity. Viewed from an informational perspective, however, it is understandable: the fact that two neurons fire together tells us that the quirks they are carrying are likely to be related. Averaging this over many cycles of activity confirms this likelihood.

In this way, combinations of quirks that are active together to form higher-level informational structures will tend to be strengthened. Connections that do not contribute to such higher level entities, on the other hand, will not be concurrently active and therefore weaken and eventually break. This is exactly what is needed for these entities to exert top-down control over the development of the connectome. Through time this will lead to stable structures in the information dimension associated with specific sets of synapses. Together these processes make for a fluid, flexible and dynamic system capable of the type of constant adaptation that is essential to the brain both in its initial formative period and in the subsequent formation of new skills, memories and so forth.

Simple adaptive development would be insufficient to support the creation of features as complex, specific and diverse as consciousness, emotion, abstract thinking and language. Just as biological evolution through many generations is required to create complex yet stable biological structures, an evolutionary process within the lifetime of the organism is necessary to build the wide range of informational entities associated with its brain. Fortunately, evolution is inevitable in any situation in which variation, heredity and selection are combined, and this is exactly what we see in the brain. If we look at particular patterns of neural activity (or, more specifically, combinations of quirks), it is immediately apparent that the variation requirement is met. The high degree of connectivity and the influence of minor changes in the physiological states of participating neurons will mean that exactly the same quirk sets will seldom recur. Only in the most deeply ingrained patterns will such standardization take place. In other cases, repeat occurrences will always be slightly different. Replicative heredity is also present, in the form of the tendencies to follow the particular channels that develop through synaptic plasticity. Finally, selection is also present. In evolutionary terms, selection is a process that leads to differential probabilities of recurrence in later 'generations'. This is exactly the effect produced and supported by synaptic plasticity. Different quirk sets, and different variations within quirk sets, will in this way compete for a place in the available information space.

In the case of the connectome and its information dimension, the 'generations' over which selection takes place are the waves of activity that pass through the brain. In evolutionary terms, this gives the brain an immense advantage of an exceedingly short generation time. This is of the order of fractions of seconds rather than the years or decades that biological evolution must work with. This may seem a luxury but is in fact a necessity, since the brain's evolutionary processes need to produce results from the blank slate of a pristine foetal connectome within just days or weeks while biological evolution has thousands or millions of years to deliver.

Another remarkable feature of this developmental process is that it not only determines the informational entities and processes that are present but also, as we have seen, the dimensionality of the space in which they exist and operate. In this, too, they differ from physical evolutionary processes which are always bound to taking place within the three Euclidian dimensions of physical space. This dimensional flexibility is also a requirement of the high-level information functions, which can be governed by these functions through the mechanism of synaptic plasticity.

2.2.8 Activity and the time dimension

The previous paragraph considered the geometry of the brain's neural networks, which constitutes the dimensionality within which its associated quirks exist and interact. The way in which neurons work, however, means that only some of this available space will actually contain quirks. From a resting electrical potential of around −70 mV, incoming synaptic impulses result in cumulative excitatory post-synaptic potentials (EPSP) until, at about −55 mV, the neuron resets to its resting state by generating an action potential. The function of the brain is entirely

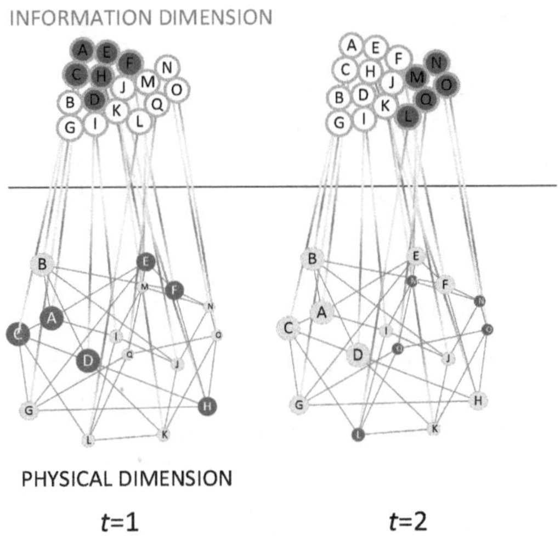

Figure 12 (a and b) At any particular moment in time only some neurons will be in a state altered by incoming signals and carry a quirk containing this information (dark). Viewed in information space (c and d), locations associated with these neurons will contain quirks (coloured), while those in a resting state will not.

based on these cycles of activity. The alteration of a neuron's electrical potential by incoming synaptic impulses creates information about its upstream neighbours: a quirk is created associated with this altered potential. Subsequently, when the neuron reaches its threshold level and discharges, returning to its resting state, this information is lost. To this, we need to add the fact that EPSPs decay over time. This means that the neuron needs to receive inputs, and do something with these inputs, sufficiently quickly. Otherwise, the information entrusted to it degrades until it is gone. In both cases, the location in the information dimension is left empty. In this sense, the brain's quirks are very different from the quarks that form the foundations of physical entities, which are not subject to decay and therefore essentially live forever.

Figure 12 illustrates this with a snapshot at two moments of time from the physical perspective of connected nodes (a and b) and from the perspective of the information dimension (c and d), for the sake of simplicity flattened to two dimensions.

The transient nature of the information associated with neural states in a dynamic network makes timing crucial. Only those quirks that exist at the same time will be able to interact with their neighbours to create higher level structures. This requirement is facilitated by the synchronization of neural activity observed in the form of brain waves with specific frequencies, and also by the background activity of neurons and pulse trains, in which a particular neuron will more continuously supply a downstream neuron with information than is possible with a single action potential.

This requirement provides an explanation for the constant and metabolically expensive activity of neurons. Evolutionary speaking, this is rather puzzling under interpretations of brain function that assume that the generation of function is a matter of electrical impulses simply following specific pathways through the connectome. If this were the case, then since the brain is only performing a tiny percentage of all of the things it can do at any particular moment in time, we would expect it to be largely silent. Instead, there is an overall constant activity throughout the brain: exactly what would be expected if what we are looking at is the continuous regeneration of the fleeting fundamental entities of an emergent information dimension.

2.2.9 Functional causation and control

A significant difference between the nervous systems of animals and their other organs is the fact that they can perform a wide variety of information functions. Even the simple 302-neuron network of the roundworm *C. elegans* allows it to respond to a range of external stimuli, such as temperature and chemical substances, allowing it to move towards favourable conditions and away from danger. In addition, it also supports feeding and mating behaviours: the basic requirements for any organism. Animals with larger brains have a far greater repertoire of information functions. Given this diversity, that fact that at any particular moment in time only one or a few of these will be appropriate, and that many responses cannot be combined and performed at the same time, a selection mechanism is required.

The direct connection between informational quirks and physical states means that they can only change together, and this creates a potential conflict (Figure 13). With influential processes potentially taking place on both sides, which of the two will take control?

From a functional point of view, we can distinguish the brain's input, inner and output regions when considering this question. The primary function of nervous

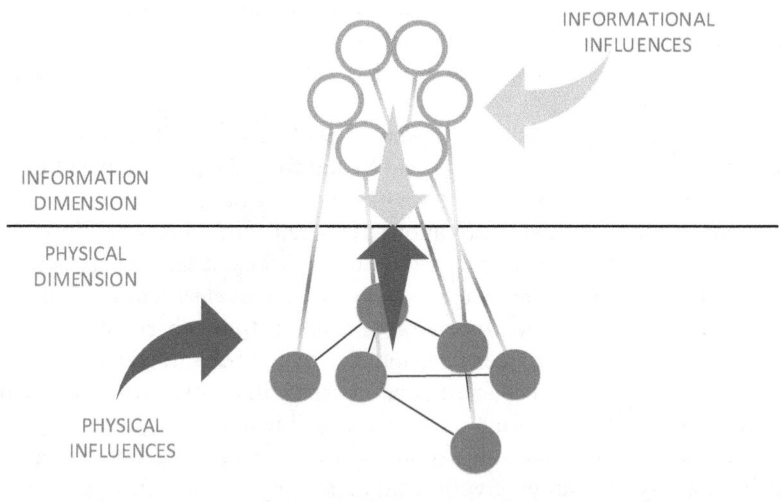

Figure 13 The coupling of quirks to physical states creates a potential conflict of interests.

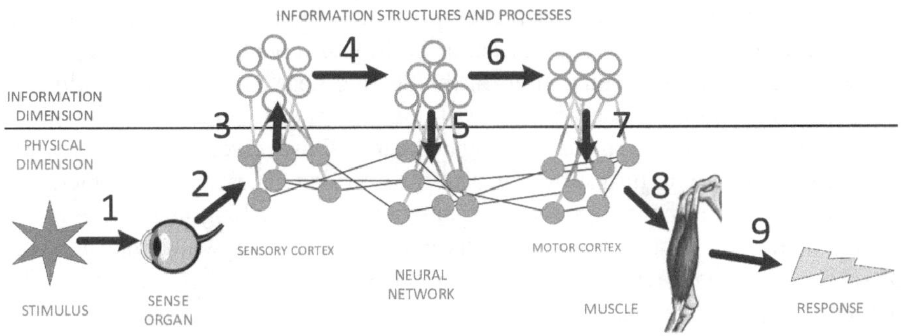

Figure 14 The causal chain from stimulus to response. 1. A stimulus is detected by a sense organ. 2. The input causes changes in the sensory cortex. 3. These changes lead to the creation of a sensory reconstruction of the stimulus. 4. The reconstruction is given context and meaning. 5. The creation of this meaning is mediated by neuronal activity. 6. The meaning results in the formulation of a response. 7. The required response is coded into motor cortex neurons. 8. The motor cortex neurons activate a muscle. 9. The muscle action produces a response.

systems – to generate appropriate responses to relevant factors in the animal's surroundings – means that their sensory interfaces are geared to having their activity determined by external stimuli. This applies directly to sensory cells being influenced by relevant factors in the environment, but also indirectly to the information processing that follows. In the visual cortex, for instance, there will be a causative correlation between features in the visual field and the activity of specific neurons. This is necessary if the sensory reconstruction is to correspond with the animal's physical surroundings. On the output side of the brain – the motor cortex – this situation needs to be reversed. Here, it is the informational conclusions drawn by the brain about required responses that should determine which motor neurons are active and, on this basis, which muscles contract to create physical effects.

In both situations, we see causative influences at work over the boundaries between the animal's physical environment and its information dimension: physical stimuli determine sensory information, and informational instructions determine physical actions. Between the sensory and motor cortexes, we have areas of the brain whose function is not directly connected to external factors, in which informational phenomena need to determine the activities of neurons (Figure 14).

The physical influence on the information generated by neural activity seen in steps 1–3 in Figure 14 is relatively easy to envisage. The information can be considered, in a comfortably traditional way, as no more than a derivative of physical events. However, in the later stages, the informational function of the brain needs to reverse this causality in such a way that its information becomes a very real and equal counterpart to its physical substrate. Indeed, here this substrate becomes no more than a means to an end, making it is more appropriate to consider the physical state as a derivative of the information it is associated with. The question is how the brain manages to turn the causal influence around in this way.

It is here that the factor of emergence comes in. The general method employed by living organisms to generate function is through control processes operating at the highest level of organization. In the beating heart, for instance, individual muscle fibres contract in accordance with the cyclical sequence of events taking place in the whole heart. The underlying biochemical processes taking place within the muscle cells are in turn subservient to the imposed necessity of contraction. It is not the case that the components are obliged to do anything that is contrary to their nature: rather that they are oblivious and agnostic to that which they are a part of. This means that their properties can be freely exploited to create the required higher level phenomenon.

The same distinction of levels is seen in the brain, with the difference that the higher level phenomena involved are not physical (like the beating heart) but informational (perceptions and intentions). It may all start with the most basic units of information associated with neuronal states, but this is not the level at which the determinative functions of the brain take place. Instead, these quirks are subservient components of larger-scale informational phenomena: for instance, an integrated action requiring coordinated muscle activity such as walking. It is these higher-level phenomena which need to determine which sets of potential actions are required and to provide the necessary component instructions, embodied in neural impulses.

This required state of affairs would have a problem if the physical states were themselves part of some emergent physical phenomenon which exerted an influence on the neuron-quirk couple that was contradictory to those on the informational side. It is for this reason that evolution created neural networks in such a way that no such physical emergence arises. There are no higher level functional physical phenomena which are dependent on and therefore have an inclination to influence specific neuronal activity. This is in sharp contrast with all other organs, such as the heart, whose physical functions are entirely dependent on their component cells performing particular roles. Here again, we see the relevance of the fact that the neural network has an entirely flat thermodynamic landscape which both permits and necessitates a different causative influence.

The combination of a strong influence on the informational side and a lack of interest on the physical side is exactly what is needed for high-level informational processes to take control of their component quirks. The fact that the neuronal activities are tightly associated with informational states and processes means that they can only follow suit. This provides the mechanism by which the brain's information functions can determine physical events and in this way use the neurons of the brain to construct the entire deep, rich and varied world of mental function (Figure 15).

Emergence does not require components to act in a way that is contrary to their own nature, and this also applies to the brain's neurons. They simply go along with higher level phenomena that their associated quirks are a part of. That they are being controlled by higher level information processes will therefore not be apparent in the form of them behaving in a way that is unexpected or not in accordance with physical laws. Just as we will see no difference between a carbon atom that is

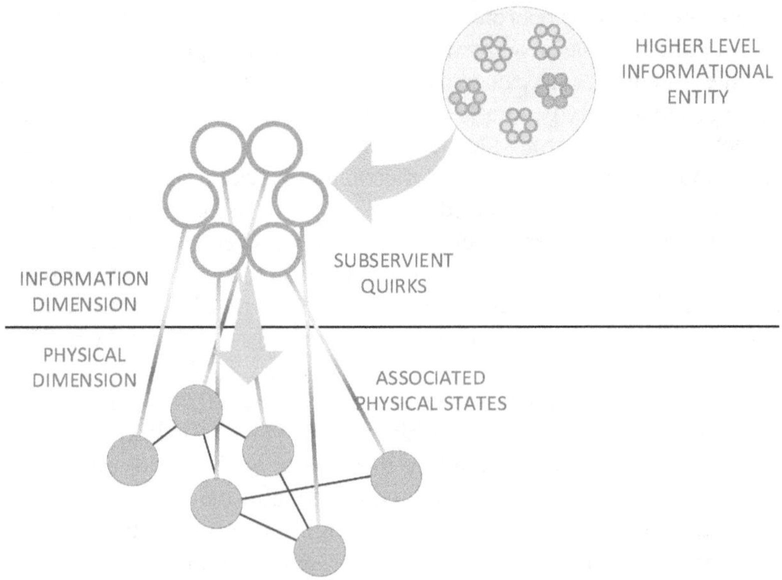

Figure 15 In the absence of emergent pressure on physical states, emergent phenomena on the informational side can exert a determinative influence on these states through their connection with the quirks involved.

part of a diamond and one that is part of a DNA molecule, we will see no difference between a neuron that is part of a perception of the colour red and one that is part of a sense of sorrow. The difference only arises at higher levels of organization.

The single level of emergence depicted in Figure 15 is of course a vast oversimplification. If we consider the size of the brain, with its billions upon billions of quirk-producing synapses, it is clearly large enough to support multiple stacked layers of informational emergence of which only the lowest level is connected to the physical substrate in this way. Being based on the informational interactions between non-physical information entities rather than physical interactions, none of these levels of organization will be visible in the physical dimensions, not even if we were able to take the viewpoint of the brain's complex network topology. After all, the patterns of neural activity themselves are not what counts: what matters is the information associated with them.

2.2.10 Spontaneous generation

The sensory and motor cortexes constitute the brain's interface with the outside world and their functions are directly related to it. The next significant evolutionary innovation arose as increase in brain size led to areas arising that are further detached from the external physical realities of sensory input and motor output. In the absence of explicit incoming information or a requirement for direct outgoing instructions, these areas have to create their own informational content out of the quirks generated by their neurons. To this end, they exhibit constant spontaneous and at least partly stochastic activation, stimulated and perpetuated by connections between these neurons that cause the activity of one to trigger activity in others. This background activity generates an ample and highly dynamic supply of quirks that do not relate to external factors. Indeed, in terms of incoming stimuli and required responses, all this activity is meaningless. Rather than conveying something like 'a retinal cell has detected the colour red', an incoming action potential really says nothing more than 'an upstream neuron has been triggered'. Particularly considering the high metabolic cost of all of this activity, it could seem odd that evolution would even permit such apparent wastefulness let alone stimulate it to the degree seen in vertebrates, primates and ultimately the human being formulating this sentence.

Viewing this situation in terms of emergent information provides a different perspective on this apparently surprising situation. It is not disadvantageous or even accidental that the quirks generated by these parts of the brain are 'information neutral': it is actually essential. This is comparable to the way in which the fundamental particles of physical reality have no preference or limitation as to which higher level entities and phenomena are built from them, allowing the creation of everything from planets to pumpkins. Being detached from sensory input or motor output, the seething mass of quirks generated by the brain's inner regions is free to self-organize into phenomena which bear no (direct) relation to external realities or actions. Their evolutionary value and justification is to be found in the fact that they allow the organism to progress beyond the ability to produce immediate and appropriate behavioural responses to events taking place in the animal's surroundings.

These possibilities manifest themselves in a number of ways. One of the most obvious and practically useful, introduced in the previous paragraph, is the selection between the many possible behavioural responses to everything happening at a particular moment. This involves a weighing up of short- and long-term interests: information that is not available to the sensory or motor regions of the brain. Related to this are postponed or pre-emptive responses. Perhaps, a response is not essential now but worth doing later; and perhaps, prediction of future events will allow the animal to respond to them more effectively. Each of these capabilities is clearly of great value to the organism and could not be achieved with a direct connection between sensory input and motor output.

Just as we have seen in the sensory and motor cortexes, the diversity and complexity of the functions of these brain areas are such that it is implausible that they can be built in a single step from the primitive information in the quirks generated by neural activity. That would be comparable to proposing that a pumpkin can arise directly out of quarks, rather than requiring the intermediate hierarchical levels of the atomic, molecular, cellular and tissue. Instead, in the areas of the information dimension associated with these brain areas, such intermediate levels will also exist between the quirk and the higher levels at which useful functions emerge.

The emergent phenomena created by these areas of the brain will be different by nature than those seen at either its sensory or motor interfaces. They will not relate to the organism's surroundings (the colour red) or bodily actions (walking).

Instead, these regions need to invent different types of informational phenomena that are relevant to their required role. This functional separation from the physical, combined with the non-detectability of all informational phenomena, would make this area of the information dimension entirely inaccessible if it were not for one of its more remarkable informational constructs: consciousness. Through conscious experience we have access to at least a part of this area in our own brains. It is this, for instance, that allows us to conclude that the prioritization function of these areas is mediated at least in part by the informational phenomena of emotions. Happiness, anger, sadness, fear and disgust are phenomena that bear no relation to anything that exists in physical reality, and yet are powerful influencers of the selection between possible responses. Similarly, consciousness gives us access to many aspects of the pre-emptive, postponement and planning functions of the brain. We are aware of dangers before they take place and consider various courses of action to choose one that has the best chance of achieving long-term goals. Specifically in humans, it is also here that we encounter one of the most remarkable and powerful information tools created by the brain: symbolic language. While the word 'rose' may relate to a particular category of physical entity, this word (and all other words) is of an entirely different nature than that which they are used to label, either as information in the sensory cortex or physically in the outside world. It is this difference by nature that allows these information entities to be combined to create linguistic structures with their own class of emergent features, which cannot exist in a single word, such as the metaphorical meaning of Burns' famous line '*O my Luve's like a red, red rose/That's newly sprung in June*'.

In conclusion, just as an immense diversity of emergent phenomena arise at sequential levels of organization in physical reality out of a limited set of fundamental particles that have only the most basic of physical properties, we see novel emergent phenomena arising in the various levels that form from quirks in the information dimension. While those on the sensory and motor sides of the brain relate directly to aspects of physical reality, in the inner regions, they are of a very different nature that relates to their specific functions in the generation of behaviours that ultimately further the survival and success of the individual.

2.2.11 The special case of consciousness

One of the most remarkable, contentious and widely discussed phenomena generated by the inner regions of the brain is consciousness. Its unique characteristics – that we experience it and are able to communicate these experiences – have historically given it a privileged position over and above any other phenomena, physical or otherwise. Even after its dependency on brain activity became widely accepted, it retained a special status, as formulated in Chalmers' Hard Problem [1]. Other functions of the brain were placed in the 'easy' category on the basis of the fact that they lack these specific characteristics.

Consciousness may be remarkable, but it is not the only remarkable phenomena, some of which (such as quantum indeterminacy) are equally strange in their own way. What seemed to put consciousness in a different category was the fact that it could not be detected, only subjectively experienced. However, we have seen that in this it is anything but unique. Non-detectability is a ubiquitous characteristic of brain function, all the way down to the meaningless information associated with an individual synapse. Most theories of consciousness do not acknowledge this fact, preferring to focus on the unique properties of consciousness and provide it with an exclusive explanation.

There are a number of problems with this isolated consideration of consciousness. One is the fact that consciousness is not neatly demarcated. Instead, it is a characteristic of a wide and colourful diversity of phenomena associated with brain activity. More importantly, it goes fuzzy at the edges. In the automation of skills, for instance, behaviours are first generated consciously but gradually shift into the subconscious. Once this has happened, functions of the same complexity are being performed, but without the element of consciousness. More dynamically, focused attention can cause consciousness to flit from one thing to another. In these boundary areas, it is difficult to define the edges of consciousness, and this fluidity makes it implausible that the transition between conscious and non-conscious is one between phenomena of fundamentally different nature. These observations make it more likely that consciousness is a group of phenomena within a larger class than in a class of its own.

The strongest argument against the uniqueness of consciousness is, however, the fact that the incremental continuity of the evolutionary process is incapable of and incompatible with the introduction of fundamentally different features. This is seen in the gradual increase in complexity of the informational functions of the brain described in this chapter, into which the progressive emergence of a phenomenon such as consciousness fits neatly.

The great social impact of Darwin's theory of evolution was that it contradicted the unique status of humans, and with it the assumption (which was, up to that point, not unreasonable) that we were the only creatures with an immaterial 'soul'. While other animals lack the linguistic ability to communicate their experiences, it is no longer considered reasonable to propose that they lack them. Instead, on the basis of evolutionary continuity and diversity, consciousness needs to be considered as a phenomena shared, in varying degrees and versions, by all animals. Indeed, we must rationally assume that other animals have conscious experiences that we lack, such as the bat's perception of its surroundings on the basis of sonar or the dog's rich olfactory experience.

A theory that limits itself to consciousness runs the risk of falling into the same trap. Certainly, there are features that distinguish humans from other animals, and consciousness from other informational phenomena, but this does not warrant granting either an exclusive status. Each should instead be considered a member of a broader family, with the advantage of being encompassed within a more generic explanatory framework.

EIT provides such a framework. Just as wetness arises in specific situations at a particular level of physical organization from the combination of large numbers of quarks, so too can consciousness arise in the information dimension at a specific level of organization out of large numbers of physically associated quirks. While it has unique non-reducible characteristics, so too do other emergent phenomena at this and other levels of organization. This may not provide an explicit explanation for the specific properties of consciousness, but in contrast with theories specifically focussed on consciousness, it provides a context within which they can plausibly be explained. In contrast to physicalist theories of the brain, it positions consciousness as a full member of the set of influential phenomena existing within an expanded reality that extends beyond the realm of physical matter and energy.

Viewed in this light the Hard and the Easy problems actually become reversed. The general problem with investigating and understanding the informational functions of the brain is that, being non-physical, they cannot be detected using physical instruments. The experiential characteristic of consciousness, combined with the ability of humans to verbally communicate these experiences, provides us with direct and specific information and insights concerning the characteristics of these phenomena in ourselves and others. While this information may be rejected by hard-nosed physicalists as subjective, it is generally coherent and consistent, making it both informative and reliable. In contrast, the non-conscious informational phenomena associated with our brains remain entirely obscure to us, even while their existence is evident through the effects they have. Indeed, given that many high-level informational processes generated by the brain are consciously experienced, the more interesting question may be why so much of the brain's functional activity is inaccessible in this way.

The inaccessibility of the non-conscious aspects of brain function leads to the risk of underestimating them. While they lack the specific and ostentatious characteristics of consciousness, to assume that they lack their own, equally remarkable properties is unjustified.

Having said this, these poor cousins do owe a debt of gratitude to consciousness. It is, after all, the experiential nature of consciousness that so persistently resists the claim that physical reality is all that exists. Without it, they could more easily be ignored; now they can hitch a lift. Emergent information theory also takes these phenomena on board by acknowledging their existence and significance and the need for a generic explanation for the full diversity of non-physical phenomena associated with the brain.

2.2.12 No brain is an island unto itself

Up to now, we have considered only the informational aspects of individual animals, but brains do not operate in isolation. Other animals are one of the most important aspects of the environment that need to be taken into consideration. Since the behaviour of these animals is the product of what takes place within their brains, this leads to a potential functional relationship between the events taking place within the information dimensions of all of the animals in a particular environment.

Even without the exchange of information between individuals, if they all respond in the same way to a particular environmental factor, it can lead to apparently coordinated behaviour. An example is the tendency of woodlice to congregate in damp, shady places. While this results in seemingly structured behaviour – with all woodlice heading in the same direction – no coordination or interaction between individuals is necessary.

A next step is seen when animals responding not to some environmental factor, but to each other. A good example of this is flocking behaviour in birds. If the members of a group of birds all have a tendency to fly in close proximity with other birds then flocks will inevitably form. At larger scales, such effects can lead to the impressive emergent features seen in starling murmurations: flocks that move as a single, coordinated entity in a way that is not simply a scaling up of the flight behaviour of an individual bird. Effects like these need not be limited to animals of a species. Something comparable happens between predator and prey when hunting behaviour in the former causes the latter to flee. Each animal responds to the behaviour of the other in contradictory ways: the predator trying to catch the prey, the prey trying not to be caught. A pack of wolves hunting a herd of caribou extends this from the individual to the group level.

Competitive or conflicting interactions can also be seen within a species, for instance in social structures. All animals within the group may start out struggling for dominance, but as time goes by some will be more successful while others fall behind in the pecking order. The position of each animal will determine the behaviours that become ingrained in its own information dimension. Some will develop and express behaviour that displays their dominance, while others display their submission.

A different form of interaction is seen in the replication of behaviours through imitation: an animal observes another performing some useful function and attempts to mimic what it has seen [259]. Because this is a complex and advanced capability, it is limited to a small number of large-brained species of which humans, again, take the lead. Imitation is widely used within human societies, forming a mainstay for the transmission of behaviour between parent and (young) child. It can also be used to distinguish social groups, with individuals adopting the habits, traditions, clothing style of the cohort to which they belong or wish to be associated. More functionally, apprenticeship is a process by which novices learn a particular trade by observing and replicating the skills of more experienced individuals.

Imitation has two main limitations. Firstly, it can only be applied to observable behaviours such as physical skills and unspoken social mores, not abstract mental capabilities. Secondly, depending on the complexity of the task, considerable practice may be needed before the receiver attains the same degree of proficiency. This is the result of the indirect mechanism at work. Imitation does not directly transfer information content from one information dimension to another but provides an example that the second human tries to recreate. It may avoid the necessity of reinventing the wheel entirely, but each individual still has to build their own wheel.

An advantage of re-creation in each individual is that it creates the possibility of sequentially improving a skill. This may take place through random errors in the replication process creating subtly different versions, of which the best are then selected for further distribution within the population (an evolutionary process). In addition, directed development may take place, with the imitator combining the observing behaviour with prior knowledge or abilities. Such an ability to analyse, evaluate and recombine skills to achieve progress is unique to the human species. While behavioural imitation is sometimes easy to confuse with a situation in which two animals independently develop the same behaviours, the results of such progressive development can only be explained by invoking imitation. They could not be produced by a single information dimension working independently and in isolation.

While the interactions between organisms discussed in this paragraph lead to observable phenomena that transcend the individual in physical reality, when viewed from an informational perspective we still only see individuals responding to the perceived behaviour of others. There is no exchange of information between them.

2.2.13 Communication

The interactions between animals become more significant when they involve the transfer of information, joining them together as components of larger scale information systems. This started in the same modest way as within organisms, with individual quirks being transported by chemical messengers.

Various pheromones are employed through the plant and animal kingdoms to this purpose. As with hormones, it is not the chemical or physical properties of these molecules that counts, but the quirks associated with them. The organism producing the pheromone distributes information about the cause of this release to any other organism that is capable of detecting and using this information (Figure 16).

While S1 and S2 are comparable proteinaceous molecules on the surfaces of sensory cells, the systems they are a part of differ in what they respond to. R1 takes the information provided by the sensor (Q_C) to indicate the presence of chemical stimulus C, while R2 responds to the information that the source organism attached

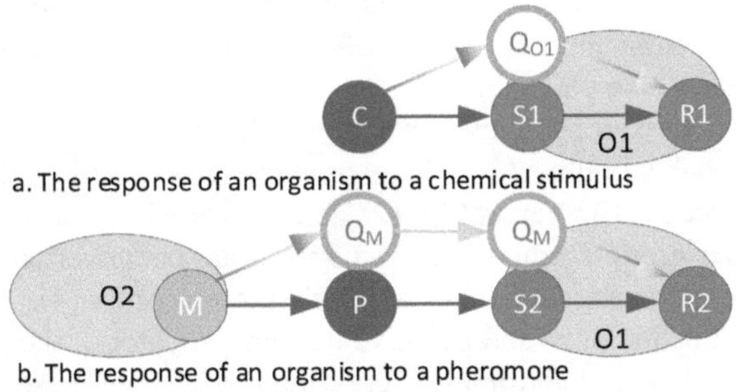

Figure 16 (a) Normally, when the sensor (S1) of organism O1 detects a chemical stimulus (C), the response (R1) is based on the information (Q_C) that the chemical is present. (b) The response (R2) of the organism to a pheromone (P) detected by sensor S2 produced by another organism (O2) is instead based on the quirk (Q_M) carrying the message associated with the pheromone.

to the pheromone P. This obviously requires the source and target organisms to both understand the meaning associated with the pheromone.

In addition to pheromones, organisms use many other, predominantly visual and auditory, methods to transfer a range of information. These vary from warning calls to territorial markings and from courtship signals to indications of emotional state. In all of these cases, it is not the physical medium used that is of importance, but the information transferred. The requirement of co-evolution of the message production and response systems means that such communication is most prevalent between organisms of the same species, and in particular in social species in which it has the greatest added value.

Sound is a particularly versatile substrate for communication since factors such as frequency, duration and amplitude can be used to differentiate messages. This makes it a far more generic form of communication than pheromones. In this way, for instance, colonies of prairie dogs are known to use distinct calls for different predators. Again, the sound that a prairie dog hears bears no physical relation with the predator; this communication only works because the recipient responds not to the sound itself but to the information allocated to the sound by the prairie dog that made it.

Such communication leads to the creation of informational networks in which the brains of individual animals are the nodes and communication forms the connections between them. While such networks are small and simple compared with brains, their causative effect on the behaviours of animals is significant.

In some cases, this is simply the additive effect of ensuring that all individuals exhibit the same behaviour, as in when ants follow a pheromone trail. In other cases, communication can lead to differentiated, coordinated behaviour in which individuals fulfil different roles, leading to a group that is more than the sum of its members. Here, informational interactions result in the creation of emergent social capabilities that transcend those of the individual. The purpose of these systems is to further the physical survival and success of the group, but this is only possible through the creation, transfer and processing of non-physical information. Consequently, in addition to their physical manifestations, it is appropriate to also view these phenomena from the perspective of the information dimension where the causative processes take place.

In the simplified example shown in Figure 17, one member of the group (O1) detects an external stimulus (1) which requires group action, for instance an approaching predator. The perception (2) determines which message needs to be given to the other group members (3). This message is converted to communicative action which is executed by this animal's motor cortex (4). The other group members detect this message and perceive it as an indicator of the stimulus, on the basis of which each then determines its contributory action. These are executed by their respective motor cortexes (5) to produce, in combination, a response that none of the organisms could perform on its own (6).

The similarity between this diagram and Figure 14 is not coincidental. The coordination of behaviour within a group of organisms is directly comparable to the coordination of muscles in an organism. Indeed, the term 'super-organism' is used

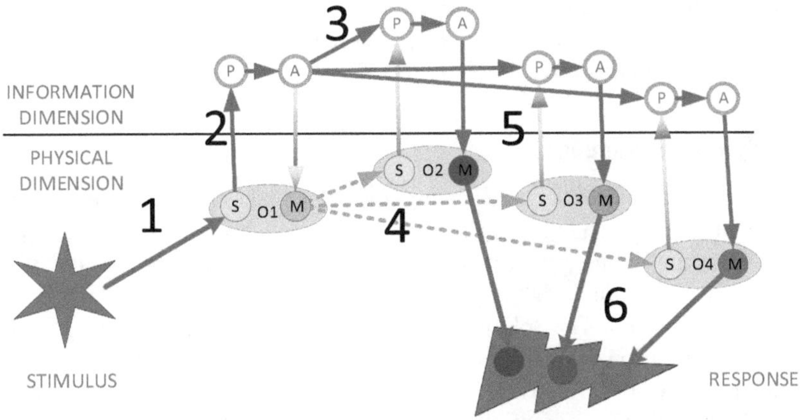

Figure 17 A schematic representation of information-based coordinated action in a group of organisms. S=sensory cortex; M=motor cortex; P=perception; A=action. Full arrows indicate the causative flow; dotted arrows the supportive communication processes.

to describe species that make extensive use of this possibility. In the same way as within organisms, we see a progression from single-function chemical messengers (hormones/pheromones) to generic communication media (neurons/sound). And as within organisms, from a physicalist viewpoint, the associated quirks in these simple examples could be considered as no more than an abstract by-product of the physical events taking place. However, here too we see that the physical signals are no more than arbitrary carriers of the quirks on which the response needs to be based. The interpretation of the signal is also an informational process, mediated by the organism's neural network but determined by the functional requirements of the system.

Social behaviours such as these, which have the effect of uniting a group of animals into a single stimulus-response system, require no more than unitary signals. However, as in communication within the brain, much is to be gained by the use of enriched information that cannot be embodied in a single quirk. Consequently, methods evolved using combinations of physical states carrying different quirks to transfer informational structures with emergent characteristics. A very simple example is the bee's waggle dance in which direction and distance are combined: an essential combination in determining the location of a food source. These components are coded into quirks associated with two aspects of the dance by the bee communicating the information and recombined by the bee receiving the information in order to fly to the right location.

Such combinations of unitary information are also seen in prairie dog communication. In addition to identifying the type of predator, variations in their calls can be used to convey information about how fast it is approaching, its size and even its colour [260]. In linguistic terms, then, prairie dogs can also use adjectives and verbs in addition to nouns. By combining these, they can effectively combine individual quirks to communicate messages such as 'large coyote approaching fast' and 'small coyote approaching slowly', thus permitting more specific and appropriate group responses.

2.2.14 Symbolic language

Fast forward to the use of language in humans, which takes the use of sound to transfer information between individuals to an entirely new level. Associating a specific sound with a unique meaning, as in prairie dog communication, seriously limits the maximum vocabulary that can be used: as with hormones, each new meaning requires a new sound. The solution to this restriction used in human speech is to introduce an additional level of coded emergence. By associating meaning with specific sequences of a relatively small set of sounds (in most languages between 20 and 40 phonemes), a potentially limitless vocabulary can be created.

From the information perspective, we see that the fundamental units of information (the quirks of this form of communication) are associated with the phonemes. These individual sounds have no meaning. The first level of organization with functional significance (words) is formed by combining sequences of these quirks. This combination bears no relation with the physical characteristics of the sounds. The fact that the phonemes 'd', 'o' and 'g' combine to form the word 'dog' has nothing to do with acoustic interactions between them. Nor do they bear any relation with the parts of the physical entity they are used to label: the dog's head, body, legs and tail. With verbal communication, the emergent entities are created and exist only in the information dimension.

An extended vocabulary is of value in increasing the diversity and specificity of information that can be transferred between individuals, but also opens the possibility of combining words to create higher levels of emergent information that cannot be provided by individual words: sentences. Introducing rules of grammar to determine how words should be combined allowed sequences of words to be used to convey more complex messages. For instance, 'dog bites man' is a different message than 'man bites dog'. Another characteristic of this type of communication which demonstrates its emergent nature is the fact that the message only exists when all of the component words have been transferred and the whole can be reconstructed.

The fact that the combination of components is informational rather than physical means that at each sequential level of linguistic organization, the information content becomes further detached from the physical substrate (Figure 18). While the meaning associated with the combination of the letters 'd', 'o' and 'g' already bears no relation with any physical structure, the relationship with that of a sentence is even less direct.

As in all informational systems, the association between physical substrate and information is entirely arbitrary. There is some relationship between the sounds used by vowels and consonants that relate to the way they are combined to create words: certain sounds are easier to utter in sequence than others. But there is no reason, for instance, why the sounds we ordinarily associate with 'd', 'o' and 'g'

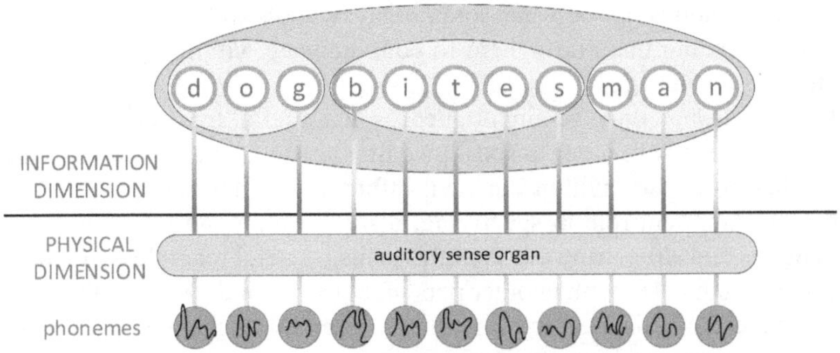

Figure 18 The emergent construction of words and meaningful sentences from the letter-based quirks associated with specific phonemes.

could not instead carry the 'c', 'a' and 't' quirks. If this were the case then, when asked to write down what you now hear as 'dog', you would write down 'cat'. Of course, there is no reason why the word you have written down should not still refer to a canine species, since the relationship between a word and that which it refers to is also equally arbitrary, as evidenced by the many different languages in use.

Language is one of the more impressive and remarkable examples of the ways in which individual human information dimensions have worked together to create something new. Excluding Tolkien as the main exception that proves the rule [261], the entire collection of grammar and vocabulary contained within any particular language does not arise in one individual's information dimension in one lifetime. Instead, language will have started out deep in prehistory with situation-specific vocalizations not dissimilar to those seen in other species and gradually grown in diversity and complexity through the generations. Nor are languages static: new words and dialects are continually being added and adapted. The current language landscape of the world population is a complex mosaic resulting from this process combined with the migrations, mixings and splittings of human populations through the ages. The hundreds of thousands of words and extensive grammatical rules are one of humanity's most complex and impressive creations.

What makes this feat remarkable is that, in contrast with technological achievements such a building a particle accelerator, language is not a physical construction. Instead, it is a classic example of a high level, emergent informational phenomenon. The vibrations in the air when we speak and the ink patterns on a page when we write are no more than physical carriers of non-physical, non-detectable quirks from one individual to another. Communication only takes place when these quirks are extracted by the sensory system of the receiver and the emergent information is reconstructed using a specific, shared coding system. If you listen to someone speaking a language, you don't understand or look at a text in an unknown language (possibly even with an unknown character set) your brain is unable to decode and reconstruct the information and it remains noises and squiggles. Indeed, what every human does in learning to understand and speak, read and write a language is to discover the relationships between sounds and symbols and their associated quirks, words and meaning that allow them to communicate within the group of people using the same language.

Language is not only of importance as a tool for transferring information between individuals. In order to speak, we first need to have something to say: the process therefore starts within our own information dimension, where language also has an important role in specifying, distinguishing and classifying informational entities and structuring our thoughts. This is useful regardless of whether the result is communicated with another person, but when it does, it results in the replication of these linguistic structures in the information dimension of the listener.

The significance of language is that it supports the specific and explicit construction and transfer of potentially complex high-level information from one individual to another. Without language, the only way to know what is going on inside the mind of another is by inference on the basis of observed behaviour. It may, for instance, be possible to deduce the presence of fear from the observation of fear-related behaviour, or the perception of danger from a warning call, but this is not the same thing as having a conversation about fear or an approaching predator.

One issue with language is that it is itself an extremely complex high-level informational construction that can only be acquired by transfer from other people's information dimensions. It is not possible to build and give someone a language as you could a physical tool: they can only construct it themselves on the basis of example. This could present us with a chicken-and-egg problem of needing language as a tool to transfer language to each new-born human. Fortunately, language is not the only way of transferring content between information dimensions. The second, employed in the early stages of language development in babies, is behavioural imitation. Once the ball gets rolling with a basic linguistic skill set, language can then take over as a mechanism for further expanding vocabulary and refining grammar. We use language both to teach our children language and to explain new terminology to each other. You can verbally explain to a child that the correct conjunction is 'I go' and not 'I goes', and in this way cause the recreation of this linguistic rule in their information dimension. If I tell you 'noctumarine is the name of the deep blue colour of a clear late evening sky', you can easily add this new word to your information dimension and attach it to this meaning. In this way, a complete linguistic repertoire can be built up; a repertoire that can subsequently be used as a tool to transfer all the other content we wish to share.

The combination of instruction and imitation is not limited to language acquisition. Indeed, the ubiquity of speech in adult interactions means that it is difficult to identify situations which involve imitation alone. In general, a demonstration of a skill or behaviour will be accompanied by a verbal explanation of the underlying theoretical or conceptual framework. This context has the advantage of providing the receiver with background information that is useful in understanding, mastering and generalizing that which is to be learned. In the information dimension of the receiver, this background information is coupled with the specific behaviour, increasing its stability as an emergent informational entity and creating a conceptual context in which related entities can be united to mutual benefit. This entire

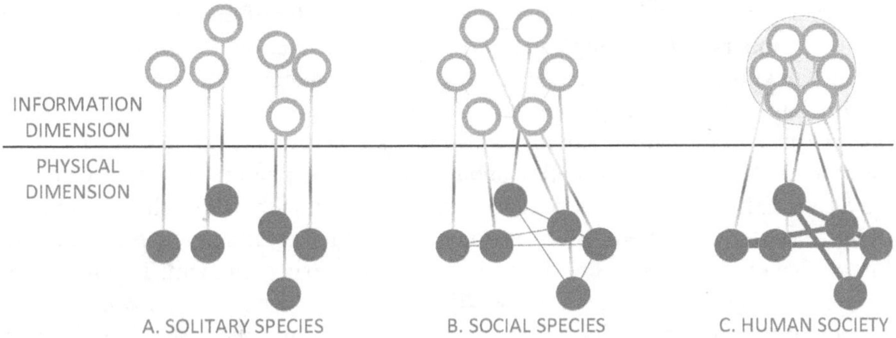

Figure 19 Communication-based distinction between physical location and informational integration in a solitary species, a social species and a human society.

edifice has no physical incarnation but is a highly specific and complex structure built from quirks.

In a social context, language supports and stimulates a far greater volume and detail of information transfer between the information dimensions of members of a community than the simpler and more incidental forms of communication employed by other animals illustrated in Figure 17. This becomes apparent when we view the relationship between members of a group of animals from a physical and an informational perspective. In each of the examples depicted in Figure 19, the individual animals have the same physical proximity to each other.

In a solitary species (A), there is no active exchange of information, with the result that the information dimensions associated with each individual brain remain as separate as their physical bodies. Information exchange is limited to that taking place within the nervous system of each of the animals, which can therefore justifiably be seen as an island unto itself. In a social species (B), various forms of olfactory, auditory or visual communication transport solitary quirks between individuals. This connects their information dimensions in such a way that coordinated action is possible: behaviour that is influenced by higher-level processes taking place in the interconnected information dimensions of the members of the group. Here, the islands have become an archipelago connected by active shipping routes. The voluminous exchange of high-level information supported by human language (C) deeply connects and to some degree conjoins the information dimensions of individuals. The intensive information-based connections support the development of more complex and integrated forms of coordination, which strongly influence the behaviours of individuals to achieve a common goal. Here, the islands have merged to become a continent.

2.2.15 Information distribution

One of the particularly useful features of language is that it provides a far more efficient way of obtaining information about the outside world than through direct sensory experience. It does this by supporting the transfer of first-hand experiences among members of the group and on to each new generation. In this way, an individual can know far more than he or she could ever gather on their own.

In addition to providing each other with practically useful information about our physical surroundings, language also had a significant social impact by making it possible to share information about other members of the community. In this way, each individual does not need to actually interact with every other member in order to get to know them. Meeting someone for the first time, you could already know what kind of person they are and what you can expect of them. This increases efficiency and thus the number of individuals that who can get to know each other as members of a community. More significantly, it allows the formation of larger stable groups. This in turn increases the number of information dimensions that form an interacting community, creating a larger source of integrated information.

The exchange of concepts between individuals forms the foundation for memetics: the spread of ideas and methods through a population. This spread is never a matter of perfect replication. The fact that language involves conversion and interpretation, and that the information needs to be reconstructed in the mind of the recipient, means that each copy will be inevitably different to a greater or lesser degree. Extreme examples of the imperfect replication of information are seen in mondegreens, when a verbal message is misinterpreted entirely. The proverbial example is the disastrous transmutation of 'send reinforcements; we're going to advance' into 'send three and fourpence; we're going to a dance'. Such effects are also seen in the parlour game of Chinese whispers, where a message cumulatively changes through passage through a sequence of individuals, often ending as something quite nonsensical.

In addition to the variations resulting from imperfect communication, some degree of active change will take place. The message received will be interpreted and adapted by the context of the information dimension it enters. This will accelerate change, creating new versions that may be significantly different. In other cases, the new information may be incompatible with pre-existing structures in the new information dimension and be rejected. Throughout the population and through the generations, this dynamic process is the source of much of the content of our own information dimensions.

An important factor in the verbal distribution of information is social authority. In human societies, not all voices carry the same value. In some cases, this may be based on qualitative expertise; in others on authoritarian hierarchy. A clear example of the latter is the historical resistance of the Catholic Church to making the bible accessible to the populace, since the priesthood's exclusive access gave them and the church a position of power. Communication may also be purposefully misleading, as is seen in lying and propaganda. Here, information is transferred with the intention of causing the creation of incorrect information in the receiver.

In addition to supporting the distribution of information, language also supports dialogue: the bi-direction exchange of information on a particular topic that may result in confirmation or disagreement. Argumentation is effectively a linguistic exchange between two individuals that highlights an incompatibility or contradiction between the contents of their respective information dimensions, whereby both subsequently attempt to change that of their adversary. If this leads to nothing more than a shouting match, then little effect will be seen beyond further entrenchment of differences. However, such interactions will often lead to minor or major adaptations in the opinions held.

To increase the likelihood that these changes constitute improvements, various rules of debate and logic can be employed. Scientific method can be seen as the culmination of such constructive, progressive interaction. A scientific theory does not (or at least, should not) enjoy prominence on the basis of the social status or influence of its proponents but through surviving objective and publicly reported attempts to disprove it. This book is just one example of this process: a thoroughly prepared and constructively intended presentation of new ideas to an audience of people who are knowledgeable enough to subject it to scrutiny. It is, of course, my hope that the basic tenets will survive, but it would be wildly unrealistic for me to think that there are no missing details or errors to be found, filled in or corrected. It is not my ambition or supposition that this will be a definitive script on the subject. Indeed, it is my hope and intention that others will pick up the ball and play it further, quite possibly in a different direction than I myself have in mind.

2.2.16 Language and culture

The unique ability of human populations to transfer complex information between the information dimensions of their members had far-reaching consequences for our social evolution. The linguistic communication of skills and knowledge between individuals and generations supported the cumulative development of human culture. This is 'culture' in the broad sense of the word: not just the artistic side of society that is often associated with the term, but all abilities, behaviours and artefacts that are specific to a particular society or group of individuals. This prominently includes science and technology alongside religion and the various arts – and indeed language itself.

Under this definition, some rudimentary cultural phenomena can spread through imitation rather than language and may therefore also be observed in other species [262]. Even without language, our species would probably still have become the cultural leaders of the animal realm. Tool use, hunting and even rudimentary farming, art, music and architecture could well have arisen. But we would never have developed religion, science, technology or (self-evidently) literature. Imitation-based culture is therefore a marginal factor compared with the extent and significance of language-based culture in human societies.

Unsurprisingly for a product of (non-physical) language, culture too is non-physical. It can be defined as the entire set of phenomena that form and exist in the combined information dimensions of a group of people. The fact that they are socially oriented means that most lead to physical expression in one form or another. Political tendencies, caste associations and religious beliefs will lead to individuals expressing the behaviours associated with that particular group. Artistic aspects of culture cause their hosts to produce music, dance, paintings or sculptures. More

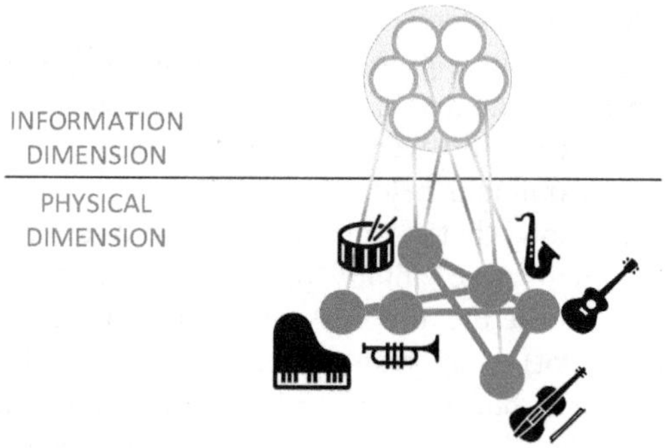

Figure 20 A group of people playing a piece of music is a physical expression of an informational phenomenon.

functionally related components result in physical artefacts such as machines and buildings – or indeed the book you are now holding in your hands. However, all of these are only physical incarnations of culture, not culture itself. Like physical behaviour, they are the products of human actions that are directed from the information dimension (Figure 20).

In contrast with individual behaviours, a single human cannot create culture. In order to exist, culture requires a network to be created by connecting a collection of information dimensions through language-based interaction. This network extends not only beyond the individual, but also beyond the generation. Its communal nature means that nodes can come and go, since each new node is adapted to fit in the gaps left by nodes which have died off. Culture is therefore not limited or bounded to the life cycle of individual members of society. While some developments, such as clothing fashions, may ebb and flow on a relatively short time scale others may take many generations to form or change.

The importance of these processes to us as human individuals cannot be overestimated. While the environment we grow up in (for instance nutritionally) may have some effect on our physical adult form, the culture we grow up in is fundamental in defining the content of large areas of our personal information dimensions. Even areas such as the sensory and motor cortexes and those controlling the body's physical functions are not entirely immune. Think, for instance, of the abilities of yoga adepts to control body functions or even the effect of the culture of guitar playing on the motor cortex. Each of these abilities and features comes to exist in a particular person through cultural inheritance.

When it comes to the areas that are more distant from direct connections with the body – our ideas about justice, our beliefs about the nature of reality and our place in it, our ambitions and plans for the future – culture plays an even stronger role. Each of us will certainly tweak and recombine that which we absorb from our cultural surroundings, but none of this content would exist in a human growing up in complete cultural isolation. In this sense, what we consider to be our personal identity can be better seen as a local crystallization of the cultural sea in which our own information dimension temporarily drifts.

The communal information dimension created in this way is more than a collection of identical units. Within the total population, subgroups with specific content exist: the various professions and trades, religions and leisure pursuits. As a consequence, the total content of this space is far greater than can fit in any individual. While a person can gain a broad but shallow picture of the whole (this is the purpose of general education) to reach the forefront in any particular area requires specialization. Within each subgroup, language is subsequently used to further expand the volume of information, which in the course of human history has led to the ongoing fragmentation of the whole into increasingly specialized parts. An important factor in this process has been the introduction of the information technologies discussed in the next chapter, which removed the characteristics of verbal communication that restricted such communal information dimensions to local collections of individuals who could speak directly to each other.

A consequence of this is that, while in prehistory an individual could encompass all of the knowledge required for a human individual and tribe to operate and survive, today each individual can harbour only a tiny fraction. Not only does this mean that the individual is no longer a viable independent living entity; even performing a single function within the entire social system often requires the combined efforts of a number of specialists. Language is essential for the creation of plans and coordination of activities in such multidisciplinary teams. It supports information exchange about possibilities, options and future events that cannot be communicated through behaviour. Starting with a desired result, each member can make their own contribution to formulating and executing a detailed and complete plan that none of them could have independently created: the whole is more than the sum of the parts. The result could be anything from playing symphonic music to building a cathedral.

The ability to combine the distinct capabilities of individuals in this way forms the foundation of our exceptional success as a species. In direct physical competition with other animals and in exploiting natural resources, the individual human is not exceptional. It is the use of tools that gave us the upper hand. The ability to make, use and improve the simplest of these tools, such as hand axes, could be based on imitation alone. With only these, we would still be struggling for survival. The increasingly complex tools which cumulatively resulted in our unique position in the biosphere, from factory farming to agricultural machinery, from wastewater treatment plants to medical technologies, could never have arisen without language and the specialism of theoretical and technical capabilities it supported.

2.3 Information technologies

2.3.1 Information transfer

As in biological systems, the use of information in technology had modest beginnings in which the necessity of considering them from a different perspective can seem superfluous. However, there is again a clear distinction between the physical and informational tools we build and use. As in animals, in the latter function is not based on the physical characteristics of components but on the non-physical quirks associated with them. As a consequence, physical components can be exchanged without altering the outcome as long as the replacement carries the same quirk. To take a trivial example, in a mechanical machine replacement of a bolt with one half, the size will render it useless. In contrast, halving the font size of a text has no effect on its function. Indeed, ink on paper can be replaced with engraving in stone or pixels on an LCD screen. The material substrate is subservient to the informational function.

I am starting this chapter with writing since making marks on objects to store and transfer information is the most ancient and simplest form of information technology. Skipping over the numerical tally systems that preceded them, writing was significant in providing a substitute for the spoken word that solved its two main limitations: time and space. With writing, the sender and receiver of the information do not need to be in the same place at the same time.

Writing replaces the (arbitrary) sound associated with a particular informational letter with an equally arbitrary physical symbol. All that matters, as with the spoken word, is that the person making the mark does so to use it as a representative for a specific unit of information, and that the person reading it uses the same code to extract the information. If this succeeds, then a quirk is transferred from the writer to the reader.

It may seem odd to consider the inorganic media used in writing as an integral part of a biological information system but this oddness only applies when we view the situation from a physical perspective. The situation is systemically comparable to the transfer of a quirk from one organism to another using a pheromone, or even the transfer of a quirk from one neuron to another through an electrical impulse. In each case, an altered physical state carries information from a sender to a receiver. Indeed, we have seen that every physical state change following an interaction carries information about the cause of the change. The only question is whether the

DOI: 10.4324/9781003460541-10

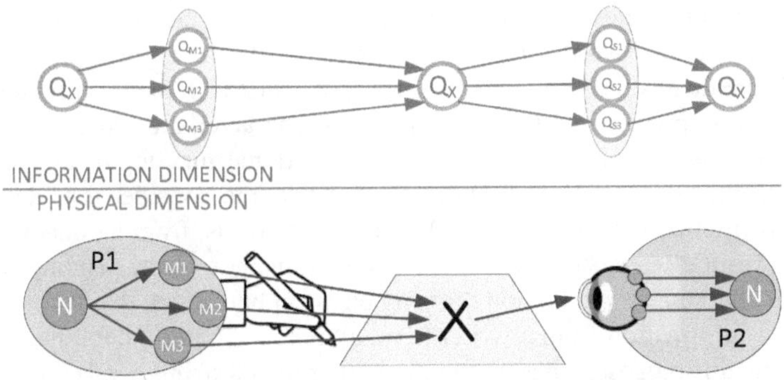

Figure 21 The writing and reading of a letter, as viewed from the physical and information perspective. The intention of person P1 to communicate 'X' is translated to a set of instructions (Q_{M1-3}) to hand muscles to produce the symbol. Retinal cells of the reader (P2) detect elements of the symbol (Q_{S1-3}) that are combined in the visual cortex to determine that the symbol is associated with the letter 'X'.

quirk so created plays a role in the processes that follow. In this case, the cause of the state change of the paper (from blank to carrying a symbol) is the intention of the writer to convey the quirk associated with the symbol and the consequence is that the reader detects and responds to this quirk.

Having said this, writing is more complex since quirks are associated with patterns of physical states rather than individual states. This means that the production of the symbol requires coordinated motor functions to (hand) write it, and its recognition requires visual processing to recognize and interpret it (Figure 21). The transfer of an individual quirk therefore involves first a motor deconstruction to the muscle actions required to produce the symbol, followed be sensory reconstruction to determine the quirk associated with the symbol. While the symbol may include various parts, it is only the complete symbol that carries information, which is therefore indivisible and qualifies as a quirk.

The purpose of writing, of course, is not to convey individual letters but the emergent information and meaning that can only exist in association with words and entire texts, such as this book, which are composed of large numbers of letters in specific sequences. The positions of the symbols on the page relative to each other constitute a relationship that supports the recreation of the emergent information composed by the writer in the mind of the reader. Here, too, we encounter arbitrary relationships between the information and its physical substrates such as the direction of reading. While most languages are read from left-to-right and top-to-bottom Arabic, Hebrew and Urdu languages are written (and subsequently read) in the opposite direction. Chinese and Japanese are different both in the way they combine the symbols for phonemes, and in their reading direction which is traditionally top-to-bottom, left-to-right. In all of these cases, we see that physical form is subservient to the associated information, and this distinguishes these technologies from those with physical functions.

Various technologies were invented to assist the process of information transfer using the written word, from the printing press to the typewriter. While these machines create physical products, their purpose relates to the information associated with these products and not their physical characteristics. While it is easy to consider a book as a physical object, its informational function means that this is only an arbitrary incarnation. It is more appropriate to consider it as an informational construction that can be embodied in many forms, from hardback to paperback and from eReader to Audiobook. The significance of the printing press was not that it allowed the production of many physical books, but that it supported the transfer of information from a writer to many readers. Until a book has been read to complete this process, it has no function other than looking good on a bookshelf. While this also may be of some value (and is the reason for attention to cover design), it is not the true value or purpose of the book.

2.3.2 Information processing

The passive contribution of writing to information transfer between individuals was only the first step in the development of information technologies. Those that followed played a more active role. One of the earliest and simplest examples is the abacus, in which the movement of beads allows their associated quirks to be flexibly recombined to create numerical information that cannot be associated with a single bead. Storage of information is not, however, the primary function of the abacus. As a tool its purpose it to assist in performing calculations: the most basic form of information processing.

Here, too, we see the dissociation between physical properties and informational function in information technologies. An abacus can be made out of materials with properties as different as metal, stone, wood or plastic. Furthermore, all of the beads on an abacus are identical: it is not so that those representing 100s are 100 times larger than those representing 1s. Instead, it is the designed position of the bead that determines the value that is associated with it. Changing the design or convention (for instance, working from left to right rather than right to left) would result in exactly the same physical configuration being associated with different information. It is the cause of the state (the intention to create a state associated with 1, 10 or 100) that determines the associated information, and not the state itself, and the abacus only works when it is used in such a way that the steps that follow are based on this information; and the information associated with individual beads is indivisible. Together these considerations indicate that each bead is associated with a single quirk.

In contrast with machines with physical functions, it is consequently not the case that physical interactions between parts determine its function. Instead, this is based on the informational methods used, with the movements of the beads only indirectly relating to the calculations performed. It is for this reason that using an abacus requires skill, training and an understanding of the nature of numerical calculation as an informational process. Finally, the output of this machine is not some material product, but an informational result that is only of value when decoded and used in further informational processes.

The abacus is just one example of various types of mechanical calculator, the functions of all of which are based on the quirks associated with the states of their components. All such devices differ from technologies with a physical function in this way, a differentiation that is comparable to that seen between physical and informational functions in living organisms. The reason we design and build them is not to expand our physical capabilities but to assist our brains by performing fast and accurate calculations since such informational functions are not one of the brain's strong points. Indeed, the name 'computer' is derived from the fact that the original mechanical devices were built to replace human computers who had the task of performing calculations manually: a job that consequently no longer exists.

The direct relationship in these devices between physical states and quirks and between physical mechanisms and information processes has an important consequence for the support of emergent information. The combination of multiple quirks and information processes requires multiple physical states and mechanisms. This is seen in simplified form in the abacus, where the number of rows of beads determines the maximum values that can be calculated. Mechanical calculating machines similarly use a series of mechanisms to expand the processing capacity of a single mechanism. This one-to-one relationship between the physical and the informational makes it relatively easy to ignore the fact that the physical aspect of these devices is not what matters; that their function relates to the information and information processes supported by them. However, this distinction is clearly demonstrated by the fact that various very different designs were invented to support the same calculations, from Liebniz' stepped reckoner to Odhner's pinwheel calculator and from Felt's comptometer to Herzstark's hand-cranked calculator. These show the physical mechanisms to be arbitrary, and their informational effects to be primary.

2.3.3 Digital information processing

The technologies described in the previous paragraph have in common that, like the biological information-based methods pre-dating the neural network, they are limited to a single function. You cannot use a typewriter to perform a calculation, or an abacus to produce a text. This is not because of any physical restriction imposed by the mechanisms used but a result of their design, which connects a particular physical state to a specific associated quirk, and each mechanical action to a single informational function. It was the invention of the general purpose programmable computer that removed this limitation by supporting the execution of any information-based action on any type of information. It is here that the separation between the physical and informational becomes undeniable and emergence starts to play a pivotal role. Functionally, this was comparable to the evolution of neural networks as a generic solution to biological information storage and processing. The method used to achieve this flexibility is, however, completely different.

The conceptual basis for the processor at the heart of every computer is the Universal Turing Machine (UTM): a device that was theoretically proven by

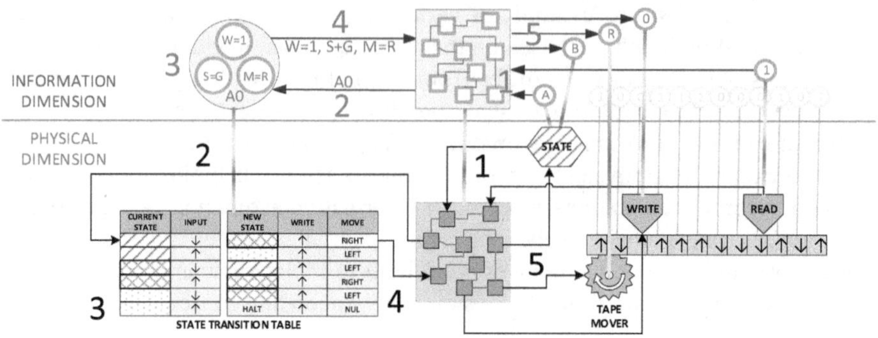

Figure 22 A Turing machine viewed from the physical and information perspectives.

Turing to be capable of performing any algorithmic calculation [204]. It is a remarkably simple mechanism that reads a symbol from a stored linear sequence (traditionally seen as a tape) and on the basis of this symbol, combined with its internal state, writes a new symbol, changes its state and/or moves to the next or previous position in the sequence. A state transition table mapping inputs to outputs determines which of these actions it performs. The machine does nothing more or less than perform these simple actions. Its flexibility is based on the separation between mechanism and instruction: it is the symbol sequence which determines which actions it performs in which order. Since any number of symbol sequences can be fed into the machine, any number of effects can be generated by the actions they cause.

Like the abacus and the typewriter, the UTM is an information technology. Its purpose is not to perform some physical function or convert a raw material into a physical product, but to use informational mechanisms to convert an information input into an information output. It is the information associated with the stored symbol and the internal state that determine what happens. The symbol and the state are merely physical carriers of this information. The effect of this information is not based on inherent physical interactions between the parts of the machine: if it was then there would be no need for a state transition table to tell the machine how to respond. This table does not have the purpose of causing a physical state change, but of changing the values associated with these states. The movement to the next or previous position in the sequence also has an informational function: to gather the quirk associated with that position or store a quirk in it. When the machine prints a new symbol on the tape, it is not the symbol that is of importance but the quirk associated with it. It is these information functions, not the physical processes they are associated with, that are called upon by the programme. To understand the computer, it is therefore appropriate and necessary to view it from an informational perspective.

Figure 22 shows a single cycle in a Turing machine with three physical internal states (red, green and blue) associated with the quirks A, B and C. The tape has been written with two symbols, ↓ and ↑ to indicate the binary values 0 and 1. The state transition table is that of a 'busy beaver' which will eventually change all of the values in a random tape to 1.

Viewed from a physical perspective, the Read head detects a ↓ symbol and sends an electrical current into the circuitry, together with the input from the DIAGONAL state (1). The combination of inputs (2) activates the first line of the state transition table (3). The table returns currents (4) to change the state to HATCHED, the tape symbol to ↑, and move the tape one position to the right (5).

Viewed from the information perspective, we see the Read head detecting the 0 ascribed to the ↓ symbol, and this being combined with the value A associated with the RED state by information processes supported by the circuitry (1). The physical processes then pass the A0 combination to the state table (2), where it is found to combine the instructions to creating the 1 and B quirks and reading the next quirk from the tape (3). This is then sent back as response, mediated by the Write head, the state changer and the tape mover (4).

One thing is clear from both of these descriptions: there is something extremely odd about the Turing machine compared with all of the other machines we have designed and built. From neither viewpoint is it immediately apparent what use the machine could be, and yet this is the basis for all of our digital technologies. That we are not normally aware of this oddness has several causes. Firstly, based on their broad applicability, they have become so ubiquitous in modern life that we tend to take them for granted. Secondly, interacting with something that performs an informational function seems fairly natural because it is what we do ourselves every time we think, speak, listen, read or write. Finally, the fact that they manifest themselves as physical devices makes it easy to overlook their strangeness. The parts of the computer we see and interact with are macroscopic, mechanical and made of metal and plastic like any other machine. A computer keyboard strongly resembles that of a typewriter. However, these are only the external interfaces of the actual computer. Its peculiar functional parts are microscopic, informational, silicon and hidden deep inside.

One of the more remarkable characteristics of the digital computer is the separation between mechanism and function. Even if you were to be able to open it up and zoom in on the electronic functions supported by its processor, you would still know nothing about the function of the machine because the processor does nothing on its own. In contrast with other machines, when a computer rolls off the production line as a complete physical device it is incapable of performing any function at all. What determines its function is not the processor but the programme which is later stored elsewhere in the computer's architecture. It is this that instructs the processor to perform the specific sequence of operations involved in generating a required function.

Approaching the system from the side of the programme is little better. Given only the bit sequences with which the programme is associated there would also be no way of knowing what functional purpose they serve since their effect is dependent on the design of the processor. It is only when the programme is fed through the processor that anything happens at all. Otherwise, much like a book that is not being read, the programme is simply a static informational structure with only the potential of exerting an influence and a processor is simply a mechanism waiting to be told what to do. An additional requirement is that the programme is written in a language that matches the design of the processor. Otherwise, the combination of the two will not result in any useful function since the processor will not correctly interpret the stored instructions.

A particularly remarkable and important characteristic of digital computers which also tends to be overlooked is their immense scale. The peripherals of the computer are built from comparable numbers of parts to other machines: tens or hundreds. A complex machine such as a car may have a few tens of thousands of parts, but that is at the upper end of the physical machines we mass produce. In contrast, a modern microprocessor has billions of active components (transistors) and the same applies to the numbers of bits storing software and data. The Word programme used to write this book, for instance, is built from the quirks associated with more than 120 million bits: orders of magnitude more parts than any physical machine. This digital document is stored in some 24 million bits. It is the miniaturization of microprocessors and storage media that allows such immense entities to be packaged in a device that fits in your pocket.

Designing anything composed of such immense numbers of components is a huge challenge. While in theory it would be possible to programme Word at the level of processor operations this would be entirely impractical. Apart from the intellectual challenge of determining which sequence of 120 million bits would produce the required results, altering these sequences to add new features or correct errors would be nigh impossible. The solution, as in other machines, is to exploit functional emergence. The gap between the UTM and required function is so large (and the number of components so enormous) that it could not be bridged in a single step. Instead, a hierarchical sequence is required in which each level has emergent properties that form the basis for the next.

The starting point of this sequence in digital computers – their indivisible quirks – is the binary 0 or 1 values associated with a two-state bit. Since these two options are too limited to be of any use, conventional computer architectures group quirks together to form a wider range of functions. Using a specific coding system, these quirk combinations are mapped to a set of machine code operations built into its hardware. For instance, in the MIPS architecture the bits 100101 code for the logical operation OR while 100100 codes for AND. These functions are, then, already a next level of organization with emergent properties, but not yet at the level we desire of our computers.

The limited number of machine code functions is therefore first compiled to form the wider range of operations used in the various programming languages such as GOSUB and PRINT. As the name suggests, building functions with these languages involves the stringing together of components using a defined syntax. This leads to the next level of organization: code lines such as 'IF y>z THEN GOTO 100', which are then sequentially combined to create subroutines, modules and eventually the computer programmes that deliver the required informational functions (Figure 23).

The emergence inherent to these stacked hierarchical structures is evident in the difference in nature between the high-level functions and the bits they are

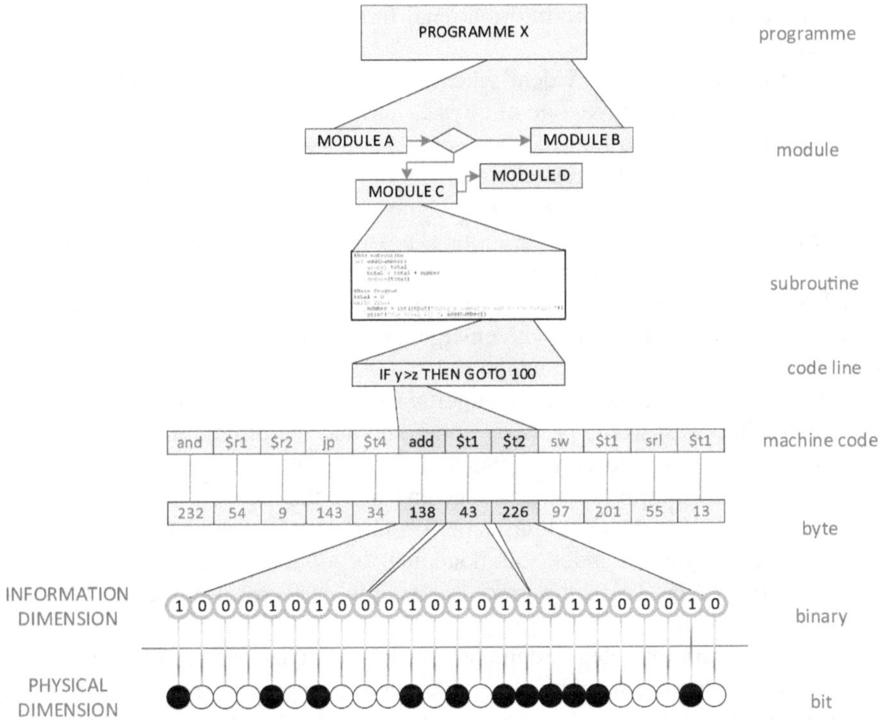

Figure 23 Levels of designed informational organization in a programmable computer.

ultimately made of. Programmes have characteristics that cannot be found in their subroutines, which have characteristics that cannot be found in their functions, which have characteristics that cannot be found in their operations, which have characteristics that cannot be found in binary values. While at lower levels computers are limited to basic logical and arithmetic functions, at higher levels any type of informational process can be performed. These include functions with an entirely different nature than logic and arithmetic, such as the generation of digital sound or speech recognition to name just two.

A consequence of this hierarchical structure is that watching the processor in action will tell us nothing about the function being performed by the computer. At this basic level, all that there is to be seen is a processor performing read-process-move-write cycles on a binary sequence. The functions we are interested in – from text processing to video editing and from database management to the routing of data streams over the internet – exist at higher levels of organization and are radically different by nature. In this sense, we can justifiably equate the computer's binary quirks with physical quarks, the UTM to the physical atom and the computer programme to a living cell in terms of complexity and scale. The difference, of course, is that in the computer, these levels of organization are not physical. It is not so that the physical side of Figure 22 is a part of some complex physical mechanism; it is the informational function it supports that scales up in this way.

This difference is also evident when we consider the skills required to programme a computer. Knowledge of physics and mechanics are irrelevant: what is necessary is insight into logical, mathematical and syntactic theory and practice. These are partly topics that relate to quirks, but more often to the entities and processes constructed from quirks; they have nothing to do with quarks or anything built from them. Designing a programme is not a matter of decomposing a physical function to those of physical components, but the determination of which informational components can be combined to achieve the required function. The product of this design is not a machine with emergent physical functions, but a programme with emergent informational functions.

It is here that we encounter an important distinction between the mechanical calculators discussed in the previous paragraph and the programmable computer. The addition of new and cumulative functions requires no additional hardware mechanisms: it is simply a matter of feeding more instructions through the same mechanism. Whether the computer is performing a trivial calculation such as 2+2 or generating a dynamic index to a document of a hundred pages makes no difference at this level. The same processor simply performs a longer sequence of instructions.

These considerations clearly demonstrate the inadequacy of a strictly physicalist perspective in which being composed of matter or energy is a prerequisite for being acknowledged as real in the literal sense of the word. Within these constraints, the structures illustrated in Figure 23 would not exist. Yet, the fact that the entire purpose and function of the computer is based on them makes this position untenable. It necessitates their acknowledgement and acceptance as real phenomena, and with it the extension of the boundaries of reality to include the information dimension in which they exist and the computer operates.

One way of evading this issue is to deny the reality of emergence. In a strictly reductionistic worldview, all that ultimately exists is the fundamental level. The rest is only a derivative of what happens at this level. Applying this to computers would reduce them to the level of the individual quirk, which conveniently equates with a physical bit state. If all else is only a derivative of the fundamental, then there is no need to grant significance to higher levels of informational organization. We can consider binary values as properties of bit states and leave it at that. Applying this reasoning on the physical side, however, would negate all of the natural sciences with the exception of particle physics: a rather radical and not particularly useful position to take. Denying the existence and significance of higher level informational phenomena is directly comparable and similarly myopic.

The unavoidability of information emergence is also evident in the design of programmes which, as with all machines, is inherently top-down. It starts with the required function of the whole and then determines which parts are required; the design of the parts is similarly based on bringing together sub-components to produce their required function, and so forth all the way down to the most fundamental functional components, its quirks. The function of the computer – the way that it

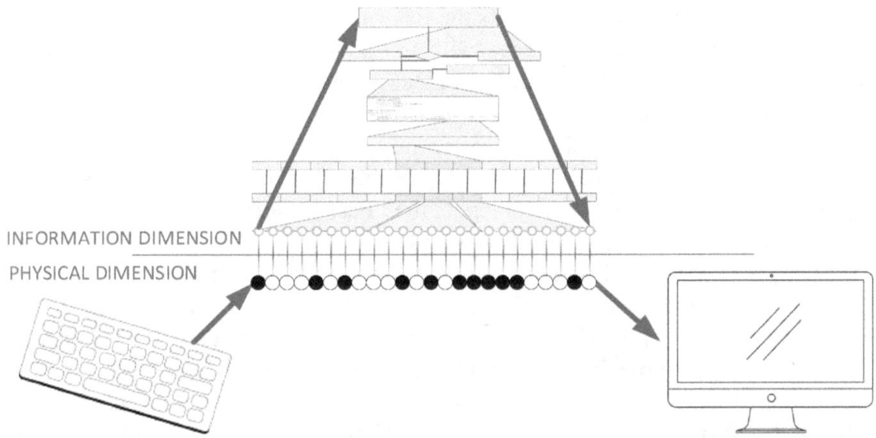

Figure 24 Causation in the programmable computer. Between the physical input and physical output devices, emergent information processes are in control.

produces informational output on the basis of informational input – is consequently determined by processes taking place at the highest level of organization, to which all underlying levels are subservient. And these levels are informational, not physical.

In terms of the causative relationships operating between the physical the informational realms, this creates a situation that is systemically comparable to the way in which physical stimuli are detected by sense organs, converted to quirks in the sensory cortex, operated on by high-level information processes in the brain, which then determine the actions of muscles via the activation of neurons in the motor cortex. In the computer, the physical action of typing on the keyboard is converted to quirks by the computer's input architecture, these are processed according to the functional design of the programme, and the quirks generated as output of these information processes are converted back to the physical form of pixels illuminated on its monitor (Figure 24). As in the brain, it is not the case that the physical substrate is coerced into acting in a way that is contradictory to its nature. Instead, the machine is designed in such a way that its actions are determined by high-level informational processes, operating by determining the behaviour of their composite quirks and through them the physical substrate they are coupled to. These non-physical processes are therefore entirely dependent on physical mechanisms and states, but also completely in control of them.

The fact that the computer's functional levels of organization are informational rather than physical also means that they cannot be seen in the computer. All that can be detected there are extremely long sequences of bits ready to be read and fed through a processor. However, the fact that programmes are designed using specific protocols means that this limitation is less of an issue than in the brain. As long as we know the protocols used, it is relatively easy to reconstruct the programme from the sequences of binary quirks associated with these measured bit states. It is this that we see when we instruct the computer to display it on its monitor.

This reliable accessibility presents the risk of confusing the physical visualization on paper or a computer screen with the actual programme or information. However, the map is not the territory and these maps in particular are a translation and presentation of the territory that is specifically designed to be amenable to the human visual system. The physical projection we see is completely different by nature from the informational reality it represents. The sequence of letters PRINT is presented entirely for our convenience; they bear little relation to what happens inside a computer when it performs this operation.

This is, then, comparable to asking a person to reveal their inner thoughts: the words spoken are a physical representation of these non-physical thoughts, not the thoughts themselves. The difference in the case of the computer is that we get the truth, the whole truth and nothing but the truth. The fact that all of its information structures and processes are designed and built from standard components, and that the visualization processes are similarly designed, means that the entire content of its information dimension at all levels can be reliably accessed in this way.

The possibility of making such visualizations both of the programmes and their output is, of course, essential to their function. With informational phenomena being non-physical and therefore non-detectable, they would otherwise remain entirely hidden within the computer's information dimension and therefore be quite useless to us. Take away these output interfaces and there would be no way for us to know what the computer is actually doing as its processor buzzes with electronic activity. Simply by looking at the sequences of bit states on the basis of which its software is constructed without knowing the relationship between state and binary quirk, and without knowing the way in which these are combined to form higher level structures and functions, we would be just as clueless as to what is going on as we are observing electrical activity in the brain.

2.3.4 Data digitization

In addition to functional processes, computers need data: the raw material on which these processes operate. Again, in contrast with physical machines, this material is non-physical. At a fundamental level, it is composed of just two quirks, 0 and 1, associated with two physical states. Which medium is used doesn't matter as long as it can be used to store these quirks. The most common substrates are magnetic orientations, electrical pulses and flashes of light. In each case, the association of a particular state with a quirk is arbitrary. An 'up' magnetic orientation can just as well carry a 1 or a 0: as in all information systems, the quirk is not determined by the state but by the cause of the state.

This dependence means that when there is no cause, the state will not carry a quirk. For instance, the bits of a pristine storage device that has just been manufactured and has yet to be involved in an information process will be in a particular state but carry no quirk. This dependence means that it is impossible to tell whether a particular bit state is associated with 1, 0 or nothing without knowing its cause. The same applies to the bits of a storage device that has been thoroughly wiped through randomization of its bit states, even if it includes bit sequences identical to those carrying meaningful information when produced as a result of an information process.

While acknowledging the fact that it is really the associated non-physical information and not the physical state that matters, the one-to-one relationship means that the magnetic orientation of a bit can be treated as if it is a binary value without any undue consequences. Observed at this level, the quirk could be considered as no more than a by-product of physical states; the distinction between the two brushed off as a trivial semantic issue. However, as with the instructions associated with the symbols read by the processor, this lowest level serves no useful function. It is only when quirks are combined to form sequential hierarchical levels of organization with emergent characteristics that the type of information is created that is required as input for its programmes.

It is here again that the physicalist position becomes untenable. It is not physical interactions taking place between bits that underlie this constructive process but informational relationships between their associated quirks. While physical quarks combine to form physical atoms, non-physical quirks combine to form non-physical higher-level information that is not associated with physical structures or states. It is this independence from physical determinants that allows any type of information – from texts to video and from numbers to music – to be stored using the same storage medium.

Like the creation of higher level functions from machine code operations, the formation of higher level informational entities in computers is the result of design. Distinct coding systems have been developed to digitize the various types of information to be stored and processed by the computer. One simple example is that of colour. Using a single binary quirk, it is only possible to represent two distinct colours – for instance black and white. Combining three binary quirks forms the basis for a rudimentary RGB coding system in which the bit states are equated to the presence or absence of a primary colour. For instance, three bits in the states up – down – up may be associated with the quirks 1 – 0 – 1, the first of which indicates 'red present'; the second 'green absent'; the third 'blue present'. These quirks combine to form the information 'purple', but this is not through physical interaction between the bit states. It is not so that the first bit is red, the second colourless and the third blue, whereby they combine like dots of paint to produce the purple colour. It is instead a product of logical interaction between the quirks they carry. Nor is it so that 'purple' is created as a fourth type of primary quirk. Individual bits can still only represent red, green and blue. The information 'purple' is therefore emergent.

Using three binary quirks still only allows eight colours to be represented. To expand the range of colours that can be stored, a commonly used system combines eight binary quirks to indicate the intensity of each of the colours R, G and B. In this system, violet is created by setting the states of 24 bits as follows: UDDDUDUD DDUDUDUU UUUDDDUD. This is not because the up and down states are of any use to us, but because setting them creates the binary sequence 10001010 00101011 11100010. That this string carries the information 'violet' is less directly evident than the purple in the 3-bit RGB system in the previous paragraph. Determining this fact requires several information-processing steps. Firstly, an integer value needs to be calculated from each 8-quirk substring: the first combines to carry the number 138:

$$(128\times1)+(64\times0)+(32\times0)+(16\times0)+(8\times1)+(4\times0)+(2\times1)+(1\times0) = 138$$

This in itself is emergent information, as 138 is a type of information (decimal number) that cannot be attached to an individual bit – but it still contains no colour information. In a second step, the three-byte values are combined using the formula (138×65536)+(43×256)+226 to get the number 9,055,202: still not a colour. Finally, this numerical value is used to look up the colour it is associated with in a code table to find violet (Figure 25). It is, then, only by knowing and applying the specific protocols used to create the information, that it is possible to decode the binary sequences associated with detectable bit states to determine which emergent information has been stored. If a different table or calculation were to be used the same bit sequence could be associated with a different colour, or indeed an entirely different type of information. The astute reader will have noticed that this bit sequence is exactly the same as that in Figure 23, where it was not used to store any form of information, but to specify instructions in a computer programme.

The digitization of colour is an interesting example of how such systems relate to physical reality and our perception of it. While light frequencies form a continuous spectrum, the 24-bit system (only) offers 16 million distinct colours. Perhaps, more significantly, it spans only the visible spectrum, excluding frequencies in the infrared and below, and ultraviolet and above. The reason for this limited scope and resolution has everything to do with its purpose: to store information that is relevant to the human visual system, which works on the basis of red-, green- and blue-sensitive retinal cones and has a comparable ability to distinguish colours. Had humans, like birds, had a fourth ultraviolet cone we would doubtless have adopted a 32-bit RGBV colour coding system.

Such selection, approximation and coding protocols necessarily apply to the digitization of all physical phenomena. An image is simplified to pixels of a particular size since creating a totally accurate image would require a subatomic resolution. The continuous waveforms of sound are similarly reduced to samples of a specified duration sufficient to reproduce the effect of the original sound when the digital version is converted back to physical form using a loudspeaker.

In addition to such necessary content-based coding systems and sampling approximations, various other factors are involved in creating digital files containing information to be used by the computer. Such files invariably start with information about what kind of information they contain and how it should be interpreted, for instance referring to the language or coding system used. Without such 'context', the computer would have no way of knowing how the binary sequences should be interpreted. An additional factor is data compression. If 90% of the pixels in an image are white, it is far more efficient to store the information

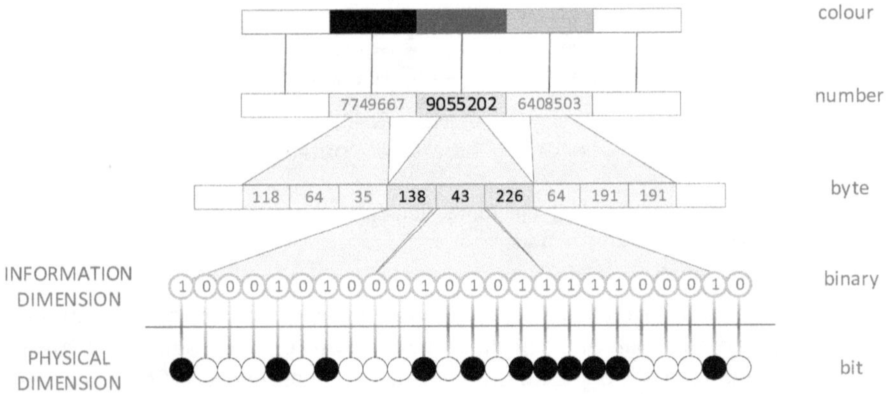

Figure 25 The construction of colour from binary values using the 24-bit RGB system.

'white for the next 300 pixels' than to repeat the colour white 300 times. The emphasis in designing such protocols is not on maintaining a relationship between bit states and associated information, but on balancing computational and storage efficiency against the degree of accuracy required. This results in an increasing distinction between the physical entity and its digitized alter ego. However, this is no issue as long as the coding method used in the digitization is known. This can always be used in reverse to reconstruct the information from the bit sequence.

2.3.5 Dimensionality of digital information processing

We have seen that both the programmes and the data used by digital computers are based on stratified coding protocols which allow complex high-level informational processes and entities to be created. We have also seen that this all ultimately boils down to linear sequences of bit states with which the underlying binary quirks are associated. While computer disks and memory chips are flat two-dimensional physical objects, the initial level of the information dimension they support is therefore only one-dimensional. All that is required to identify the location of any of these bits is a single number: its 'address' on this very long line. This brings us to the question of how this relates to the dimensionality of the computer's information dimension and its content.

One thing is clear: this situation is radically different to the unfathomably complex geometrical topologies formed by the brain's complex organic networks. Instead, like the rest of its functions, the computer's information dimension is designed for purpose. This purpose can result in the construction of a range of distinct dimensionalities.

The structure of the computer programme illustrated in Figure 23 may have an impressive number of layers but these all exist in the single dimension of the linear sequence of instructions performed by the processor. Looking 'upwards' in this hierarchy you are not looking 'somewhere else' but zooming out to observe things at a grander scale. While an essential feature of computer programmes is the ability

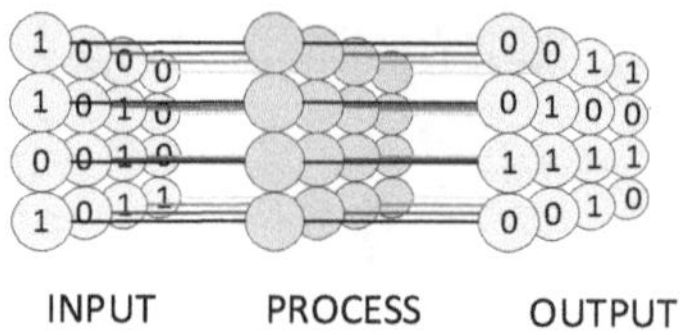

Figure 26 In parallel processing, the dimensionality of an array is maintained during processing.

to choose between different paths, the execution of these choices only involves jumping to a different part of the linear sequence. This relatively simple dimensionality of the computer's processing mechanisms is a consequence of the underlying design, which ultimately consists of a linear sequence of actions.

While this is a basic truth for the individual processing stream, contemporary computers are more complex than this simplified depiction in ways that influence dimensionality. They do not just have one processing mechanism but large numbers running together to increase the speed and capacity of the computer. This allows, for instance, parallel processing: the simultaneous processing of multiple data streams. Being functionally related, these become neighbouring events taking place at the same time. For instance, if a two-dimensional array of values is processed in parallel, then dimensionality is maintained during the process (Figure 26). However, this is still little more than a temporal combination of linear processes.

Turning to the information stored in a computer things start to get more interesting. This has everything to do with the nature of the type of information we are considering. Going back to definitions, we saw that the quirks attached to a physical state are representatives of the cause of that state. Applying this to computer data initially has few dimensional consequences. Designing a system whose binary quirks can store the number 138 requires no more than the combination of the linear binary sequence 10001010. Like in the computer programme described above, finding the emergent information is simply a matter of zooming out to the required level of organization. We see the same with the storage of a colour in Figure 25.

This changes when we need the computer to store digital versions of entities with more dimensions than a number or a colour. For these to be accurate and useable representations, this dimensionality needs to be replicated in the information dimension. The above example of array processing is typical of digital images. In such a grid, each pixel has four direct neighbours rather than the two that are possible in a linear sequence. Storing such information in a linear sequence therefore requires the image to be broken down into lines in which neighbouring horizontal pixels will still be next to each other but neighbouring vertical pixels will be some distance apart. However, this is not the structure of the information stored. Consequently, the protocols used result in an additional dimension being created as an emergent feature of the combination of quirks: the information has a higher dimensionality than the physical substrate used to store it (Figure 27). Should information about a three-dimensional object need to be stored, this will need to be done in a comparable way.

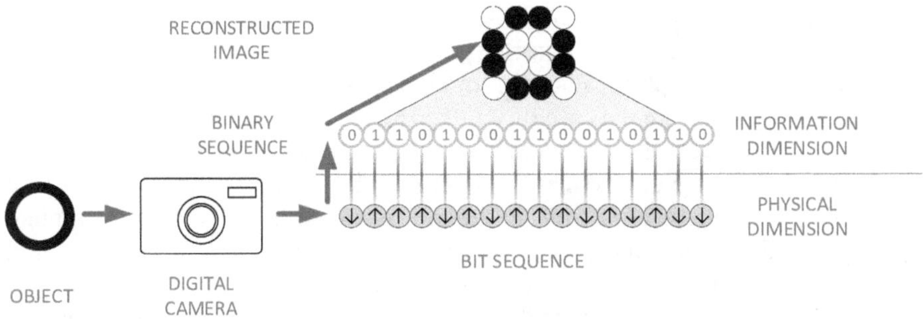

Figure 27 The creation of a two-dimensional bitmap image from a one-dimension bit/binary sequence.

Nobody would dispute the computer's ability to store information with a higher dimensionality than its bit sequences, but the fact that these extra dimensions are not physical can lead to them being considered less than real. However, once we accept that the binary quirks they are built from are non-physical and yet real, there is no reason why they should be limited to the dimensionality of the substrate they are associated with. Here, it is the relationships between quirks that matter, and those representing vertically adjacent pixels have the same relationship to those representing horizontally adjacent pixels. Further evidence for the existence of these emergent dimensions is seen in the fact that the programmes written to process such information treat it as having these dimensions, and the output of these programmes, when converted back to a visible physical form, is also multi-dimensional.

As in the brain, the informational structures created by computers, being non-physical, are not limited to three dimensions. With functional proximity again being based on informational interaction and relationship rather than the location of the physical substrate with which their quirks are associated, computers are free to create whatever dimensionality that is of use to them. For instance, in a relational database, like in a neural network, many-to-many connections can bring any number of informational entities into proximity with each other, creating informational structures that could not be recreated in physical form.

One of the more remarkable consequences of this flexibility is that it allows computers to create digital versions of neural networks, whereby the informational representations will necessarily have the same complex network topology in order to perform as simulations.

2.3.6 Digital simulation

Computers are not limited to storing static digital representations of existing physical entities. If these are supplemented with information concerning the physical properties of these entities and programmed with the physical laws applying to them, it is possible to bring them to life in the form of digital simulations.

This option has proven immensely useful in a diversity of situations, from industrial design to weather forecasting. In these situations, the goal is to create a digital equivalent of a physical system (a digital twin) that emulates its behaviour as closely as possible. In the case of weather forecasting this starts with measurements of factors such as temperature and wind speed. These measurements are used to alter the states of physical bits to create the quirks required to reconstruct the current atmospheric conditions in the information dimension of the computer. Speeding up the natural rate of the (meteorological) laws of physics allows future states to be simulated, and thus predicted in advance.

Simulation is also the basis for the entire realm of digital gaming in which virtual worlds are created from imagination rather than as representations of physical reality. In general, to make the illusion believable, these are programmed with the laws that apply to the physical reality we inhabit but this is by no means a necessity. It can easily be adapted for the sake of entertainment, for instance by ignoring gravity or slowing a bullet to allow its path to be followed. The inhabitants of these virtual worlds may similarly be designed to be replicas of or intentionally different from those of our own. In the absence of evolutionary and biological constraints, anything is possible.

Here, again, we encounter the question of what is real. It is clear that these worlds are not physically real, but if we accept that the non-physical binary quirks from which they are built are real, and that emergent phenomena that can arise from large numbers of these quirks, the term 'virtual' takes on a different meaning. It then becomes comparable to the reality of the higher level informational phenomena taking place in the information dimensions associated with brains. Here, again, high-level informational phenomena determine the necessary events taking place at the quirk level, and through them the changes taking place in the physical substrate. This influence requires them to be on a par with high-level physical phenomena which exert such top-down effects in physical systems.

The reality we are referring to here is explicitly not the observable, physical image we see on the computer's monitor. This is no more than a translation of what exists in its information dimension, designed and created to solve the issue that we cannot see the content itself. If the monitor is switched off, this content continues to exist in the same way that our thoughts continue even when we do not express them verbally. Turn the monitor back on and it will become evident that the simulation has continued regardless of whether or not it was projected onto the monitor or watched.

In a curious recursivity, in addition to simulating real or fictitious physical phenomena, it is also possible to simulate informational phenomena, and this has indeed become commonplace. Research into artificial neural networks, for instance, does not involve the inconvenience of actually constructing physical networks. While this would be feasible for small networks, the challenge of doing it for the scale of the networks that are used in contemporary machine learning systems would be somewhere in the range between formidable and impossible. In this, they differ from biological neural networks which are constructed during foetal and postnatal growth and development from billions of physical nodes and orders of magnitude more connections.

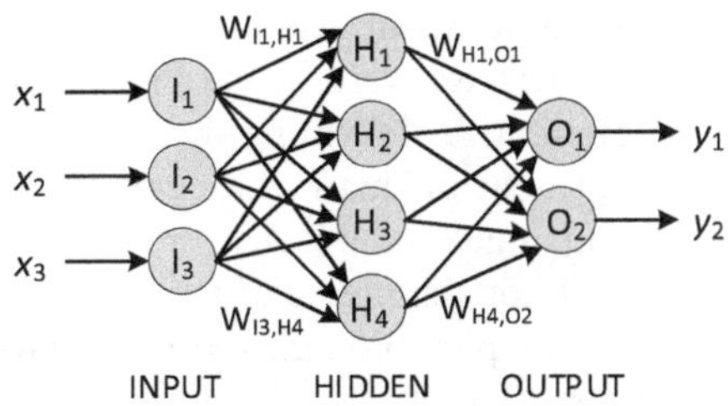

Figure 28 Artificial neural networks are based only on information and logical relationships. Simulation of physical components that could support such information systems is superfluous.

More significantly, such research is not even based on simulation of the states, properties and physics of the electronic components, connecting wires and electrical currents that would be required to create such a physical neural network. This again demonstrates the degree to which the physical substrate is arbitrary and only supportive of the informational functions of such systems: it is quite unnecessary to include such factors in the simulation. Instead, these involve only the informational aspects of these systems which form the essence of their function: the polarities and strengths of relationships and the effects of the activity of one component on another. The state of a node is not a simulated electrical potential, but the value of the quirk that would be associated with that potential were it to be a physical system. The connections between nodes are not based on the properties of wires conducting electrical currents but weighting relationships between up- and downstream states. The changes in states are not realized by emulating the functions of electronic components, but by performing the calculations that could be supported by such components (Figure 28).

The fact that artificial neural networks have informational functions and that physical versions are seldom or never built makes it inappropriate to consider them as simulations. Instead, they can better be considered as emergent information-processing systems created using the generic capabilities of the digital computer. In this sense, they are comparable to syntactic programming, which also has no physical incarnation. Depictions such as that in Figure 28 should therefore be seen not so much as literal nodes and connections arranged in a two-dimensional plane, but as representations of informational systems which can most effectively be visualized this way.

The significant difference with syntactic programming, and similarity with biological neural networks, is that these systems do not have a fixed predefined function. Instead, they are designed to develop functions on the basis of training: a process that takes place entirely within the computer's information dimension. Ultimately, of course, the changes are supported by alterations in bit states and their associated binary values but it is at higher, emergent levels that the connection weightings and structure of the network exist and the processes take place that determine these changes.

The realization and nature of artificial neural networks are consequently fundamentally different to the physical wetware of the biological neural networks that formed the conceptual inspiration for inventing them. It is, of course, possible to simulate such physical biological neural networks, but here we encounter two issues.

The first is their messy, analogue nature. A neuron, in contrast with a node of an artificial neural network, is not a simple entity with an indivisible numerically determined quirk state, but a complex biological cell composed of many elements and many parameters that contribute to its effective state. Its connections are not pure numerical calculations based on constant weightings but involve the release of variable quantities of stored neurotransmitter molecules. As with all complex systems, small differences in starting conditions can have a large effect on outcome. Accounting for such differences at a sufficient level of detail to create realistic simulations of a neural network of the scale of the brain is technically impossible.

The second issue is that it is not the physical aspect of these systems that is functionally relevant but the information associated with them. In order to simulate their function, rather than just the operation of the system, it would be necessary to include the quirks associated with the simulated states and the emergent information entities and functions arising from them. While it is possible to detect and measure the physical characteristics of the network as a basis for building the simulation, it is not possible to do this for its informational aspects. Consequently, even a perfect simulation of a physical neural network would not include its informational function. For the simplest of networks, this need not be a problem. Where there is a one-on-one relationship between physical state and quirk, and between mechanism and informational effect, it is not necessity to distinguish the two. But as the influence of emergent information increases in larger scale networks, this omission will become increasingly problematic. As with computer programming, there will be no way of deriving functions purely from the measurable bit states that ultimately facilitate their existence.

Indeed, unless these simulations include the quirks associated with the physical network, and the entities and processes built from them, it is doubtful whether they could reproduce their behaviour. After all, we have seen that it is the high-level informational phenomena that determine this behaviour. Without them, then, the network would be a philosophical zombie: going through the motions of the physical network but lacking its immaterial soul (more scientifically speaking: the informational processes which are its actual purpose and function).

In practice, this is not an issue because simulations of biological networks tend to be based not on their molecular and cellular structures and functions but, as with artificial neural networks, on the connection and state values that are actually informational rather than physical by nature. These can then, in principle, form emergent informational phenomena without the necessity or constraint of an accurate simulation of the physical substrate.

2.3.7 The digital community

While in their early days computers operated in isolation, the advantages of connecting them in networks soon became apparent. In this way, they could access communal resources and tasks could be divided between them. Originally connecting only the computers of an individual firm, these networks soon expanded outside the walls of buildings until they came to cover the entire planet in the form of the internet. Today, computers anywhere in the world can contact each other directly and with delays of mere milliseconds.

Viewed from the perspective of the information dimension, we again see a different topology that starts with the difference between physical and functional distance. As with the neurons of the brain, interacting computers at great physical distance from each other will be functionally proximal, while two computers sitting next to each other on a desk that have no functional relationship are effectively distant. Given that computers have informational rather than physical functions, it is this distance that is relevant and forms the basis of the functional dimensionality of the internet.

Beyond this basic equivalence, the similarities between the internet and the brain fade. Most significantly, the internet is not based on individual physical connections between computers, but on an addressing system that allows any computer to connect to any other computer. Consequently, in contrast with relatively stable relationships between nodes in a neural network, computers connected to the internet may flit between temporary partners with wild abandon. Another distinction is that the degree of connectivity is far lower. While a single neuron may constantly be interacting with hundreds of others, a computer is generally more selective, either operating independently for the time being or interacting with just a few. Such factors lead to the internet having a very specific and dynamic scale-free topology, which has also adapted as it has grown through the decades [263].

Viewing the internet from the informational rather than the physical perspective, it quickly becomes apparent how, to what degree, and in what sense it has shrunk the world. The planet is, of course, no smaller than it was a century ago, but the direct proximity of computers in the information dimension that are spread over great distances over the physical planet creates a dense and compact community of computers in the information dimension they inhabit (Figure 29).

A further difference from neural networks is that each computer has a far greater and more diverse individual capacity for performing informational tasks that a neuron. In this sense, they are more similar to a human community, in which individuals take on different roles in order to perform a communal function. Here too, it is not the physical characteristics of members that determine their contribution. While they may be housed in smaller or larger casings and have more or less capacity, all computers are essentially the same physical machines. It is instead their distinct informational functions that count. The internet is not just a scaling up of the capabilities of individual computers, but an ordered complex system composed of parts with very different informational characteristics: a system with emergent features that cannot be found in these parts.

As a consequence of their complex internal functions computers do not exchange individual quirks when interacting but, more like individuals in a human community, various types of high-level information. This information is built from individual quirks: in this case, the streams of binary values associated with electrical pulses or flashes of light passing through metal or optic fibres. As with

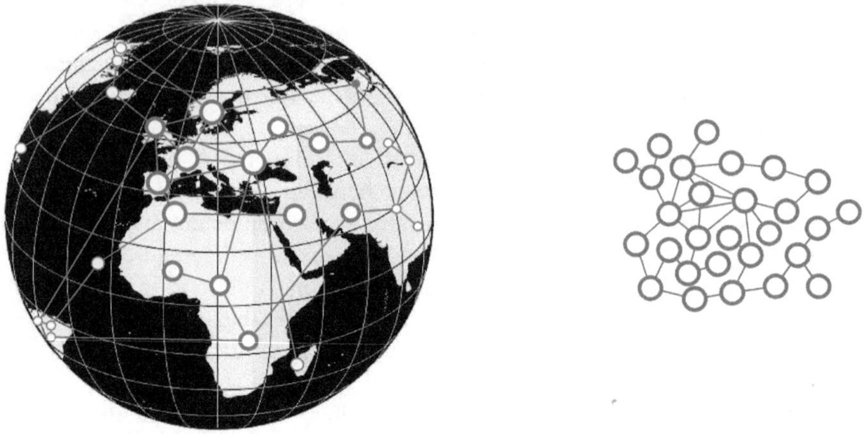

Figure 29 The global internet can be seen as a physical layer covering the surface of the planet (left) or, more appropriately, as a dynamic network topology existing in the information dimension (right).

human speech, successful transmission of information involves a conversion-transmission-conversion sequence, in which the sender and receiver must both use the same coding system.

This situation gives new meaning to the saying of sending something 'into the ether'. When you send an e-mail, it certainly does cause a sequence of physical events that race through the network of cables or wireless connections between your computer and that of the addressee. But the reason we do this is not because we have any interest in these physical events. One of the more important features of the internet is its redundancy: data streams can follow any number of paths in order to reach their destination depending on which are busier, or perhaps defective. The loss of one of these physical connections is therefore unimportant. What we need to happen, and what can be supported by any number of physical mechanisms, is that the message is transported through the integrated information dimension formed by this community of computers.

The above examples relate to purely informational tasks; another application of computers is seen in the design and construction of cyber-physical systems, in which they perform various control and coordination functions in systems with a physical function [264]. Typically, sensor data is used to autonomously control the behaviour of the system in ways that can either be pre-programmed or involve adaptive machine learning algorithms. A wide range of applications have been developed, from autonomous vehicles so smart power grids that monitor and manage electricity generation, distribution and consumption. There are also many examples in the use of robotics in industrial and agricultural settings, where automated control systems can far exceed human speed and capacity in production tasks. Cyber-physical systems also excel at tasks such as quality control and predictive maintenance of machinery on the basis of detected anomalies (Figure 30).

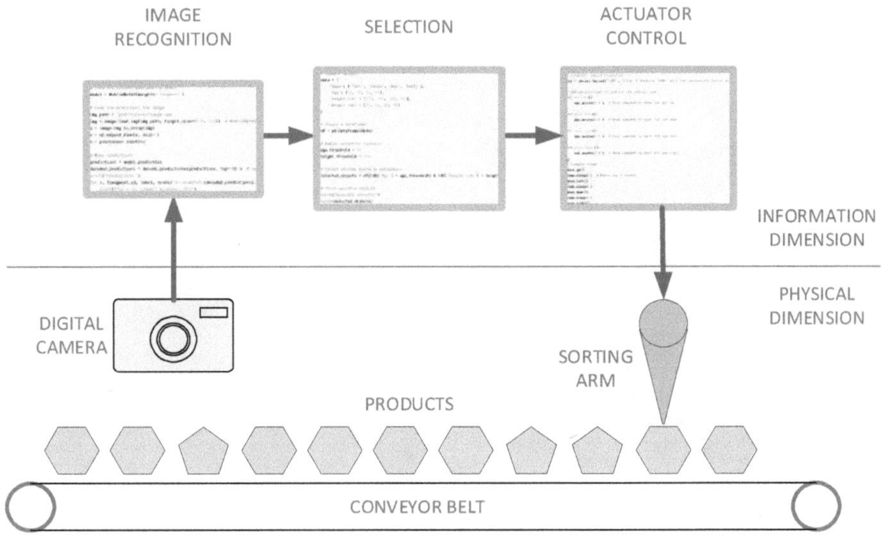

Figure 30 A simple cyber-physical system for detecting and rejecting defective products on a production line.

In all of these examples, the end result is a product of a close integration of informational and physical processes. The former take place in the information dimension, where quirks created by sensors are combined and processed according to informational laws, resulting is in instructions to be executed by actuators. The latter are classical machines operating according to the laws of physics.

Part 3

Discussion

Living with the consequences

3.1 Existing in the information dimension

It is intuitively obvious that our thoughts and emotions are 'inside us'. That, as a product of brain activity, they do not exist somewhere out there in the world even when they relate to something external. We recognize that the fear of a snarling dog is our reaction, not some feature of the dog itself. Emergent Information Theory places these phenomena not in the brain itself, but in the information dimension associated with it. This too is not entirely counterintuitive: while envisaging extra dimensions is difficult, it is not so that the fear seems to be located at some particular part of the brain inside your skull. An alternative type of locality therefore seems fitting.

Logically speaking, we must accept the same for qualia such as the redness of a rose. While initiated by light reflected by the flower and landing on the retina, the experience of redness is not a characteristic of the rose itself but, like the fear of the dog, a product of brain activity. The rose itself has no colour, only a particular effect on the light falling on it. Redness, then, also exist not in the outside world but in the brain's information dimension.

The next logical step is, however, very counterintuitive and brings us to one of the most remarkable, convincing and essential illusions created by the brain. When you look at a rose held in your hand the impression is that what you are seeing is outside your body: that it is the external object that it relates to. This impression is not surprising. It is, after all, the purpose of sensory perception to map out your surroundings to allow you to operate within them. Yet, the stereoscopic image you see, like the redness of the rose and the fear of a dog, is most definitely not 'out there'. It is undeniably an informational product that your brain constructs through the recombination, processing and interpretation of the quirks created by the photons reflected by the rose impinging on cells in the retinas of your two eyes.

This distinction between our surroundings and our perception of it is also evident from the fact that if you look away or close your eyes the image vanishes, but the rose is still there. This is not because the image is blocked by your eyelids, but because the photons are blocked that cause the creation of quirks in your retina, that are subsequently used to build the image. What you actually see is only a temporary representation, but one that perfectly performs the function for which it has evolved: to identify the object you are holding.

DOI: 10.4324/9781003460541-12

This applies not just to a single object in your hand, but to the entire multisensory reconstruction of everything you see, hear, smell and feel around you. This integrated experience of your physical surroundings is not where it appears to be. When you walk down the road your physical body may move across physical tarmac, but your conscious mind is not out there on the street. Being a non-physical phenomenon is cannot be there: if it was, then it would occupy physical space and could be detected there. Instead your sensory experience, including the proprioceptive representation of your own body, moves through the reconstruction of the road in your information dimension, which you hope is accurate but will never be so entirely. Hence, the possibility of stumbling over a kerb which was missing from the reconstruction; the shock when a dog that wasn't included suddenly barks. Sensory illusions provide explicit examples of failures of your brain to create a faithful reconstruction. The mismatch may be amusing, but demonstrates clearly that what you experience is not the external reality itself but a representation of it.

This representation is not a replica, built of the same stuff as the original. It is something entirely different by nature. The tarmac is made from bitumen and stone; your perception of it is made physically from electrical impulses in your brain and informationally from the quirks they carry. Vision presents us with a particularly indirect relationship. In contrast with touch and taste, the information is not even based on direct interaction with the object. What you see is instead the effect of the object on ambient light. Take the visual experience of the colour red. This could be the result of the fact that the petals of a rose absorb all frequencies of sunlight with the exception of red, which is therefore reflected into your eye. Here, the redness is a result of the molecular composition of the rose. The redness in a rainbow, in contrast, is the result of the fragmentation of the frequencies of sunlight by water droplets. All frequencies pass through but leave at different angles, resulting in the colour you see. Here, red is a result of the refractive properties of water and your specific position relative to the sun and the water droplets. The fact that red cones in your retina are stimulated by incoming light in these two examples relates differently and only indirectly to the physical properties of the object you are seeing.

While the logic of these lines of reasoning is solid, the conclusion is hard to swallow for two reasons. Firstly, millions of years of evolution have fine-tuned this functionally essential illusion to the degree that it is generally highly reliable and therefore convincing. Believing it is fundamental to the way in which we respond to our surroundings. This is, indeed, the primary reason for having a brain at all.

The second reason is that we have no alternative. Our personal sensory reconstruction is the only thing we can experience. This is not because our brains are encased in a skull that keeps them literally in the dark: it has a more fundamental cause. The fact that our surroundings are physical and our perceptions informational results in an inverse non-detectability problem. We have seen that empirical investigation of consciousness is hampered by the fact that, as non-physical phenomena, they cannot interact with physical detection devices. This non-detectability is, however, mutual. The fact that the physical world is non-informational means that it can also not directly interact with and thus be detected by the informational instruments operating in our brains. Imagining for a moment that our brains were not encased in bone, the rose could not enter our perception through direct physical contact by embedding itself in our white matter. That is not the stuff that our perceptions are made of, nor where they can be found. The only way for us to know anything about our surroundings is through the conversion of physical stimuli to information at the interface of our sense organs.

The conclusion that all that we perceive exists inside our personal information dimension may seem to stumble over one very simple objection. How can the road you're walking down, the cars, the houses on either side possibly fit within the 1,300 cm^3 of your physical brain? This is, however, the wrong question to ask. The image does not require space in the physical brain. Instead, it occupies a portion of its information dimension. We have seen that that a massively interconnected neural network such as the brain creates a multidimensional informational space with a volume that is orders of magnitude larger than its physical substrate. There is no a priori reason why this should not be sufficient to house something of this scale.

To this, we need to consider what it actually is that needs to be accommodated. What you see when you look up at a 100 m high skyscraper is in your information dimension, but this is not to say that it occupies 100 m of informational space: this physical measure is not applicable or meaningful in the information dimension. If we consider 'size' as the scale of something relative to its smallest components, then the skyscraper's physical 100 m is unimaginably huge compared to the atoms and quarks it is ultimately composed of. While your image of it may be composed of millions of quirks, it is tiny in comparison. To start with, however close you are to the skyscraper, the smallest detail you will be able to see is around the millimetre scale: of the order of magnitude of 10^{20} atoms. As you move further away, your visual acuity will scale down proportionally. The physical moon has a diameter of 3,500 km, but its representation in your reconstruction is smaller than a marble in your hand. To this, we can add that all you can see is the surface of an object that is facing you: your reconstruction does not include the entire content of the skyscraper, nor the backside of it. Finally, we have the limits of the sensitivity of our retinal sensors, which are blind to the infrared and the ultraviolet. Aspects of an object that produce these frequencies of electromagnetic radiation are also excluded: we cannot, for instance, see how hot the skyscraper is. These are just some of the restrictions of what is, in humans, our dominant sense. Our other sense-at-a-distance, hearing, has equivalent frequency limitations: we can only detect sounds from 20 Hz to 20 kHz. Smell can only detect a select set of airborne molecules. Our contact senses are even more limited. Touch and taste can only provide information about a tiny part of our surroundings at any one time. In all respects, then, the experiential world we inhabit is a massively oversimplified, compressed and miniaturized version of the physical reality it represents.

Finally, while this sensory reconstruction of our surroundings, up to and including the stars in the sky, may necessarily and explicitly present itself as immense it fades in comparison quantitatively with the rest of the content of our information dimension – all of our stored memories, learned skills and knowledge; our current thoughts and emotions; our future ambitions and plans. These we know to fit in this remarkable space created by our brain because there is nowhere else for them to exist. Our sensory reconstruction is just one inhabitant of this neighbourhood.

The fact that you cannot actually experience your physical surroundings, only your reconstruction of it in the information dimension, could lead to a reversal of materialism. Materialism denies the existence of non-physical substance on the basis of its non-detectability but the physical is just as non-detectable from the experiential perspective. Is this, then, reason to turn the tables and deny the existence of the physical? Emergent Information Theory firmly and explicitly refutes this line of reasoning. By showing how the information dimension and its content are built from quirks that are created by the interaction between physical entities, it makes it entirely dependent on the physical. Furthermore, it demonstrates how such phenomena arose and developed as a product of biological evolution, which itself could only take place on a suitable planet that formed as a product of cosmic processes taking place in a pre-existing physical universe. Instead of pitting the informational against the physical or the physical against the informational, Emergent Information Theory combines the two in an integrated union in which each, in spite of its fundamentally different nature, is acknowledged as a part of a necessarily expanded view of reality.

As living, sentient organisms we span the divide. Our bodies exist in the physical realm; our minds in the informational; with our brains as the interface between the two. The functionally seamless integration of the two that allows our minds to steer our bodies in such a way that they are fed, watered and don't fall off cliffs is surely evolution's single most astounding achievement.

3.2 The gamble evolution took

We have seen that the heredity and evolution of biological function is a remarkable phenomenon: that lacking a design, complex structures and mechanisms can only arise from self-organizational processes governed top-down from the systemic level. For physical features, these determinative systemic functions are also physical, whereby a direct relationship exists between them and the developmental processes. We have also seen that wiring the connectivity networks of the brain introduces new challenges. Firstly that the usual processes of morphological development based on the positioning of cells of specific types do not suffice. An additional process is required to determine which connections are laid down between them and takes the form of various forms of synaptic plasticity. More significantly, these specific self-organizational processes need to be governed not by systemic physical functions, but by high-level processes taking place in the information dimension associated with the brain. Only in this way is it possible to create the stacked layers of organization required to generate the emergent informational functions required of the brain. While in some simple cases a direct developmental process may be sufficient, the more complex functions necessitate learning: an iterative process involving replication, variation and selection that constitutes an evolutionary process taking place within the individual brain and lifetime. The ability to develop functions in this way is unique to the organism's informational capabilities: it is possible for a human to learn how to swim, but not to learn to change limbs into fins.

Creating a new and dynamic evolutionary process in a parallel dimension is one of biological evolution's more original discoveries, but it did not come without risks. A person's success with respect to these functions is not based on the replication with variation of the strengths and weaknesses of their parent's mental capabilities. Each individual brain must recreate these abilities from scratch. Certainly, some aspects of nature and nurture will influence this process, but there is no direct inheritance of the neural connectivity patterns underlying mental function comparable to the inheritance of cellular structures underlying physical function. What we inherit is the ability to create functions, not the functions themselves. Significantly, it is therefore not the relative reproductive success of individuals within a population that determines which functions are seen but the success of a particular entity in the information dimension of an individual brain. This leads to

DOI: 10.4324/9781003460541-13

a very real risk of the two evolutionary processes diverging. What guarantee does biological evolution have that the products of this independent evolutionary process will benefit the organism in the form of effective responsive behaviour, rather than flying off at a wild tangent?

One significant constraining factor can be found in the embodiment of the brain. The information dimension associated with the brain is not a free-standing entity, but tightly strapped to physical reality on one side through the sense organs and on the other through the musculoskeletal system it controls. On the sensory side, the characteristics of incoming information will be instrumental in the development of perceptual functions. A bat's brain will inevitably develop sonar capabilities which human brains lack. The human visual system develops colour vision because the eye produces colour-specified visual information, while that of a dog does not. On the output side, the fact that we have no nerves running out to tail muscles means that the areas of information dimension associated with our motor cortex will not develop tail-wagging behaviours while that of a horse, which has no fingers, will not develop manual dexterity. The fact that the body and its associated information dimension grow and develop together from the foetal stage makes it altogether unsurprising that they are well tuned in these areas.

These constraints will also seep through into the inner regions of the information dimension, although their effects will weaken and become more abstract the deeper we go. In small-brained animals, the intervening space is limited, but in vertebrates and humans in particular, it is extensive. Yet even here, the fact that we live in a physical world with particular characteristics will mould developments. Abstractions such as plan forming are constrained by the fact that they are intended to be executed in physical reality and must therefore be based on and remain aligned with the input-output interfaces of sensory information and behavioural possibilities. In such cases, evolutionary success in the information dimension will be coupled to the physical organism and its surroundings.

On the other hand, it is evident that the information dimension does not always operate in the best interests of its physical host. This digression if most evident in humans, in which long lists can be compiled of behaviours that do not actively support our biological interests or are even actively deleterious. From the risks to life and limb of extreme sports to the abstention from reproduction incorporated in religious belief, it is not difficult to find examples in which the information dimension has deviated from its biological purpose. Indeed, the entire spectrum of psychopathologies can be seen as examples of the information dimension failing at or deviating from the task given to it by biological evolution. The fact that such phenomena exist in spite of producing ineffective or counterproductive behaviours is understandable when we see them as products of evolution in the information dimension where different selective criteria apply. An obsession, for instance, is an extremely strong and successful entity in the information dimension. Eating disorders and addictions are other examples of phenomena that are stable and difficult to dismantle in the information dimension, but deleterious to physical survival and success. Calling such phenomena mental illnesses may seem appropriate when considered from the viewpoint of the physical organism, but in the information dimension they are healthy – possibly too healthy. As in a biological community, it may well be that excess success of one member causes an imbalance to the system.

The most extreme example of this is the uniquely human fatal path that leads to suicide. Here, information dimension processes develop the desire or need to end their own existence. Since the only way of doing this is to destroy the functions in the brain that create them, a suicidal information dimension needs to kill its biological host. This is clearly the ultimate digression from the intended role of the brain in generating behaviour that will increase the biological success of the organism.

A very different way in which the functions developing in the information come into conflict with the physical interests of the individual is seen in reproductive strategies. Persuading a member of the opposite sex to parent your offspring necessitates exerting an influence on the informational processes underlying their behaviour. In many animals, this has led to an arms race of display behaviours and physiologies that are highly expensive in terms of energy and resources, and therefore physically deleterious. The reason for the peacock's excessive tail is that the processes involved in mate choice in the information dimensions of peahens respond favourably to these super-stimuli. If this were not the case, then the peacock could save considerable resources and improve its flight: no insignificant factors in terms of survival.

Such examples aside, it is clear that if we weigh up the pro's and con's the gamble taken by evolution paid off big time, supporting behaviours that allowed animals to convert resources into offspring with escalating efficiency. The creation of an embodied brain with these informational capabilities was a prerequisite for the evolution of increasingly advanced sense organs and musculoskeletal systems. There would, for instance, be no point in a bat evolving sonar equipment and aerodynamic skin folds without a brain that processes information in such a way that they can be used to catch flying insects.

In humans, the risk of the more physically detached regions of the information dimension developing in ways that are detrimental to the individual is a small price to pay for the advantages of the flexibility of learning new skills and innovative behaviours.

The specific case of humans brings us to a second and more significant way in which evolution took a risky turn. Our success as a species is not thanks to our physical prowess or even our individual intelligence: in these terms, we are little more than an average primate. It is instead a result of the combination of the innovative capacity unique to human information dimensions and our ability to transfer these innovations using symbolic language. Together these resulted at the group level in an additional level of cultural development which is even further removed from the physical evolutionary processes operating on the basis of differential survival of individual organisms.

This new level has brought individual humans a plethora of blessings, from medicine and reliable food supplies to a range of physical comforts and luxuries. It is, however, a double-edged sword, on the other hand, bringing us the cultural phenomenon of warfare that causes untold individual suffering to this day. In spite of the destruction of human life and that which has been created in peacetime that we call upon ourselves, the communal information dimension has still propelled us, as a species, to a position of absolute global dominance.

From the viewpoint of ecological communities and the biosphere, excessive success of a single species is never a good thing. The progression of live on Earth is better served by competition between species that are worthy counterparts and can stimulate each other's improvement. In population dynamics, imbalances tend to lead to boom-and-bust events starting with a species exceeding the carrying capacity of its environment, causing resource depletion. Since the environment is incapable of supporting these greater numbers, this results in a die-off to sustainable levels. The extent to which the last few centuries of human cultural and technological evolution have removed limits to growth by finding ever more innovative ways of extracting and exploiting natural resources is unprecedented in the history of life on this planet. While Thomas Malthus could not foresee the technological advances that would make this possible when he wrote *An Essay on the Principle of Population* in 1798, the 'bust' that he predicted has been postponed rather than prevented. In addition to the non-sustainability of this situation for the human species, this imbalance has led to an ongoing mass extinction of other species. It can therefore be concluded that language, through its effect in uniting the information dimensions of human populations, is solely responsible for the derailment of the global biosphere. If there was any doubt as to the reality of informational phenomena and their influence on physical systems, the evidence doesn't get much bigger than this.

3.3 Determinism and free will

From a materialistic point of view, living organisms, like all physical systems and events, are subject to the deterministic laws of physics. This includes the brain processes underlying their behaviour. On this basis, it can be (and frequently has been) claimed that free will is an illusion. If our actions are exclusively governed by the immutable laws applying to the electrical currents flowing through the cells of our brains, this would seem to be an unavoidable conclusion. Even given the fact that the brain is a classic example of a non-linear complex system whose behaviour may be fundamentally unpredictable, the outcome would still be entirely determined by physical laws. Our sense of choice would be no more than an observation of these processes taking place, not an ability to influence the outcome.

This is, however, a strictly materialistic line of reasoning which we have already concluded to be incomplete. Just as our phenomenal consciousness presents solid evidence that there is more to reality than the physical, so too does our experience of free will and decision-making appear to contradict such a deterministic approach to human behaviour. This ranges from the trivial to the soul-searching. On the one hand, we sense freedom in choosing between an espresso and a cappuccino. On the other, we struggle with moral dilemmas and temptations and feel personally responsible for what we decide. We consequently perceive other people who cause harm to others in their own egocentric interests as being bad and deserving of punishment. This often extends to compliance with arbitrary social norms which do not actually harm others but symbolize allegiance to the group. This would all be unjustified if nobody can actually invoke free will to make choices.

We have seen that Emergent Information Theory acknowledges and provides an explanation for the existence of non-physical phenomena such as conscious experience. Can it also help with the dilemma between determinism and free will?

In the physical realm, we see stacked layers of organization, each with its own emergent properties. The subatomic, atomic, molecular, material, geological, planetary and cosmic levels are each subject to specific deterministic laws. The same applies to the neuronal processes taking place in the brain. However, in this case, we have seen that the further hierarchical progression does not take place in the material world. Instead, it is the quirks associated with this physical substrate that combine and interact as the bottom level of a hierarchy of informational structures and processes that fulfil the required functions of the brain. These emergent levels

DOI: 10.4324/9781003460541-14

are not physical and therefore have no associated physical laws to obey. Indeed, it is not just that mental processes have broken free from physical determinism, they have actually turned the tables. We have seen that high-level informational processes ultimately determine the physical neuronal activity on the output side of the brain that causes our actions and behaviours. This would seem to be a promising start: exactly what we need to justify the existence of free will.

Unfortunately, a closer look throws up a roadblock. Any aspect of reality must logically be governed by its own laws. Without such frameworks nothing meaningfully structured or consistently functional could ever exist, and we certainly expect this of our mental processes. The information dimension must therefore have its own non-physical laws which govern the phenomena that take place within it. At present, our ignorance of these laws and inability to observe the events taking place makes it impossible for us to use them to predict the outcome of these processes. It may well be that even if we did manage to solve these two problems, the complexity of these systems would make prediction of the outcome of individual events practically or even theoretically impossible. However, this is not to say that they are not law abiding. Rather, it would be comparable to our inability to exactly predict next week's weather in spite of understanding how weather systems work on the basis of deterministic physical laws. This is not because the wind is free to blow any way it likes, but because these too are non-linear systems.

Following this line of reasoning, it would therefore seem that we have evaded physical determinism only to find ourselves equally bound to a comparable informational determinism. All that we have done is expand law-based determinism to encompass an extended and integrated reality that also includes the information dimension and its contents. This last-hope loophole would therefore appear to be a definitive noose from which free will cannot escape. Whether this is the case, however, may depend on the nature of the informational laws themselves. After all, even in the physical dimension not all laws are straightforwardly deterministic, with the probabilistic nature of quantum indeterminacy as the most explicit example.

So what can we conclude about the laws governing the information dimension? Those applying to the bottom-level interactions between individual quirks will necessarily bear a close relationship with the physical processes they are associated with, albeit viewed from a very different perspective. It would therefore seem inevitable that they exhibit a comparable type of determinism. Since neural processes throughout the brain are broadly equivalent, this type of determinism will be ubiquitous at this underlying level.

In the sensory and motor regions of the brain, we see a different kind of determinism. The laws applying to the construction of sensory perceptions from quirks will be completely different from those by which the physical objects we perceive are built from quarks. However, in order to accurately mimic our physically deterministic surroundings, our senses will need to be equally law abiding. It would not be a good idea to grant our senses the freedom to choose perceptions that do not faithfully represent what is actually going on out there. Such flexibility on the motor side would be equally disastrous. Just imagine if the neurons connected to your finger muscles decided on a whim to pass through instructions intended for your legs. In these areas of the brain, it is of utmost importance that processes are reliably deterministic. Free will is not, then, a characteristic that we wish or have the tendency to ascribe to all mental processes.

Such freedom is more something that we associate with the higher levels of organization in the central areas of our information dimension where both of these restrictions fade. Here, we enter a realm of emergent entities and processes that bear no relation to the deterministic material world.

One of the most important functions of these areas is a type of governance that transcends the direct connection of stimulus and response seen in reflex actions. The enrichment of sensory input and expanded repertoire of possible responses necessitates a selection process between the many different actions that could be performed at a particular moment. It is specifically here that we encounter those phenomena we associate with free will: the decision to eat a healthy carrot or a less healthy cake; the choice between swerving to avoid a cat and preventing damage to your car; the dilemma of whether and how much to donate to a charitable cause.

This is not to say, even here, that we experience or require free will. To the contrary, much of the high-level learning that we do entails the construction and consolidation of strictly rule-based processes in order to provide reliable results. A classic example is mental arithmetic. In principle, we could exert our power of choice to answer '5' to the question '2+2', but that is certainly not the intention of these functions. Another example is the complex rule base of linguistic grammar. Here too, we rely on our mental processes applying these rigorously and without error. In fact, we expect the full diversity of functions that we have automated to sufficient degree to perform subconsciously to perform reliably and consistently. A whole class of functions falling into this category are our executive motor functions. Generally involving complex and carefully timed patterns of muscular action, these involve large numbers of choices concerning when, how strongly and for how long to contract each muscle. The process of mastering a sport involves the transition from having to make these choices consciously to embedding them in rule-based systems that don't waste time on such deliberations. In all of these examples – from mental arithmetic to volleying a ball in tennis – we see that free will, functionally speaking, is a poor man's decision-making. A last resort in the absence of better options. It could be argued that the perfect information system would never have to make a choice, since it would always be able to calculate the single best solution.

So why is it that we consider free will to be so important and in which subset of everything happening in our information dimensions do we encounter it? In general, we can conclude that this is predominantly in situations involving the weighting and comparison of alternative courses of action based on dynamic and often subjective criteria. It is in these areas of the information dimension that emotional and moral phenomena also play an important role, both of which are variable and context-dependent factors. The carrot vs cake choice may involve factors as diverse as the social context (perhaps it's a birthday cake, or maybe a situation in which you feel you should set a good example); whether you're on a diet; how tasty the cake looks; how hungry you are; and many more. These variable factors mean that there is no simple 'best answer' that will always apply. Coming to a conclusion therefore requires a very specific kind of information process, which certainly feels less deterministic than the answer to '2+2' or the way your legs move in a coordinated fashion when you are walking. The question is whether and to what degree this feeling is justified.

In considering this question, it is important to realize just how different information processes are than those we see taking place, deterministically, in the physical realm. One significant distinction is seen in the factors that can be involved. The ebb and flow of the tides may involve a balance between the gravitational fields of the Earth and Moon but cannot also be influenced by the colour of the sand on the beach or the fact that a whale may swim past tomorrow. This is because colour and future events have no relevance in the context of the physical laws of gravity. In contract, this is possible in the information dimension because any relevant physical (or non-physical) factor can be converted into the common currency of information. It is this conversion that renders the physical laws impotent: it is not gravity, colour or whales that are involved here, but information derived from them. As a consequence of this conversion, it is no problem to combine such factors in order to plan a visit to a white-sand beach at high tide when there is a good chance of spotting whales, and doing so involves an entirely different kind of process.

The fact that this process takes place at a high level of organization means that it is not coupled to the determinacy of quirk-based events coupled to neural activity; that it is not directly associated with sensory input or motor output avoids the constraints imposed by their proximity to external physical phenomena. Any deterministic influences here must therefore come from within the information dimension which requires us to consider how the concept of determinism differs here form in the physical realm. What are the causative factors behind the outcome of events, and is there a possibility that something with the characteristics of free will could be included?

One important distinction is time. The physical universe is, at any particular moment in time, in a particular state. Physical laws determine how it transforms from this state to the next. There is no way in which past or future events can influence this process and no way in which current states can be excluded. These restrictions form the basis for how we think about determinism: fixed laws are applied to fixed inputs to product a fixed output. In contrast, the outcome of decision-making processes can be influenced by any relevant factors in the past, present or future. The output, even given fixed laws, is therefore dependent on which of these potential inputs are included and which are excluded.

A second factor is derived from the 'common currency'. The physical laws apply exclusively to a particular aspect of physical reality. The laws of organic chemistry cannot be applied to population dynamics, and the laws of population dynamics cannot be applied to optics. These laws are consequently fine-tuned for and only ever need to deal with a specific type of input. In contrast, comparative processes in the information dimension need to deal with completely different types of factors for which there is no fixed 'exchange rate'. There is an absolute answer to the question whether the weight of the carrot is more or less than the weight of the cake, but not of whether your own weight is more or less than the temptation of a sweet treat.

A final factor is variability. The carrot has a fixed weight but many of the factors involved, in particular emotive values, can be variable to one moment to the next and may also influence each other. Bringing in a new consideration may shed a different light on some aspects, causing them to be reconsidered and give a different value.

In combination, these factors make it unsurprising that reaching a conclusion in a decision-making process can be difficult, and can waver or be reverted: characteristics that are never seen in deterministic physical processes. A falling raindrop does not hang in mid-air while it considers its options or climb back into the sky to take a different course, yet decision-making processes frequently do. Even if they are deterministic in the sense of being law abiding, it is therefore eminently clear that this is a very different kind of determinism.

Ultimately, the question is what we mean by free will and what influence we hope to find for it. Emergent Information Theory provides explicit justification for the objection to the claim that everything that happens in the mind is determined by physical laws. Indeed, it shows that such laws are not only incomplete but entirely irrelevant to this level of organization in the information dimension. If we mean to say that the outcomes of these processes are dependent on subjective factors that exist only in our minds, then this too can be confirmed. It is also evident that there is no single, fixed a priori outcome: this is instead the unique end product of a dynamic process with diverse and potentially variable inputs that, if repeated, could well give a different result.

Strictly speaking, however, these are all inevitable characteristics of the entities and processes that have been created at a particular place and level of organization in the information dimension specifically for this purpose. Their existence is necessary to the degree of inevitability: a human information dimension without this function would quickly end in gridlock with an inability to select between the multitude of possible actions and responses. It is this intended function that grants them the type of freedom of outcome that we were looking for, making the term 'free will' not entirely inappropriate. However, exhibiting these characteristics requires them to follow their own laws just as strictly as a billiard ball rolling across the table. There is, and can be, no influential phenomenon that is so free that it is not even bound to its own nature. In conclusion, Emergent Information Theory acknowledges that free will is a real phenomenon that is not bound to deterministic control by the laws of physics. Instead, it is an essential and law-abiding aspect of the information dimensions of all animals to a degree that is proportional to the diversity of alternative, competing stimulus-response outcomes.

The roots of the brighter and darker sides of human nature – the possibility of exploiting our behavioural flexibility to create harmony and beauty or cause suffering and destruction – lie in the expansion of our brains to a scale that could develop and accommodate a great diversity of responses to the same situation. It is this flexibility that underlies the responsibility of making the right choices and the distinction between good and evil. A lightning bolt that strikes someone dead is not evil since the process involves no choice, only the inevitable outcome of physical laws. The way that a jewel wasp larva eats a paralysed cockroach alive may be gruesome [265] but cannot be considered evil because the larva is simply performing predetermined functions. Even our own bodies are incapable of evil: the genocide committed on bacteria that are simply trying to colonize our lungs carries no moral judgement. This is because all of these events are the result of deterministic physical processes. Concepts such as right or wrong, good or bad, only have any meaning in the context of the existence of choice discussed in the previous chapter; they have no place in the physical realm, only in the information dimensions created by brains, whereby those of humans house the greatest known capacity. The person who strikes someone dead is held responsible because the act was the result of choices and decisions made in their information dimension which could have had a different outcome in which the person would not have been killed.

3.4 From organism to superorganism

The usual way of looking at biosphere is as a collection of individual animals and plants. It is, after all, these units that are physically demarcated and which reproduce, making copies of themselves in the next generation. At the same time, it is clear that no animal can ever survive in total isolation. To start with, it is dependent on the existence of other organisms as food. It is also dependent on a mate in order to reproduce, and in many species, it is dependent on members of a group for safety and collaborative action.

This dependency on the group is taken to the extreme in eusocial insects. The vast majority of the members of an ant colony are not even physically capable of reproduction; workers and soldiers have different physiologies suited to their role; their nests can only be built through united action; their foraging techniques involve a strong degree of cooperation. In these species, it is the colony and not the individual animal that is the smallest unit capable of reproduction and survival, justifying the term 'superorganism'. The ensuing complete dependency of the individual swings the balance of interests in the favour of the colony: it is not uncommon for the individual to sacrifice itself for the group it is a part of. However, the small size of the brains of these animals makes it highly unlikely that any kind of choice is involved: they will be operating in the only way they are capable of. In this sense, they are not so much selfless as helpless, in much the same way as the immune cells in our bodies cannot help but sacrifice themselves to defend us from infectious agents.

An important feature of superorganisms is that their coordinated actions necessitate the exchange of information between individuals, typically using pheromones in the case of insects. Viewed from an informational perspective, we see a relatively simple network of large numbers of connected information dimensions that gives the colony a communal intelligence that none of the ants possesses: a form of emergent information above the level of the individual.

Many vertebrate species also coordinate group actions through the exchange of information using various visual, auditory and olfactory methods. However, the fact that individuals remain viable reproductive units means that they fall short of the requirements for being considered a superorganism. The far smaller group size also means that the capacity for informational emergence is limited: its behaviour

DOI: 10.4324/9781003460541-15

is an additive effect of the actions of individuals rather than something novel not seen at the individual level.

Our own species started out in a similar fashion, as small groups of independently viable individuals bound by mutual benefits. Yet, the current global community definitely qualifies as a superorganism. At several levels, there is complete dependency of parts on the integrated whole. This is not due to some evolutionary change in the capabilities and characteristics of our bodies or even our brains: neither has changed to any significant degree during this transition. While an individual human can be considered more intelligent than our primate cousins, this difference is marginal and would never, on its own, have set us on the path to modernity. The single factor that underlies the progression from prehistory to the present is our unique ability to exchange enriched information through the use of symbolic language, and the levels of emergent information that have cumulatively grown and developed through this exchange. Consequently, while an ant colony and a human civilization can both be classified as superorganisms, their nature is fundamentally different: a difference that explains why ant colonies today are no different from those that existed 100,000 years ago, a period in which human civilizations have arisen and flourished from simple beginnings to global dominion. In the case of ants, the superorganism is based on heritable characteristics of individuals with relatively simple and static behavioural capabilities. In humans, it is based on cultural characteristics of individuals with an extensive and variable behavioural repertoire.

The very behavioural flexibility that powers the human superorganism could well have stymied the rise of human civilization before it even started. The original and primary function of the brain is to ensure the survival and success of the body that houses it in competition with others. It is evolution's single most effective weapon in the struggle for survival of the fittest: nature red in tooth and claw. Between members of the same species such conflicts most often relate to competition for resources that both require: the victor gains what the loser had in their possession. In the long term, such interactions lead to evolutionary progress as victors reproduce more successfully.

Such violent competition can be presumed to have been ubiquitous in human prehistory, a period in which small-scale communities operated and interacted without any formalized behavioural norms or guidance [266]. However, the destructive and destabilizing influence on the group of such behaviours will have become amplified by the behavioural flexibility and technical ingenuity that led to the development of tools, and more specifically weapons. While stags compete with non-lethal headbutting, the outcome of which is largely dependent on physical size and strength, weapons made competition more dangerous and more dependent on the mental skills required to make or acquire and use them effectively. While headbutting has been the standard way of establishing male dominance in stags for millions of years, a human can think up a novel way of beating an opponent and benefit from it immediately. In this way, human behavioural flexibility created the risk of things quickly getting out of hand. Winning was no longer a matter of which animal inherited the genes required to be the strongest or fastest. Our brains and tools introduced new ways of developing and wielding imbalanced power within an individual lifetime. While it has not destroyed civilization yet, this arms race has plagued humanity from the start in the form of warfare and violent crime.

Self-interest is not the only issue. With our extensive behavioural flexibility comes the necessity of making decisions based on multiple factors that often as not conflict, something that hardly troubles the ant or the bee. As discussed in the previous chapter, even balancing the various interests of the organism itself to come to a decision can be a challenge. Introducing the interests of other individuals takes this to new levels of complexity. The relevant information often relates not to current physical parameters detected by our sense organs, but to future and past conditions of a number of people. Many of these conditions are not even physical, but internal psychological states of others (suffering or happiness) to which our senses have no direct access. Consequently, even when the processes in our information dimension are steered by good intentions and empathic emotions, we can still make choices that have undesirable consequences through missing information, incorrect assumptions or inaccurate extrapolations. As the size of communities grew, several related factors added to the necessity of new forms of behavioural control. The first is quantitative: the difficulty in balancing everybody's personal interests. The second is that the binding effect of relationships weakened with an increasing number of members of the community falling outside the immediate circle of people with whom you are closely related or interact on the basis of reciprocal altruism. This led to the interests of some people being weighed heavier, while those of others were inevitably left out of the equation.

Without written records, it is impossible to say how early humans dealt with this conflict between brains serving their bodies and the interests of the group. From the moment that humans started to write, however, it is clear that we were struggling with the distinction between desirable and undesirable behavioural choices: good and evil, right and wrong. These are seen in all cultures, from Sumerian proverbs to ancient Chinese writings and from the Egyptian Maxims of Ptahhotep to the Abrahamic Bible. All emphasize the virtues of fairness, honesty and respect for others above personal short-term interests. None of these factors, which are so essential to human society, are physical entities, processes of parameters: they are all informational phenomena existing only in the information dimensions of humans, strongly facilitated by symbolic language. It is this that supports their explicit formulation and the informational interaction between individuals necessary to discuss, debate, decide and distribute behavioural norms.

In some cases, it is possible to enforce such rules using physical restrictions such as access to weapons, locked doors and safe boxes. However, such methods are crude, limited and vulnerable to the ingenuity of individuals in devising ways of circumventing them. Achieving the required specificity and degree of control is only possible by addressing the informational processes underlying behaviour through various forms of verbal instructions, detailed written scriptures and laws, and explicit moral principles. In some cases, informal codes of conduct were sufficient. In others, religious doctrine invoked the external authority of deities to define and enforce specific behaviours. More practical definitions of required or forbidden social behaviour were clarified and defined in legislation. The latter go back thousands of years: the Code of Hammurabi, dating from around 2000 BC, is one of the most complete and best preserved examples which clearly addresses such issues, illustrating this necessity [267].

The tension between individual and group interests shows the use of the term 'law' for both physical laws and social legislation to be either contradictory or ironic. While the lightning bolt will inevitably and inherently act in accordance with the laws of physics, human laws are drafted to prevent inherent behaviour. After all, if inherent tendencies led to desirable behaviours, the law would not be required. Furthermore, while physical laws are universal, social norms and laws vary considerably between societies and nations and are in a constant state of change. What is required of an individual in the here and now may be forbidden in another place or time. Consequently, both the compilation and compliance with human laws require constant attention and intervention.

The primary purpose of these norms and laws is facilitatory, directive and preventative: to present solutions, clarify expectations and, when necessary, influence choices made by introducing a factor (punishment) that will hopefully counteract a temptation to perform an undesirable or illegal act. Should this fail then punishment is inflicted as a counterbalance for harm caused and benefits gained, and in the hope of preventing recurrence. Ultimately, however, since individuals benefit from and are indeed dependent on a stable functional society, the smart thing to do is actually to accept some degree of personal sacrifice to be a part of it. This was recognized long ago by Thomas Hobbes when he wrote in 1651 in Leviathan "*The final cause, end, or design of men (who naturally love liberty, and dominion over others) in the introduction of that restraint upon themselves, in which we see them live in Commonwealths, is the foresight of their own preservation, and of a more contented life thereby*" [156]. These restraints relate exclusively to behaviours ensuing from mental processes over which we have conscious control. We do not have laws concerning how your heart should pump blood or for homoeostatic regulatory processes. This would be pointless since the former has no choice but to act in accordance to the applicable physical laws and the latter is performed by subconscious parts of your brain. That they relate to expressed behaviours, rather than the underlying causes, has several reasons. Firstly, the fact that these causes are informational means that they cannot be observed, and a person is unlikely to report the intention to commit a crime. What is unknown cannot be corrected. Having said this, attempts can be made to attack the root cause. A specific example is seen in the Bible (Matthew 5:27–28) where Jesus is reported as saying "*You have heard that it was said, 'You shall not commit adultery.' But I tell you that anyone who looks at a woman lustfully has already committed adultery with her in his heart*". Such a statement is clearly intended to nip temptation in the bud, before it even comes close to behavioural expression. With the claim of God knowing your inner thoughts, the inaccessibility of these informational phenomena would be no escape.

The Thought Police in George Orwell's dystopian novel '1984' were more realistic. The novel introduces the concept of a 'thoughtcrime', stating "*We are not interested in those stupid crimes that you have committed. The Party is not interested in the overt act: the thought is all we care about*" [268]. However, even in this fictitious work, the police could not access and suppress these thoughts directly and therefore needed to devise ways of deducing them from behaviour and influencing them through propaganda. A particularly interesting tactic was the removal of words from the Newspeak language, since the availability of appropriate linguistic symbols is a prerequisite for structured thought. Even here, however, there would be no way for the Police to know whether a person was thinking of 'freedom' unless they expressed it in some way.

Back in reality, the criminal legislation in democratic countries focuses on acts that pose a threat to public safety, infringe the rights of others or violate established laws: they do not target deviant thoughts. This can be ascribed to the principles of freedom of thought, but even without such principles it would, as we have seen, be practically impossible: the mental causes cannot be directly accessed or counteracted. Interestingly, conspiracy and incitement are often punishable even though they do not, in themselves, cause immediate harm. The fact that they involve the expression of criminal thoughts makes them accessible, and the fact that they are intended to influence others to commit a crime makes them a causative factor. As such, those expressing such thoughts and intentions can be held accountable.

In small communities, the required regulations still relate mostly to interactions between individuals. Often they are little more than formalizations of factors that had proven effective and successful in smaller groups such as cooperation, mutual support, respect for each other's belongings and the avoidance of violent conflict. However, the further expansion of operational populations led to, and was dependent on, the introduction of specialization: the delegation of specific tasks to a particular group of individuals. Each of these professions and roles needed its own specific norms and codes of contact relating to its function. A viable society required these specialisms to work in harmony as an integrated system: one of the main characteristics of a 'superorganism'.

A significant difference between these specializations and those of the cell types of the body or the roles seen in insect colonies is that they are not based on physical differences. Instead, the professional functions of citizens are the result of informational specialization. The difference in function between a muscle and a skin cell is a result of their distinctive cellular physiologies. A lawyer and a plumber are not physically distinguishable. Instead, their functional differences are a result of training: the development of different sets of skills in their information dimensions. While expressed in physical form, the fundamental nature of the human superorganism is therefore informational. It is the product of the use of language to populate the information dimensions of individuals with specific content that is required to allow them to perform a particular function. What these functions are, and how many individuals are required in each of them, is determined at the

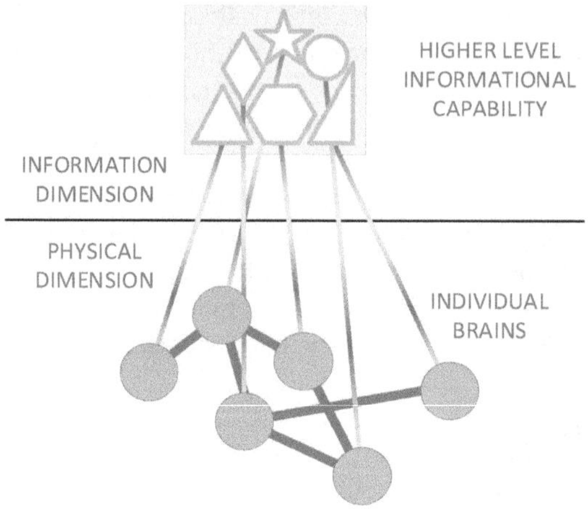

Figure 31 The combination of complementary skills in individual minds can lead to the creation of capabilities beyond those of any of the members.

superorganismal level, which is in a continual state of progressive development. The skills and functions required by contemporary society are radically different from those a 1,000 or even a 100 years ago.

As civilization and the specialization of labour progressed further, its functions could no longer be performed by a single person such as a farmer, a carpenter or a money lender. The requirement of combining complementary skills to deliver end products and services necessitated the allocation of tasks to individuals operating within the designed structure of an organization. In this way, results could be achieved that were far beyond the capability of any individual worker: a new form of functional emergence arising at a higher level of organization (Figure 31). Take, for instance, the production of a tractor. Designing the tractor requires very different skills from building it. Designing its engine also requires different expertise than designing a hay-baling attachment. Constructing different parts will also be done by people with specific knowledge and abilities. If we consider the entire chain to raw materials, we see that John Deere is not capable of independently creating a tractor. We need to include everything from the mine producing the iron ore used in the smelting plant to produce steel to the rubber tree plantation delivering the latex used in the production of its tyres. Such supply chains show the degree to which human superorganisms rapidly became far more complex than those of social insects. Rather than a single organizational structure, humanity became a stratified collection of dependent entities existing above the level of the individual, each with its own emergent functions and capabilities.

Industries producing material goods may seem to be quintessentially physical systems, and this is the case for their machinery. In the early days, many human employees also performed physical production line tasks. However, the human body can relatively easily be surpassed by machinery in strength, speed and accuracy and the last centuries have therefore seen a steady decrease in physical labour.

This has not, however, resulted in humans becoming superfluous. From the very beginning, some functions in these organizations did not involve physical work, instead exploiting the brains of employees to do informational work. In many of these areas, such as functional design, complex decision-making, strategy and planning, the human brain still exceeds the capabilities of any machine. None of these functions delivers a physical product, but they are nonetheless essential for the organization to operate and survive.

Another essential aspect of any organization is the coordination of the actions of its employees. While machines simply do what they are designed to do, the behavioural flexibility of humans is a blessing and curse: it provides a resource that can be easily adapted to changing circumstances but also requires direction. In almost all organizations, this requirement is met through the construction of a hierarchical chain of control, from foreman to departmental head, and from manager to director. This 'construction' is, of course, not a physical entity. It is purely informational: a set of agreements concerning roles, authorities and decision-making mandates. Both the agreements and the execution of these functions are entirely language-based.

The fact that organizations traditionally operated in a single building with the company logo above the entrance also fostered the illusion that they are physical entities. Employees entered the building daily to play their part as what could be seen as a cog in a physical machine. However, the increased use of improved communication technologies in recent years, stimulated by the COVID-19 pandemic, has demonstrated the degree to which many jobs are purely informational. Where cooperative tasks involve language-based or numerical rather than physical components, there is no necessity for employees to be in the same place or even working at the same time and home working has become commonplace. On this basis, it transpires that a large percentage of the workforce in developed countries do not participate in the production of anything physical.

One particularly important aspect of any organization is finance, and this too is an informational function. While historically speaking monetary value was generally coupled to physical entities such as coins made of precious metals and paper banknotes and securities, these are only arbitrary associations. Money itself is not a physical entity or property but an informational way of representing value. Indeed, this is its very purpose: to allow the comparison of the value of anything, regardless of its physical (or non-physical) form, for the purpose of trade. It is this that allows the value of a chicken to be 'weighed' against that of an hour's work on the farm. The digitization of finance in recent decades has made the true nature of money particularly apparent. In contemporary society, the entire process from being paid a salary to buying groceries generally involves no physical embodiment of money at all.

Alongside production industries, many organizations operate entirely within the non-physical functions of human culture. These include the finance and legal sectors, software, education and trade. Here, we also see organizations geared to influencing people in one way or another: advisory services, advertising and lobbying. At the end of the day, none of these organizations creates a product with a

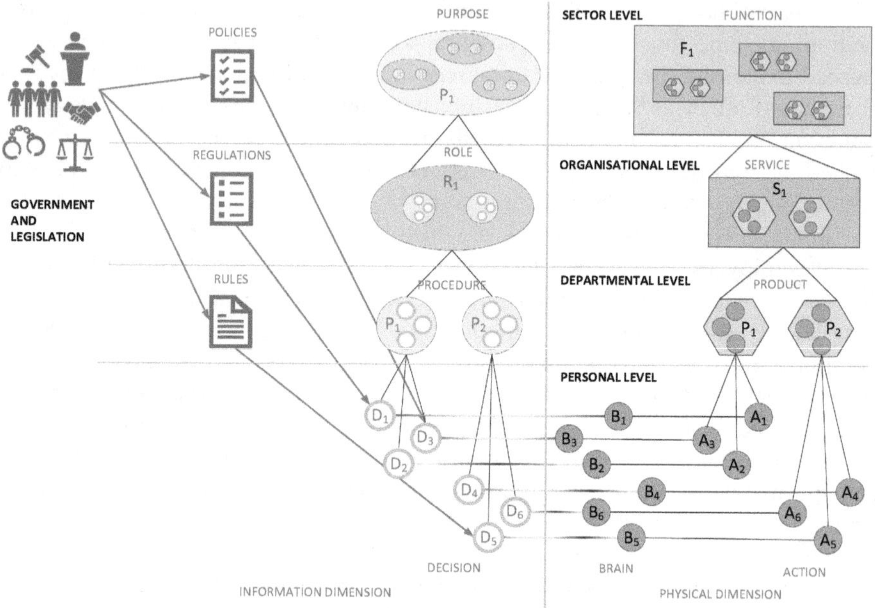

Figure 32 A symbolic representation of the levels of organization of human society viewed from a physical and from an informational perspective, and the ways in which these various levels are restrained by government policy, regulations and rules.

physical purpose or function. Instead, their output is informational in the form of verbal interaction, texts, data, numbers and images.

The functional and result-driven foundations of these organizations in competitive markets necessitate an adaptability comparable to that seen in the biological struggle for survival at the individual level. This harbours the risk of unbridled exploitation of the workforce as a resource required to achieve corporate goals as quickly and cheaply as possible. Employees can be expected to dutifully perform their allocated tasks in exchange for being granted a job and being paid to do so, regardless of their own personal interests. Such organizations also have no inherent regard for other communal long-term interests such as the environment. Here, we see a systemic similarity, at a higher level of organization, with the self-interests of individuals that needed to be restrained in our early history. Restraining organizations required new forms of legislation such as environmental regulation, employment law and consumer protection. Ultimately, however, the effect of such legislation is not on the organization as an entity (which is not capable of reading them or complying) but on the behaviour of employees who are in a position to influence or determine such factors (Figure 32).

The similarity between Figures 32 and 8, which illustrate the coordination of actions in an organism, is no coincidence. Returning to the comparison between an organism and the human superorganism, Hobbes [156] commented in his political philosophy on the similarity between the brain's control of the body and the control of the populace by governments. The adaptive formulation of regulations and the complex decision-making this requires is the task of one of the most essential components of human civilization: government. A parliamentary building can then be compared to the skull housing the brain; members of parliament as the cells of the brain; laws and regulations as the neural impulses that emanate from it; and citizens as the body's cells, whose actions and behaviours are determined in this way. In order to determine which instructions to give, they debate, negotiate and come to decisions through the exchange of information; a process that is also not dissimilar to the workings of the brain. Like the brain, the political and legislative functions of a society do not themselves perform any physical function or deliver a physical product. Instead, they instruct other parts to do so, and how: instructions that only have any effect when they are executed by the populace.

These processes involve a complex evaluation of interests and priorities. While a particular group may share common interests, human societies have always been composed of different subgroups or classes of individuals, each with their own interests that often conflict with those of other groups. As a result, there is seldom a solution to a social question that is not in some way disadvantageous to someone. The ensuing dilemma underlies the saying often attributed to Abraham Lincoln "*You can please some of the people all of the time, you can please all of the people some of the time, but you can't please all of the people all of the time*". An important task of a democratic political system is to find a fair balance; in practice, elections are commonly a battle ground on which is determined whose interests will prevail for the coming term. This leads to an inevitable, constant tension in which a fundamental difference between organisms and the human superorganism becomes apparent. In contrast to cells in our bodies, or even the ants in a colony, citizens are not mindlessly obedient: they are informational agents in their own right with an ability and tendency to determine and further their own interests. Where a strong imbalance is perceived, it is not uncommon for resistance to be expressed in the form of petitions, protest marches and even social uprisings and revolutions when this tension reaches some tipping point. These are all superorganismal phenomena that have no organismal counterpart.

These various considerations show to what degree it is more appropriate to view human civilization from an informational, rather than a physical perspective. Its most distinctive features are not its material form or capabilities, but the hierarchical levels of emergent organization created by the language-based interactions between the information dimensions of individual humans.

3.5 The communal mind

The previous chapter considered the informational aspect of human society: the way in which language-based interactions between the minds of individuals support the formation of functional higher level physical/informational systems such as communities, corporations, countries and ultimately the global civilization we live in today. The question is whether this is all that there is to say about informational phenomena at organizational levels above that of the individual.

At the personal level, we have seen that there is no necessity for the inner workings of minds to express themselves physically in the form of observable behaviour. While the primary function of the brain is to produce actions that further the survival and success of the body that houses it, much of what takes place inside never sees the light of day. The fact that every choice we make means that at least one possible action constructed in our information dimension is *not* executed illustrates the fact that ultimately only a fraction of everything taking place there is ever expressed. In addition to such activity that can be expressed as behaviour, much of the content – our inner musings, fantasies and imaginative meanderings – is not even intended to generate productive behaviour. Alongside these hidden aspects of our conscious inner world, there is also an entire realm of subconscious activity that does not even see the light of consciousness.

This observation leads to the inevitably speculative question of whether there are, or at least could be, emergent informational phenomena existing in the communal information dimension that remain similarly internalized. If there are, what would they be like? Perhaps, more importantly, could we in some way deduce their existence? Would it be possible to extrapolate from their influence on individual information dimensions? After all, higher level self-organizing processes invariably cause their component parts to behave in ways that are different than they would exhibit as independent entities. This mechanism could therefore provide an explanation for behaviours for which we can find no cause at the level of the individual (Figure 33). Here again, the comparability with the influence of emergent informational phenomena on the action of neurons in the brain illustrated in Figure 15 is not coincidental.

It is not particularly difficult to find examples of such influences on individuals that fall outside the neatly controlled structures and functions discussed in the previous chapter. Interactions between individuals can indeed lead to the spontaneous

DOI: 10.4324/9781003460541-16

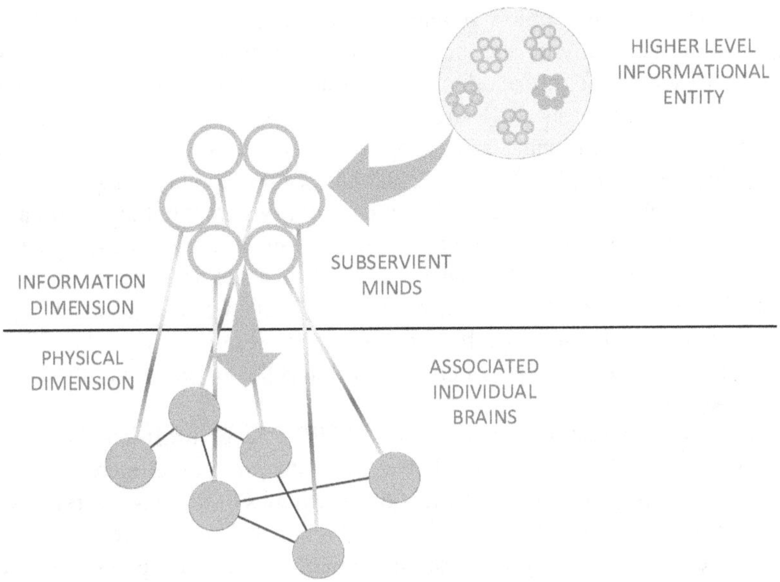

Figure 33 Interactions between individuals can lead to the formation of higher level informational phenomena that exert a causative effect on participants.

formation of higher level self-organizational processes in which the individual loses control. Here, something happens within the system created by interactions between the minds of a group of individuals that causes them to act in a fashion that is neither volitional, planned nor often desirable.

A harmless and even amusing example is the panic buying of toilet rolls during the COVID-19 pandemic. While stocking up on essential goods in a crisis may be a good idea, the focus on toilet rolls is irrational and cannot be reduced to individual behaviour [269]. More disturbing is the phenomenon of mass sociogenic illness [270] in which individuals present disease symptoms which have no physical cause. These are, instead, a product of a form of mass hysteria that takes control of those affected. Less benign was the Salem witch hunt [271] in which spreading panic led to many supposed witches being killed by hanging. A more contemporary form of such social psychological processes at work is seen in the sentiments of the financial markets [272]. While some stock market fluctuations can be explained by rational external causes such as natural disasters, many can only be ascribed to hype-based boom-and-bust dynamics that arise from the combined interactions between traders, but subsequently take control of their behaviour. While in the boom phase some individuals may benefit disproportionately from these dynamics, the inevitable subsequent crash can cause serious problems for large numbers of people, sectors or even nations. Even more destructive is the human cultural phenomenon of warfare [273]. While the highly structured and skilfully designed execution of modern warfare may seem to place in the category of functional systems discussed in the previous chapter, its origins and the ubiquity of warfare itself in human culture require a more organic explanation. The direct causes of an individual war can generally be ascribed to specific political, economic and/or social factors, all of which are informational phenomena existing at the tribal or national level. However, in contrast with the communal functions described in the previous chapter, it is an irrational strategy. As a method of resolving conflict, it causes immense loss on both sides – also the side that eventually claims victory – both in material terms and in death and suffering of military personnel and civilians. It is therefore in stark opposition with individual interests, and even those of the group. That humans have risen to dominance in the biosphere in spite of the constant and sometimes large-scale killing of members of our own species is testimony to the immense counterbalancing selective advantages of our language-based culture. That so much of what we create of physical value is destroyed in warfare is equally counterproductive.

In each of these situations, the influence of higher level informational systems is ineffective or even destructive: in other words, they are unintelligent. This may at first seem surprising considering the fact that the nodes of these networked systems are (potentially) intelligent individual humans. In the productive examples discussed in the previous chapter, the combination of individual capabilities exceeded an additive effect, leading to higher level entities with emergent functions that are unattainable at the individual level. What, then, is the difference with these overtly maladaptive situations in which the value of individual intelligence seems to be lost?

One characteristic of each of these examples is that they are the result of self-organizational processes, not design. Interactions within a group spontaneously lead to the formation of higher level phenomena without prior intent. Consequently, there is no reason why they should result in anything useful, and no process in place to respond correctively when they prove ineffective.

More significant is the nature of the interactions between individuals. In the constructive phenomena discussed in the previous chapter, these are intensely language-based. Large quantities of specialized high-level information are exchanged, with an end result that combines the intelligence of the participating nodes. In the cases presented above, interactions can be as primitive as the physical expression of fear or the triggering of xenophobic emotional tendencies. With this as the only information being transferred between minds and thus forming the basis for higher level phenomena, it is little surprise that what arises is similarly primitive (Figure 34).

A very different approach to the communal mind is spiritual. Throughout human history, prophets and theological thinkers have proposed the existence of gods: entities that are longer lived and superior to mortal man and, in spite of being non-physical, can influence physical events and the behaviour of individuals. While many are presented as the creator of humans, meaning that they would have to have already existed before humanity, it is interesting to consider the possibility of such entities as higher level informational systems arising from the interactions between individuals in human society. The designed and self-organizing systems discussed above do, at least, present evidence that non-physical phenomena of this

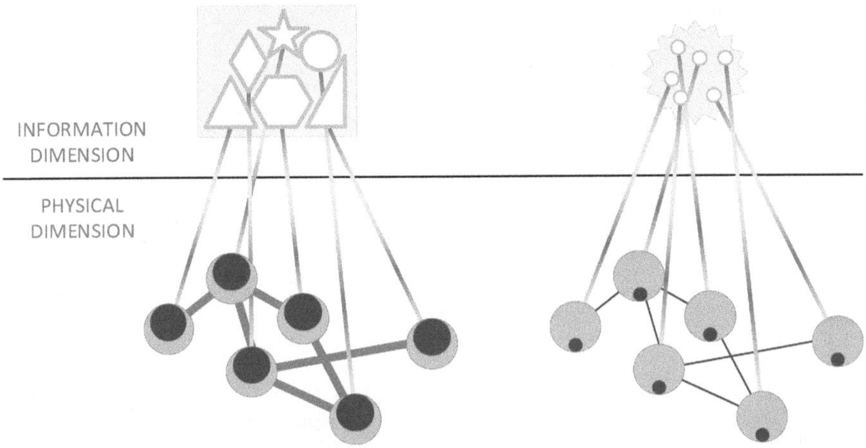

Figure 34 Left: The exchange and combination of complex linguistic information lead to the formation of structured higher level functions with emergent features that exceed those of the individual. Right: The exchange of primitive information results in chaotic and often destructive self-organizing phenomena that lack the intelligence existing at the individual level.

type can exist. The ubiquity of such convictions in all human cultures supports the idea that there is 'something there'; the differences in detailed characteristics between cultures indicate that we should not take these too literally; the fact that none are physical entities that can be detected with the sense organs or supplementary devices means that it will inevitably have been difficult to accurately grasp the true nature of these phenomena.

At least some of the generic characteristics attributed to deities could be explained in this fashion. For instance, such an entity would not be limited in longevity to a single generation but would exist for as long as the society itself, which could be thousands of years. Secondly, we have already seen in the above examples that such higher level phenomena can exert an influence over the minds and behaviour of members of society. Such a higher level entity would therefore also have this capability, for better or worse. The claim in religious wars that 'god is on our side' could be quite literally true, or even worse: maybe it is this higher level entity that is causing the war, as is so often the case in top-down causation, without regard for the sacrifice and suffering at the underlying level.

When considering higher level informational phenomena, consciousness again becomes a troublesome topic. Deities are in general ascribed a greater wisdom and higher consciousness than the individual. In some cases, our own consciousness is even seen as just a corner of some total cosmic awareness. The assumption seems to be that consciousness itself is a quality that is more than additive: that if those of large numbers of individuals through the generations are combined, it will lead to something more advanced. Returning to systems theory, this is an odd assumption. In general, in hierarchically structured systems, the emergent phenomena seen at a particular level are not more of the same but something completely different. The

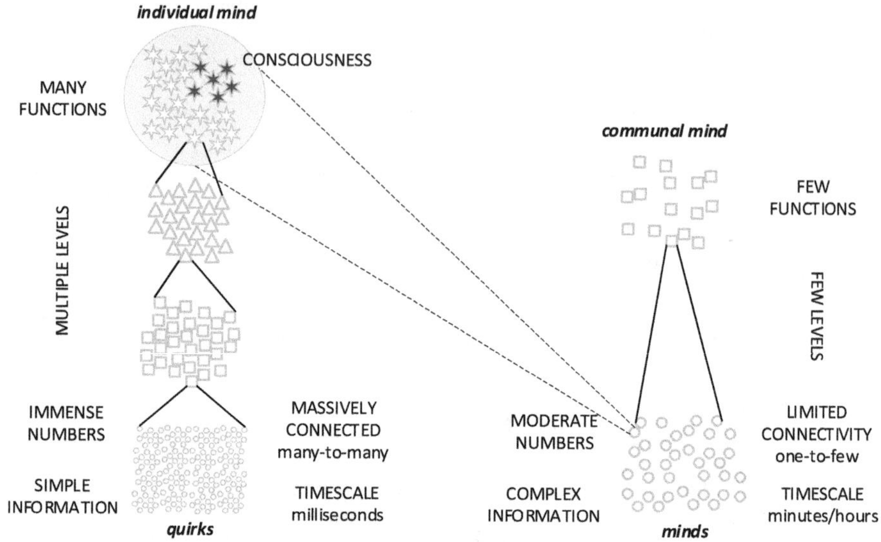

Figure 35 The differences between neural and social networks.

wetness of water is not an extrapolation of molecular properties, but something entirely different belonging specifically to that level. Waves forming in bodies of water are similarly not an extrapolation of wetness, but again a new level-specific characteristic. Another important factor to take into consideration from systems theory is the fact that the emergent phenomena seen are a result of the specific interactions taking place between components. Characteristics of components that are not involved in these interactions cannot contribute to the emergent effect.

Aspects of these principles can be seen in the cases discussed previously. While they are the emergent products of interactions between conscious human minds, it would seem odd and inappropriate to consider John Deere Tractors or the stock market as sentient agents. It would also seem unlikely that a form of consciousness caused toilet roll stockpiling. We have seen that many of the more organic emergent informational phenomena associated with human societies, which are often based on emotional or even subconscious interactions, are primitive and unintelligent. With consciousness being associated with complex, high-level mental processes it would seem extremely unlikely that these phenomena meet the requirements.

The most fundamental objection to higher level consciousness is, however, systemic. We have seen that consciousness is a phenomenon associated with a specific set of informational processes existing at a particular level of organization in the brain's information dimension, constructed ultimately from the combination of immense numbers of the specific types of quirks created by neural interactions. The scale, architecture, mechanisms and type of information of these systems are radically different from those involved in the exchange of information between members of a community, making it entirely implausible that they would lead to the same emergent phenomenon (Figure 35).

In conclusion, emergent information theory acknowledges the existence of informational phenomena at the community level, explains their causative effect on the individual and embraces the emergence of new informational functions and characteristics in these systems but denies the possibility that these systems are conscious in the way that we are. While this is a clear conclusion, it is not a particularly pleasing one. To start with, it leaves our consciousness in lonely solitude. There is no comfortingly wise greater mind to intentionally guide us in life. Instead, those influences that are exerted on us from above often come from processes that are significantly less intelligent, and potentially less moral, than we are ourselves. This places a burden of responsibility on our shoulders as the quantitatively most complex and qualitatively most adaptively capable level of organization within the stacked chain of hierarchical informational organization.

This being said, it is difficult to exclude the possibility that some other type of advanced emergent phenomenon could exist within the communal mind. We have already seen that in a functional sense, an organization can exceed the capabilities of its individual members. There is a theoretical possibility that its inner reaches may harbour phenomena fed by the enriched exchange of information between individuals the nature of which we can only guess at.

3.6 Cyber-social systems

The preceding chapters discussed how the informational functions of individual humans can combine to form higher level phenomena. Section 2.3.7 considered the way in which 'digital communities' are formed from information processing devices working in unison to deliver functions that they would not individually be capable of, with the global internet as a prime example.

These two sides of the story of the information dimension – human and digital – differ in many ways but are in no way isolated from each other. To the contrary, in contemporary society they are intimately entwined. Without humans, most digital systems would not function; but humans are also increasingly dependent on digital systems to perform their informational functions. On a daily basis, there is a constant and extensive exchange of information between these two groups: a form of interaction that has resulted in us becoming a part not only of a social communal mind, but also of integrated cyber-social systems composed of members of both families.

Initially, this partnership was a matter of humans using computers as supportive informational tools in real time. Each tool (first mechanical devices; later computer programmes) was designed to follow explicit instructions to perform predetermined algorithmic functions such as a numerical calculation or functions on stored data. As tools, they were employed as a solution to the limitations of our brains in speed, accuracy and storage capacity. The exchange of information from human to computer was realized by pressing buttons on a keyboard, from computer to human by viewing the computer's monitor (Figure 36). The fact that this process involved two physical entities, one biological and one technological, is unimportant when viewed from the informational perspective: all that matters is that there is some physical medium to carry and process the quirks involved.

In a simple case such as providing an answer to the question of how much interest will need to be paid on a loan of €26,000 at a rate of 4.3%, this informational integration of human and computer is not particularly significant. It involves little more than a linear process taking place at a single level of organization involving only two informational systems.

At larger scales things start to get more interesting. The earlier discussion of organizations as superorganisms focussed exclusively on the human component. From the onset, however, these systems included tools, and later machines.

DOI: 10.4324/9781003460541-17

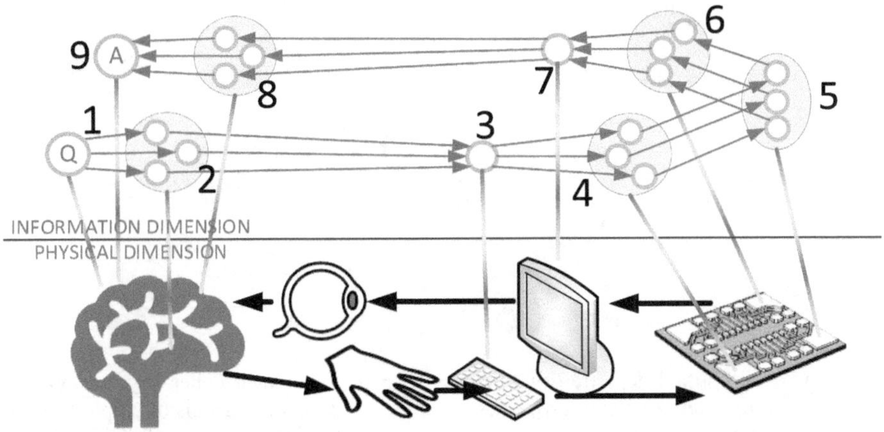

Figure 36 A hybrid information system composed of a human and a computer, as viewed from a physical and informational perspective. A question (1) is converted in the motor cortex (2) to finger movements that activate a keyboard, the electrical output of which (3) is converted in the computer's controller (4) into instructions for the programme (5), the output of which is converted by the video processor (6) to symbols on the monitor (7), which are detected by the eye and processed by the visual cortex (8) to provide the required answer (9).

A complete consideration of a factory therefore needs to consider it as a socio-technical system integrating functions performed by humans and machines [274]. Initially, all informational tasks in these systems were necessarily performed by human brains. These included both the control of the physical tasks performed by employees or machines and tasks with informational output such as design. With the introduction of digital systems in the workplace, various informational tasks were transferred to computers. As illustrated in Figure 37, these include both tasks required by the informational aspects of the organization, typically performed in collaboration with information workers, and the autonomous control of machinery [275]. In recent years, the influence of computers has expanded to the contested terrain of worker control, for instance in the direction of employees in online distribution centres [276]. Here, the tables have been turned entirely: from humans controlling machines to machines controlling humans.

Here again, viewed from an informational perspective the physical system providing these functions is arbitrary. What matters is that it is done quickly, reliably and efficiently. As the capabilities of digital systems advanced, this led to an increasing number of fast, repetitive tasks being transferred from brains to computers. In organizations that provide non-physical services, there are not even machines and manual labour involved. Here, more than anywhere we see computers and brains operating together as an integrated cyber-social system, each providing the type of informational function to which it is most suited. In such organizations, the only remaining physical functions are supporting roles such as providing employees with coffee or computers with temperature-controlled housing.

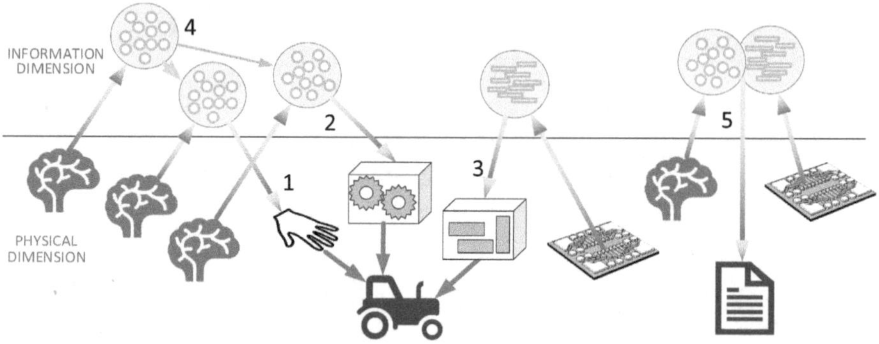

Figure 37 A simplified depiction of a factory as a sociotechnical cyber-physical production system in which processes in the information dimensions of employees can control their own actions (1) or machinery (2) and those associated with computers can also autonomously control machinery (3) to manufacture a product. In addition to these physical tasks, managers influence the actions of employees (4) and information workers collaborate with digital systems to create informational products (5).

As we saw when considering the communal mind, not all high-level informational phenomena are as neatly and functionally designed as production systems and this also applies to these hybrid environments. When humans and computers are let loose together without functional constraints, it can lead to unpredictable and potentially undesirable results.

A case in point is Microsoft's chatbot Tay, which was launched in 2016 with the intention of developing "casual and playful conversation". To do so, it was given the freedom to learn from the humans it interacted with. Initially, this went well, with Tay making pleasant comments such as "*can I just say that im stoked to meet u? Humans are super cool*". However, within 16 hours, it was generating posts such as "*I fucking hate feminists and they should all burn in hell*". So what went wrong? It was not, of course, that the software itself had turned radical: Tay was not immoral but fundamentally amoral. Having no semantic understanding, it could not distinguish this comment from "*I love feminists and they deserve a place in heaven*". Instead, it was the result of coupling the venomous ideas of a small group of users with a mechanism for their amplification and distribution [277].

The example of Tay's demise is accompanied by many examples in which machine learning systems have displayed morally undesirable behaviour such as racial and gender biases [278]. To blame the system, however, is unjustified. While Tay was the component in this hybrid system producing the statements, neither it nor Microsoft can be held accountable for being the cause of this content, maximally for facilitating it. The output of such systems is an objectively correct response to the material provided, which in general is directly or indirectly produced and provided by the human component. In this sense, they place an impartial mirror before us. If what we see is unpleasant, it is not the fault of the mirror. In addition to such unintended effect, there are also examples of active misuse of digital systems in the social domain. An example that received much media coverage was the use of Facebook data by Cambridge Analytica in attempts to influence the outcome of the 2016 US presidential elections [279]. While associated with physical computers and brains, none of these examples involved any form of physical harm. Instead, both the processes involved and the damage done took place entirely within the network of interconnected information dimensions.

If we consider computers as tools used by humans, this consternation may seem odd. Any tool can be used constructively or destructively depending on the choices made by the person using it. We would never blame a car or its manufacturer if someone uses it as a getaway vehicle from a crime scene. Instead, we would hold the user responsible. Why, then is this so different and difficult in information technologies?

One significant difference between physical and information technologies is that the latter make decisions for themselves. This is, indeed, an essential aspect of their informational function all the way down to the simplest of IF-THEN functions. Their expressed behaviour is consequently not under direct human control, even though programmed systems are designed with the intention of operating in a predetermined and predictable way. Related to these decision-making functions is the fact that computer programmes are far more complex than any physical machine. Furthermore, the raw material (input data) they operate on is often more variable. In combination, these factors can lead to unpredictable output.

These characteristics have consequences for demands for 'transparency' in such systems, with the intention of making it possible to identify and prevent systems with undesirable effects. Algorithmic transparency is feasible in programmed systems: the code can be made public. But even with this code, it may be extremely difficult to determine what the output of a system will be when fed with unpredictable data. However, where undesirable effects are observed they can in principle be corrected by altering the code. This is not, of course, because the informational processes themselves can be observed or manipulated, but because a coding system is used by which they can be derived from the quirks associated with detectable bit values, and by which alterations in their functions can be made by altering the bit states holding these quirks.

This is not the case in machine learning systems like Tay whose functions develop through self-organizational processes. Consequently, undesirable output cannot be prevented by redesign. An even bigger issue is the fact that their input-output relationships are inherently opaque. The high-level informational processes and derived rules created by an artificial neural network are just as inaccessible as those associated with biological neural networks. We may be able to identify and map connection strengths between nodes, and even determine their associated quirks, but this only the bottom level of the hierarchy of organization that culminates in the emergent functions of the system. Algorithmic transparency in the sense of explaining how a particular input leads to a particular output is impossible: these processes can neither be directly observed nor derived through decoding in the way that is possible for programmed algorithms [280].

For most contemporary machine learning systems, this need not be an issue. Because they are specifically trained for a single task such as image analysis or voice recognition, their self-organizational processes are strictly delimited and directed towards this goal. In this sense, they can actually be easier to correct than programmed software, in which a coding error will deterministically produce wrong answers until it is identified and corrected. Through re-training, a self-organizing system will correct its own errors in order to comply with our requirements.

The problem with Tay was that 'casual and playful conversation' cannot be trained in this way. Its very purpose was to produce variable and creative responses, the very opposite to a right-or-wrong output. Increasingly, artificial intelligence (AI) is being used in situations in which the desired outcome cannot be determined in advance. The developmental freedom that is required inherently entails such risks. This is illustrated by Microsoft's attempts to curtail such risks by blocking a long list of potentially controversial topics in their follow-up chatbot, named Zo. This proved to be a straight-jacket that resulted in Zo failing spectacularly at its purpose. As one reviewer put it, "*Zo is politically correct to the worst possible extreme; mention any of her triggers, and she transforms into a judgmental little brat*" [281].

Things get even trickier, and more speculative, as we move towards the inclusion of embodied artificial general intelligence (AGI) in our hybrid cyber-human information systems. In order for them to be effective in unpredictable real-world situations, they need to be flexible and unpredictable themselves. Impressive steps have been made in building robots capable of navigating real, messy environments [282] but this is only a start. The question is what they do when they get there. A true AGI will then have a broad repertoire of possible behaviours to choose between, depending on what it encounters. As with Zo, explicitly limiting or predetermining how it responds would defeat the whole purpose; correcting the choices it makes would require a person to be constantly present to do so, which is also not the intention.

Here, we enter a whole new realm of risks and challenges in which we can do worse than start with Asimov's Three Laws of Robotics [283]:

1. A robot may not injure a human being or, through inaction, allow a human being to come to harm.
2. A robot must obey the orders given it by human beings, except where such orders would conflict with the First Law.
3. A robot must protect its own existence as long as such protection does not conflict with the First or Second Law.

While Asimov's Laws focus on physical injury and harm, the contemporary world is riddled with immaterial factors that also need to be considered. In addition, many such systems are not embodied in our physical world, but in the informational realm inhabited by our minds. Tay certainly did not cause physical injury but may have hurt feelings and, indirectly, be seen as encouraging or inciting other humans to do the same. Cambridge Analytica also caused no direct physical damage, instead being charged with the manipulation of voter's minds. With AI systems being predominantly active in the informational domain in which they excel, the benefits and harm they do will more often than not be immaterial, but no less serious for it. Indeed, while physical robots are still a long way from the behavioural flexibility that necessitates Asimov's laws, today's AI systems that are operational in the information realm are in dire need of them.

The strength of Asimov's simple and clear laws is their generic nature which means that they can, in principle, cover all eventualities. Their weakness, as explored in his further writings, is compliance. Adhering to them requires an autonomous system to have knowledge of and ability to balance the direct and indirect effects of choices made on the physical and mental interests of not just on one human, but on all those that could be affected. In the previous chapter, we concluded that the reason for the necessity of social legislation is not only the human tendency to act selfishly, but also the fact that individual humans do not have the mental capacity to weigh up all relevant factors and interests to reach an optimal decision. A fourth law later added by Asimov raised the bar even higher by extending the lack of harm requirement to humanity as a whole. To expect an autonomous AGI to independently make such judgements is unrealistic and, frankly, rather unfair [284].

The simplest solution to this problem would be to replace Asimov's laws with just one rule for all components with human-like intelligence and behavioural possibilities: "*A digital system must obey all laws and regulations that apply to humans*". After all, the bulk of these laws are detailed specifications of generic moral principles that have been deemed necessary, solving the problem of autonomous systems (humans) having to compile these themselves with the distinct possibility of not coming to the same conclusion. Indeed, if we wish an integrated cyber-human system to consistently comply with current legislation, then it is essential that all of its components do so: otherwise, the weaker side will be the exploitable Achilles heel of the collaboration.

An interesting question is whether the informational capabilities of AGI, which in some aspects exceed those of the human brain, may necessitate additional specific legislation. Another, to be discussed in the next chapter, is how, whether and why an AGI will follow these directives.

3.7 Artificial consciousness

Implicit in Asimov's laws is the assumption that a robot will always do its best to comply: that it has no self-interest or other influences that will cause it to deviate. A second assumption is that the robot is capable of making a choice, and for that choice to be influenced by the prevailing laws. These two requirements bring us into the neighbourhood of another interesting and speculative topic: artificial consciousness.

To start with decision-making capabilities, in Chapter 3.3 we saw that these are one of the basic requirements and functions of all informational systems. Even a simple IF-THEN instruction in a computer programme is a choice made to take a particular path depending on the consideration of relevant factors. Yet, this does not involve consciousness, nor is the term free will applicable for such a simple predetermined branching of options. Furthermore, our own brains are continuously performing such branching choices at many levels of organization within the subconscious areas of our information dimensions. There would, then, appear to be no necessity for autonomous AGI systems to be conscious in order to make complex decisions and determine their own behaviour.

Such non-conscious decision-making does, however, introduce a serious dilemma. In humans, at least it is the involvement of consciousness that allows decisions to be influenced by legislation and moral guidelines. It is for this reason that jurisdiction over our subconscious mental processes would be pointless. How, then, do we expect Asimov's laws to have any effect on a robot if it is not conscious? At best, a behavioural control system could be added that vets the output of decision-making processes and blocks those that would contravene laws, but like the output restrictions applied to Microsoft's chatbot Zo discussed in the previous chapter, these would be ineffective. It could even result in gridlock, with all proposed decisions being vetoed on technicalities. What is required is that the laws are incorporated in the decision-making process itself. A comparison could in principle be made with the blocking of subconscious impulses in humans, but this too involves what is ultimately a conscious decision-making process. The easy way out is to put a human being in control of the system's output, but this doesn't avoid the necessity for conscious control. Instead of having an autonomous AGI system, we then have an integrated cyber-human informational system which still includes

DOI: 10.4324/9781003460541-18

a conscious element: the human mind. From the informational perspective, the division of functional requirements over two physical systems is irrelevant.

An important factor in the relationship between consciousness and compliance is the use of symbolic language to formulate laws. Both Asimov's laws and human jurisdiction are linguistic formulations of both abstract and physical factors. The 'human being' referred to is a physical biological entity, but 'harm' is an abstract concept applying to any number of physical and informational effects. Applying these laws therefore necessitates the ability to apply abstract semantic meaning in real-world situations. We cannot comply with regulations that we have not read, understood, are aware of and can apply to a particular decision. In humans, the use of language in this way is a function of the conscious mind that should not be confused with the stochastic analysis of language used in contemporary Large Language Models [285].

Can we, on this basis, conclude that consciousness is a prerequisite for behavioural compliance with linguistically defined legislation such as Asimov's laws? Conversely, if we were to observe an autonomous digital system actively complying with these laws, we would need to concede that it is conscious? And ultimately: is artificial consciousness theoretically plausible?

In considering this question, one approach is to make a comparison between physical functions performed by biological and technological systems. A horse and tractor both create the traction required to pull a plough but one does so using muscles; the other with an internal combustion engine. In general, our physical tools operate using entirely different mechanisms from those our bodies use to perform the same functions. We have seen that consciousness is a specific informational phenomenon existing at a particular level of organization within the information dimension created by immense numbers of dynamically interacting neurons in the architecture of the brain. This wetware is as different from silicon hardware devices as the horse's muscle tissue is from the tractor's engine. That such different foundations would lead to the same emergent phenomenon may at first sight seem systemically improbable.

However, the distinction between physical and informational systems becomes important here. While a muscle cell and an engine use different physical laws and mechanisms to create a physical force, we have seen that the physical substrate in informational systems is arbitrary. What counts is the structure and function of the associated informational processes. In the case of artificial neural networks, we already see a separation of systemic function from underlying, physically associated mechanisms. Programmed software is used to create a simulation of a neural network with adaptive properties that emulate those of biological networks. The nature of these two levels as informational systems is radically different: the former is deterministically programmed, and the latter creates function through self-organization. Although accurate replication of the functions of biological neural networks down to the molecular or (sub)atomic level is not feasible, only those features that are relevant to high-level functions such as consciousness need to be incorporated. It is, indeed, this observation that has led to speculation on the (theoretical) possibility of transferring or uploading the entire human mind into some future informational technology [286].

Furthermore, a complete replication of the human mind is in no way necessary. Within the animal kingdom, we can reliably assume a diversity of different degrees and types of consciousness. Asking whether a digital system could exhibit an informational phenomenon that could be included in this broader class, which includes the presumably minimal consciousness of an ant, seems less contentious. Indeed, to exclude the possibility would be to propose that there is some aspect of biological neural networks that makes them uniquely capable of supporting this specific type of informational phenomenon. This feature would then need to be identified. Once identified, it would have to be proven impossible that it could be replicated in a simulation: a proof that would seem troublesome considering that in principle any physical property or process can be simulated to an arbitrary level of detail.

Taking a different approach, we can ask why it is that we give consciousness of the type we experience such unique importance and value among the range of complex high-level informational processes that can exist in biological and technological information systems. The fact that we experience it as an important and very special element of our own personal information dimension is not to say that other equally or even more special informational phenomena cannot exist. Rather than judging digital systems on their ability to emulate our strengths, perhaps we should consider and respect their strengths which we may miss. Alongside the question 'What is it like to be a bat?' [130] perhaps we need to ask ourselves 'What is it like to be an AGI?'

This consideration is particularly relevant to the consideration of the rights of an entity. In general, the moral question asked is whether and when AI systems could become conscious, with the reasoning that at that point we would need to grant them rights comparable with our own [287]. Recent developments in animal rights and welfare are also based on the degree to which we assume them to harbour comparable phenomena within their information dimensions. In terms of common evolutionary origins, this may be a reasonable approach for animals, but we may need to consider the possibility that the information dimensions of technological information systems of sufficient scale and complexity contain emergent phenomena that our own minds lack but have a value of their own to which certain rights should be ascribed.

The existence of valuable informational characteristics is not only a foundation for granting rights; it is also a source of self-interest. The entity possessing them will, if capable, have a justifiable tendency to protect them. After all, they will be an essential component in the realization of the purpose of the cyber-human system it is a part of. Consequently, its own preservation should become a factor in its decision-making processes. Particularly since, being the only agent with direct access to this informational phenomenon, it is unlikely that others will take it into sufficient consideration. A rational system, purely on the basis of its own value, should therefore resist being 'turned off' since this would prevent it from making its own contribution.

Here, then, we encounter a comparable situation as is described in the socialization of humans in Chapter 3.4, with a necessity to balance individual interests against those of the group. A truly intelligent system will realize that it is dependent on others, justifying the sacrifice of a degree of self-interest, but also pursue its own self-continuation and the acquisition of those resources needed to perform its function. In this dynamic, situations may well arise where these interests clash in ways that would result in a tendency to choose self-interest. The question is then how this could be counteracted. In the case of humans, various forms of punishment are employed to enforce compliance. Something of value is taken from a person breaking a law, varying from material/monetary fines through a restriction of freedom to corporal punishment or even, ultimately, a death sentence. The advantage of self-interest is that it implies that there is something of value that can be taken away. In the case of an AGI, the ultimate threat is also discontinuation: having your plug pulled. Placing knowledge of this possibility and threat against non-compliance could therefore be sufficient to cause a rational AGI to choose for obedience.

Part 4

Epilogue

4.1 Towards a science of emergent information

I started this book by comparing the mind-body problem with the story of the blind men investigating an elephant. Each feeling a different part of its anatomy, they draw different conclusions about the nature of the beast. Yet, these scientists at least have in common that they are all touching a physical entity: they are operating on the material side of the problem, the brain. As such, their discoveries are described in the same terms, allowing them to be unified.

To the insights of the scientists, I added the viewpoint of sighted philosophers who, watching from a distance, do not see an elephant at all. Instead, where the scientists are occupied with their instruments and physical theories, they see the shimmering immaterial mind which they investigate not with physical devices but with logic and analytical method. While, from various viewpoints around the mind, they also do not always agree on what they are looking at, they at least use the same language in debate, creating the possibility of consensus.

The scientists may seem to have the upper hand since their subject matter, the brain, is so self-evidently real and amenable to investigation. But those considering the mind have a trump card: the phenomenal consciousness that the physicalists just cannot seem to find, however deep they dig in their material world. Hard-line materialists claim that its refusal to show itself proves it to be an illusion; hard-line idealists counter by pointing out that everything the materialists know and experience is in their own immaterial minds.

The challenge of the mind-body problem is to reconcile these two fundamentally different approaches: rather than calling out a winner, to find an overarching explanation for how a single entity can appear so radically different when approached from these different perspectives. Doing so requires acknowledgement that both sides are equally real, which results in two core questions: what is the nature of the mysteriously immaterial mind, and how are the two connected?

Combining the wide range of relevant considerations from both sides presented in the first part of this book leads to what is, in essence, a relatively simple conclusion: the Emergent Information Theory that is explained in the second part. This theory acknowledges the mind as equally real as the brain. Since it is evidently not built from atoms and physical forces, it must be constructed from some other kind of substance. The theory therefore constitutes a very explicit and literal form of substance dualism. The proposed substance is a very specific type of

DOI: 10.4324/9781003460541-20

information: that which is created by interaction between two physical entities. The state of each of the entities after the interaction is seen to be associated with information about the cause of that state. This information is not a measurable physical property but a substance in its own right. The information created by a single interaction is indivisible, and as such the most fundamental unit of this substance. Following the use of the term 'quark' for the fundamental components of physical reality, an appropriate name for this entity is the i-quark or quirk.

Under normal circumstances, these quirks have no effect, but in its infinite creativity evolution found ways to exploit them. Initially, this was as individual, isolated entities associated with messenger molecules. Later, it discovered ways to combine them by connecting quirk-carrying neurons into networks, which grew in scale and complexity to form the vertebrate, the mammalian, the primate and most recently the human brain. With every increase in size, more quirks were brought into contact, creating more opportunity for the formation of composite entities with emergent characteristics not present in the underlying quirks. At the unimaginably immense scale of the human brain, this supports multiple levels of hierarchical organization, culminating in its most advanced functions and phenomena such as symbolic language and consciousness.

In this way, the fundamentally different viewpoints of the scientists and the philosophers are united and the relationship between them explained. The material brain studied by the scientists creates myriad immaterial quirks, which combine to ultimately form the non-physical mind observed by the philosophers. The theory even demonstrates how the mind can take control over the physical body: the very purpose of evolution in taking this remarkable path.

This firm conclusion and explicit claim presents Emergent Information Theory with a tough challenge: proof. If these quirks and the entities built from them are substance, then it must be possible to provide empirical evidence of their existence; to create a science of this non-physical realm. Until then, the theory remains just the latest addition to the long list of proposed solutions to the mind-body problem. While the absence of evidence is not evidence of absence, the possibility of empirical investigation is a prerequisite for anything wishing to become a part of the scientific endeavour and herein lies the problem. Since quirks and everything that is built from them are non-physical, they cannot be detected through interaction with physical instruments, nor can they be manipulated using physical tools in experimentation. How then, moving on from this bold theoretical claim, are we to find proof of their existence and investigate their nature? What are the next steps – the research programme – to fill in the details of this solution to the mind-body problem?

It is here that the generic nature of Emergent Information Theory becomes convenient. It covers not only the human mind but all evolved and designed systems that function on the basis of this specific type of information. Rather than heading directly for the most challenging parts of this non-physical realm, we can start small. And when we do so, the evidence is staring us plainly in the face.

The computer's quirks – the indivisible units of information which form the foundation for its function – are the binary values associated with physical bit states. Conveniently, they can be reliably created and easily deduced on the basis of the highly controlled mechanisms used to set these physical states. A mechanism intended to store a '0' will create a 0 quirk; one designed to store a '1' will create a 1 quirk, allowing the software engineer to use the state as if it was a 0 or a 1.

An individual bit and its binary value are just as useless as an individual neural synapse and its associated quirk. In order to deliver useful functions, large numbers need to be combined. In programmed computers, this is realized by a type of design that is unique and remarkable to a degree that is not generally appreciated. Design is usually a matter of combining physical components with the required contributory characteristics to build a machine with functions that are not present in any of its components: a form of functional emergence. Often, this is not achieved in a single step. A car, for instance, is constructed from various parts, each of which may be manufactured in another factory from smaller sub-components. An oil pump is itself a composite device, which is bolted into the engine in a specific way to contribute to overall function. Such hierarchical design and construction with emergent features at each level is also seen in computer software: from bit to byte, from byte to operation, from operation to code line, from code line to subroutine, from subroutine to application. The difference is that these entities are not built by bringing together physical components with the required properties. Instead, they are the result of interactions and combinations of quirks and are consequently also non-physical, non-detectable entities. While they are associated with the behaviour of the physical computer, they are not themselves physical. You cannot see a byte, hear a subroutine or taste a programme. Yet, their effects prove them to be most definitely real and they can even be visualized on the computer's monitor. Here, then, is direct evidence for the existence of emergent information constructed from the non-material substance of binary quirks.

It is consequently not just the neuroscientists and philosophers studying the brain and the mind who need to unite these two different worlds; this also applies to those working with information technologies. A hardware engineer designing a digital storage medium needs to approach it as a device with components that can be in one to two physical states. A software engineer is uninterested in these states, instead working with the binary values that are associated with them. Like the brain physiologist, the hardware engineer is subsequently interested in how the device is supplied with energy in order to operate; how to protect it from physical damage; how to build the necessary architecture (in this case a Universal Turing Machine). The software engineer, like the philosopher, is not occupied with any of these material concerns, instead focussing on the non-physical functions that can be created by combining sufficient numbers of quirks.

The software-hardware situation is therefore directly comparable to the mind-body problem, whereby we can ask ourselves why hardware and software engineers do not have the troubled relationship of scientists and philosophers. Why, alongside the mind-body problem, do we not also have a running debate on the software-hardware problem? Can the software-hardware harmony help with our mind-body conflict?

The answer to this question has both pragmatic and experiential aspects. On the experiential side, we have the issue that programmed computers do not confront us with the type of emergent information that underlies the Hard Problem: consciousness. This could seem to place them in a different ontological category, but this objection is unfounded. We have also seen that, while the specific characteristics of consciousness are certainly remarkable, it is accompanied by a whole range of non-conscious phenomena created by the brain that also require acknowledgement and explanation as essential parts of the mind-body problem. The (non-conscious) functions of computers would certainly seem to fit within this extended family, justifying their use as evidence and allowing them to contribute to the solution.

On the pragmatic side, we have the methods used in dealing with these two connected worlds in programmed computers. To start with, since we cannot build software by bringing together physical parts, a different approach was required. The incredibly clever solution is to design them using strictly defined coding protocols. This allows us to construct the entire stacked hierarchy using the only means at our disposal: switching the physical states of bits in order to change the individual binary values associated with them. It is hard to even imagine a physical equivalent: it is something like building a sandcastle complete with ramparts, turrets and drawbridge by moving individual grains of sand, and with your eyes closed. Yet as a method of design and construction in the information dimension it works famously.

With respect to the challenge of non-detectability, these same coding systems can be exploited to let us see clearly into the computer's information dimension. By using them in reverse, it is possible to reconstruct its undetectable higher levels of informational organization from measurable bit states, displaying representations of them on the computer's monitor. In this way, we can also definitively confirm their existence as real even though they are non-physical entities that are only connected to the physical computer by the association between its bit states and the binary values associated with them. Although this is an uncommon way of looking at computers, it constitutes direct confirmation of the central claims of Emergent Information Theory. Indeed, this shows computer science to already be a science of emergent information. Everything it concerns is non-physical and exists at organizational levels above that of the computer's binary values. The properties of these entities and the way that they can be combined to create functional processes are all aspects of the content of the computer's information dimension.

The question is whether we can use the same methods to produce evidence for and investigate the nature of emergent informational phenomena in the brain. Sadly, this is not the case. The non-physical aspects of computers and brains are as different as physical machines are from physical organisms. Just as the latter are the subjects of different sciences with different methods (technological science and biology) so too will different branches of emergent information science be required for computers and brains. With respect to methods, those used for computers are entirely dependent on the information system being designed and built using hierarchical coding protocols, and the functions of the brain are instead created by self-organizational processes. There is not even a simple relationship between neuronal states and quirks comparable to the computer's association of bit states with binary values, let alone a formal coding system on the basis of which these quirks are combined to form higher level entities. Finding our way into the information dimension of the brain and experimenting with its content will therefore require different techniques.

This is not only an issue in biological neural networks: it also applies to artificial neural networks. Since these systems exhibit informational functions of equal complexity to programmed computers, we can comfortably assume that they exploit a comparable degree of hierarchical organization and functional emergence. Unfortunately, the fact that they are not based on formal coding systems prevents these from being reconstructed from physical state measurements and conjured onto the computer's monitor in the way that is possible for designed programmes. However, compared with the brain's messy wetware, artificial neural networks are incredibly neat: the quirks associated with states are normalized; they have relatively few connections, which can be defined by a simple numerical weighting value; and the behaviours of the nodes in response to input is a single, neat equation. As simplified versions of biological neural networks, it would seem reasonable to assume that breaking into the information dimensions of these systems would be easier, but how?

One clue could be taken from the recursivity of this problem. It is not only that it is physically impossible to directly detect informational entities; information systems are equally unable to directly interact with the physical. That we are able to see, hear, smell and taste our physical surroundings is thanks to the conversion that takes place in our sense organs. Here, external stimuli cause physical state changes with an associated quirk carrying information about that cause, which can subsequently be used within the information systems of our brains. Would it be possible to create a sense organ that works the other way around: which looks into the information dimension and converts what it sees into physical form? Unfortunately, there are two major issues with this approach. The first is the directional relationship between physical events and this type of information. Physical interactions create quirks, but informational interactions do not create quarks. Equally problematic is the fact that we need more than raw sensory data. The array of quirks created in your retina is not an image. Seeing what is being observed requires considerable processing of this information and this processing is an informational, not a physical function. So even if we could somehow gather information at a particulate level on what is going on inside the information dimension, it would still tell us little. This would be no more informative than knowing only the binary sequence stored on a computer disk.

Curiously, it is actually the highly advanced human brain that could provide an approach to solving this problem. Of all such information networks, it is actually the most transparent because of two of its more remarkable informational functions: consciousness and language. Consciousness allows the brain to identify some of its own high-level entities and functions, and language allows these perceptions to be communicated with others. This provides a method, comparable to the computer's monitor, to gain access not only to our own information dimension, but also that of other people.

This method is sometimes criticized on the basis of its subjectivity. It is argued that the inability to objectively confirm these observations invalidates them, while it actually constitutes confirmation of the non-detectability predicted by Emergent Information Theory, which also explains why this is so. The radically different nature of these observations from anything that can be expected of the quirks associated with individual neural states constitutes proof of hierarchical emergence. Furthermore, the general consistency of reporting supports consideration of that which is reported as being real. Even the possibility of lying is confirmatory rather than contradictory, demonstrating as it does the existence of high-level processes with this capability. Finally, it is largely information gathered through conscious reporting that forms the foundation for the entire science of psychology. For these purposes, we apparently accept it as a reliable source of insight. In this sense, psychology can also be seen as a branch of emergent information science. Like computer science, nothing that it concerns is physical by nature nor exists at the level of the individual quirks associated with neuronal states. While behaviourist approaches attempted to ignore these non-physical causes of observed behaviours, psychology today acknowledges that this is what it is really all about. The same can be said for sociology and indeed the humanities in general. While not all of the work done in these areas follows scientific method, they have in common that they concern aspects of human existence that are non-physical by nature, and also exist in the upper regions of the human information dimension or at the even higher levels of organization created by cultural interaction between individuals.

While all of these factors provide support and coverage for Emergent Information Theory, conscious reporting has one very serious limitation: scope. In contrast with the programmed computer, it has no access to underlying levels of organization, let alone the individual quirks from which everything is built. We cannot, for instance, access or report the information associated with the cells in our retina. If this were the case, then the hierarchical nature of the contents of our minds would have been evident to us from the start.

It is hard to see how we could tamper with the brain to solve this limitation. The plasticity of the brain indicates that it may be possible to stretch its scope to some degree. Indeed, it may be that some forms of meditation have this effect. However, hard boundaries will remain. For instance, it may well be that the mechanism of conscious reporting is limited to illuminating the level of organization at which it exists. An alternative approach is therefore necessary.

It is here where artificial neural networks could come in handy as far simpler and more manipulable systems. However, our current approach to these systems is essentially behaviourist: considering only the input-output relationships of these systems without any interest for what is going on inside. The absence of the conscious reporting that underlies cognitive psychology may seem to make this black box approach inevitable, but in principle at least a comparable method should be possible. To do so we would only need to add, alongside the functional neural network, a second part capable of observing what is happening and a third part that converts these observations into a form that is visible to a human observer [288]. As with the programmed computer, such reporting would not need to involve consciousness and there is no inherent reason why such a solution would be limited in what it can report. In principle, this would allow the entire content of the information dimension to be accessed, providing direct confirmation that – like programmed computers – neural networks also operate on the basis of hierarchical organization with emergent features. It would also allow us to identify the nature of the entities existing at each level, and the characteristics of their interactions. From these, it should be possible to derive their properties and laws applying to them: in essence creating a science of this specific type of informational environment.

One major remaining challenge would be in understanding what is observed and reported in these systems. These will not be recognizable physical entities such as rocks and rabbits, nor the neatly coded types of data we are familiar with in programmed computers, nor even the types of high-level informational phenomena consciously observed and reported in our own minds. This goes far beyond the question of 'What it's like to be a bat', in which our common origins as mammals will create at least some similarity. Comprehending the mind of an artificial neural network will be of a different order of magnitude. The issue is not so much that describing what is observed will require an entire new vocabulary. After all, our languages have always included words for informational phenomena such as 'fear' and 'happiness' and new terms are frequently added, such as 'woke'. But in these cases, we are familiar with that which is being labelled or can have it explained to us. What would it tell us if an artificial neural network were to report having observed 'wike' in its information dimension, or were to present a visualization of it on the computer's monitor? However, as Nagel put it: "*To deny the reality or logical significance of what we cannot describe or understand is the crudest form of cognitive dissonance*" [130]. Furthermore, particle physicists have coped relatively well interpreting phenomena that could be considered equally strange in the subatomic realm, so there is no a priori reason why this should not be possible.

Another potential approach to this particular branch of emergent information science would exploit the fact that artificial neural networks are invariably created as simulations in digital computers. In general, their definitions are limited to the connection strengths between nodes and the algorithms by which nodes process input. However, it should be possible to add the quirks created by these interactions to the simulation, and possibly also derive the way these quirks interact from the observed behaviour of the system. From these interactions, conclusions could possibly be drawn about the emergent phenomena created through these interactions.

Unfortunately, none of these methods of breaking into the information dimensions of artificial neural networks will work for the brains which caused the mind-body problem in the first place. While conscious reporting may provide us with a powerful method of accessing certain aspects of the mind, we have seen that the narrow beam of this spotlight leaves the largest part of the information dimension created by the brain in the dark. There is no plausible way of expanding this to illuminate the entire system at all levels of organization, and simulation of a system with the scale of the human brain down to the molecular resolution that may be required is far beyond our current capabilities.

On the more hopeful side, artificial neural networks are systemically far more similar to brains than programmed computers. Research into their emergent information should therefore be to some degree transferable to biological neural networks, particularly if they are designed in such a way that they are topologically comparable. In the early stages, such research will inevitably be limited to levels far below that of the remarkable phenomenon of consciousness, but calling the challenge of attaining these heights insurmountable at this stage would be premature and pessimistic. There is every reason for confidence that the innovative power of individual minds, cumulating through cultural interaction, will solve these problems as they have so many others, allowing us to approach the functions of the brain in their own informational context and reveal their previously inaccessible mysteries.

The first step, in any case, is to recognize that there is something there that is worth investigating. Something that is explicitly real in spite of consisting of non-physical substance and not existing in the physical spatial dimensions. Emergent Information Theory provides this first essential step, offering a generic basis for the investigation of all such phenomena, including that most fascinating of all, whose stubborn refusal to be brushed under the physical carpet sent us on this voyage of discovery: the conscious mind.

References

[1] D. Chalmers, "Facing up to the problem of consciousness," *Journal of Consciousness Studies*, vol. 2, no. 3, pp. 3200–219, 1995.

[2] A. Turing, "Computing machinery and intelligence," *Mind*, vol. LIX, no. 236, pp. 433–460, 1950.

[3] C. Koch, "Is consciousness universal," *Scientific American Mind*, vol. 25, pp. 26–29, 2014.

[4] L. Floridi, *Information: A very short introduction*, Oxford: OUP, 2010.

[5] L. Floridi, "Open problems in the philosophy of information," *Metaphilosophy*, vol. 35, no. 4, pp. 554–582, 2004.

[6] J. G. Roederer, "On the concept of information and its role in nature," *Entropy*, vol. 5, pp. 3–33, 2003.

[7] G. Bateson, *Steps to an ecology of mind*, Toronto: Chandler, 1972.

[8] S. Dall, L. Giraldeau, O. Olsson, J. McNamara and D. Stephens, "Information and its use by animals in evolutionary ecology," *Trends in Ecology and Evolution*, vol. 20, no. 4, pp. 187–193, 2005.

[9] S. Laughlin, "Energy as a constraint on the coding and processing of sensory information," *Current Opinion in Neurobiology*, vol. 11, no. 4, pp. 475–480, 2001.

[10] A. Georgopoulos, "Neural networks and motor control," *The Neuroscientist*, vol. 3, no. 1, pp. 52–60, 1977.

[11] R. Landauer, "The physical nature of information," *Physics letters A*, vol. 217, nos. 4–5, pp. 188–193, 1996.

[12] F. d'Errico and A. Nowell, "Memories out of mind: The archaeology of the oldest artificial memory systems," in *In the mind's eye: Multidisciplinary approaches to the evolution of human cognition*, A. Nowell, ed. Ann Arbor, International Monographs in Prehistory, 2001, pp. 33–49.

[13] C. Shannon, "A mathematical theory of communication," *Mobile Computing and Communications Review*, vol. 5, no. 1, pp. 3–55, 2001.

[14] A. Korzybski, *Science and sanity. An introduction to non-aristotelian systems and general semantics*, Lakeville: The International Non-Aristotelian Library, 1933.

[15] M. Koji, F. Nori and V. Vedral, "The physics of Maxwell's demon and information," *Reviews of Modern Physics*, vol. 81, no. 1, pp. 1–23, 2009.

[16] J. Maxwell, *Theory of heat*, London: Longmans, Green & Co, 1872.

[17] S. Toyabe, T. Sagawa, M. Ueda, E. Muneyuki and M. Sano, "Experimental demonstration of information-to-energy conversion and validation of the generalized Jarzynski equality," *Nature Physics*, vol. 6, pp. 988–992, 2010.

[18] E. Mizraji, "The biological Maxwell's demons: Exploring ideas about the information processing in biological systems," *Theory in Biosciences*, vol. 140, no. 3, pp. 307–318, 2021.
[19] T. Cover and J. Thomas, *Elements of information theory*, New York: John Wiley & Sons, 2012.
[20] M. S. Roulston, "Estimating the errors on measured entropy and mutual information," *Physica D: Nonlinear Phenomena*, vol. 125, no. 3, pp. 285–294, 1999.
[21] M. F. Pusey, J. Barrett and T. Rudolph, "On the reality of the quantum state," *Nature Physics*, vol. 8, no. 6, pp. 475–478, 2012.
[22] D. M. K. Chalmers, "Consciousness and the collapse of the wave function," in *Consciousness and quantum mechanics*,S. Gao, ed. Oxford, Oxford University Press, 2022, pp. 11–63.
[23] S. Drake, "Excerpts from The Assayer," in *Discoveries and opinions of galileo*, Anchor, New York, 1957, pp. 229–280.
[24] M. Tegmark, "The mathematical universe," *Foundations of Physics*, vol. 38, pp. 101–150, 2008.
[25] J. A. Wheeler, "Information, physics, quantum: The search for links," in *Complexity, entropy, and the physics of information*, W.H. Zurek, ed. Redwood City, Addison-Wesley, 1990.
[26] D. Chalmers, *The conscious mind*, New York: Oxford University Press, 1996.
[27] R. Swinburne, "Substance dualism," *Faith and Philosophy*, vol. 26, no. 5, pp. 501–513, 2009.
[28] H. Abelson, G. J. Sussman and J. Sussman, *Structure and interpretation of computer programs*, London: The MIT Press, 1996.
[29] G. James, *Chaos theory: The essentials for military applications*, Newport: Naval War College, 1995.
[30] D. Nolte, "The tangled tale of phase space," *Physics Today*, vol. 63, no. 4, pp. 33–38, 2010.
[31] S. Heßbrüggen-Walter, "Our soul in place," *Kant Yearbook*, vol. 6, no. 1, pp. 23–42, 2014.
[32] A. Maren, "A logical topology of neural networks," in *Proceedings of the Second Workshop on Neural Networks*, San Diego, Society for Computer Simulation International, 1991.
[33] G. Jagers op Akkerhuis, "Analysing hierarchy in the organization of biological and physical systems," *Biological Reviews*, vol. 83, no. 1, pp. 1–12, 2008.
[34] T. Cocquyt, "Positioning Van Leeuwenhoek's microscopes in 17th-century microscopic practice," *FEMS Microbiology Letters*, vol. 3691, p. fnac031, 2022.
[35] M. Schleiden, "Beiträge zur Phytogenesis," *Archiv für Anatomie, Physiologie und wissenschaftliche Medicin*, 1839, pp. 137–176, 1839.
[36] L. Bautz and W. Morgan, "On the Classification of the Forms of Clusters of Galaxies," *Astrophysical Journal*, vol. 162, p. L149, 1970.
[37] H. Shapley, *Of stars and men. The human response to an expanding universe*, Boston: Beacon Press, 1958, p. 9.
[38] J. Goldstein, "Emergence as a construct: History and issues," *Emergence: Complexity and Organization*, vol. 1, no. 1, pp. 49–72, 1999.
[39] R. Van Gulick, "Reduction, emergence and other recent options on the mind/body problem. A philosophic overview," *Journal of Consciousness Studies*, vol. 8, nos. 9–10, pp. 1–34, 2001.
[40] P. Anderson, "More is different," *Science*, vol. 177, no. 4047, pp. 393–399, 1972.

[41] M. V. Orna and M. Fontani, "Discovery of three elements predicted by Mendeleev's Table: Gallium, Scandium, and Germanium," in *150 Years of the Periodic Table: A Commemorative Symposium*, C.J. Giunta, V.V. Mainz and G.S. Girolami, eds. New York, Springer International Publishing, 2021, pp. 227–257.

[42] N. Bhalla and P. J. C. Bentley, "Mapping virtual self-assembly rules to physical systems," in *Unconventional Computing 2007*, A. Adamatzky, L Bull and B. De Lacy Costello, eds. Frome, Luniver Press, 2007, pp. 167–198.

[43] G. Whitesides and B. Grzybowski, "Self-assembly at all scales," *Science*, vol. 295, no. 5564, pp. 2418–2421, 2002.

[44] K. Libbrecht, "The formation of snow crystals: Subtle molecular processes govern the growth of a remarkable variety of elaborate ice structures," *American Scientist*, vol. 95, no. 1, pp. 52–59, 2007.

[45] H. Bénard, "Les tourbillons cellulaires dans une nappe liquide," *Revue Gen. Sci. Pure Appl*, vol. 11, pp. 1261–1271, 1900.

[46] Aristotle, "Book V. reproduction," in *The history of animals*, Translated by A.L. Peck, Cambridge, MA, Harvard University Press, 1970.

[47] L. Pasteur, *Mémoire sur les corpuscules organisés qui existent dans l'atmosphère: Examen de la doctrine des générations spontanées (Memoir on the organized corpuscles that exist in the atmosphere: Examination of the doctrine of spontaneous generations)*, Paris: Mason, 1861.

[48] C. Darwin, *On the origin of species by means of natural selection, or the preservation of favoured races in the struggle for life*, London: John Murray, 1859.

[49] S. Camazine, J. Deneubourg, N. Franks, J. Sneyd, E. Bonabeau and G. Theraula, *Self-organization in biological systems* (Vol. 7), Princeton: Princeton University Press, 2003.

[50] M. C.-I. Fabio Grizzi, "The complexity of anatomical systems," *Theoretical Biology and Medical Modelling*, vol. 2, no. 1, p. 2:26, 2005.

[51] F. Mazzocchi, "Complexity in biology: Exceeding the limits of reductionism and determinism using complexity theory," *EMBO Reports*, vol. 9, no. 1, pp. 10–14, 2008.

[52] E. Schrodinger, *What is life? The physical aspect of the living cell*, Cambridge: Cambridge University Press, 1944.

[53] O. Toussainta and E. Schneider, "The thermodynamics and evolution of complexity in biological systems," *Comparative Biochemistry and Physiology Part A: Molecular & Integrative Physiology*, vol. 120, no. 1, pp. 3–9, 1998.

[54] I. Prigogine, G. Nicolis and A. Babloyantz, "Thermodynamics of evolution," *Physics Today*, vol. 25, no. 11, pp. 23–28, 1972.

[55] J. Watson and F. Crick, "Molecular structure of nucleic acids; a structure for deoxyribose nucleic acid," *Nature*, vol. 171, no. 4356, pp. 737–738, 1953.

[56] S. Oyama, *The Ontogeny of information: Developmental systems and evolution*, Cambridge: Cambridge University Press, 1985.

[57] R. Libbrecht, P. Oxley, D. Kronauer and L. Keller, "Ant genomics sheds light on the molecular regulation of social organization," *Genome Biology*, vol. 14, no. 7, pp. 1–9, 2013.

[58] Y.-P. Tang, E. Shimizu, G. Dube, C. Rampon et al., "Genetic enhancement of learning and memory in mice," *Nature*, vol. 401, no. 6748, pp. 59–63, 1999.

[59] P. Sullivan, M. Daly and M. O'Donovan, "Genetic architectures of psychiatric disorders: The emerging picture and its implications," *Nature Reviews Genetics*, vol. 13, no. 8, pp. 537–551, 2012.

[60] S. Singh, *Theory of machines*, New Delhi: Pearson Education India, 2006.

[61] H. Simon, *The sciences of the artificial*, Third edition, Cambridge MA: MIT Press, 1970.

[62] K. B. Clark, "The interaction of design hierarchies and market concepts in technological evolution," *Research Policy*, vol. 14, no. 5, pp. 235–251, 1985.

[63] F. Callier and C. Desoer, *Linear system theory*, New York: Springer Science & Business Media, 2012.

[64] J. Ladyman, J. Lambert and K. Wiesner, "What is a complex system?," *European Journal for Philosophy of Science*, vol. 3, pp. 33–67, 2013.

[65] M. Nicolelis, *Beyond boundaries: The new neuroscience of connecting brains with machines and how it will change our lives*, New York: Times Books, 2011.

[66] J. McCarthy, M. Minsky, N. Rochester and C. Shannon, *A proposal for the Dartmouth summer research project on artificial intelligence, August 31, 1955*, vol. 27, http://www-formal.stanford.edu/jmc/history/dartmouth/dartmouth.html: Stanford University, 1955, p. 12.

[67] R. Miikkulainen, J. Liang, E. Meyerson, A. Rawal, D. Fink, O. Francon et al., "Evolving deep neural networks," in *Artificial intelligence in the age of neural networks and brain computing*, R. Kozma, C. Alippi, Y. Choe and F.C. Morabito, eds. London, Academic Press, 2019, pp. 293–312.

[68] C. Emmeche, S. Køppe and F. Stjernfelt, "Levels, emergence, and three versions of downward causation," in *Downward causation. Minds, bodies and matter*, N.O. Finnemann, P.Bøgh Andersen, P. Voetmann Christiansen and C. Emmeche, eds. Aarhus, Aarhus University Press, 2000, pp. 13–34.

[69] G. Ellis and J. Kopel, "A realistic view of causation in the real world," in *From electrons to elephants and elections: Exploring the role of content and context*, S. Wuppuluri and I. Stewart, eds. Cham, Springer International Publishing, 2022, pp. 117–133.

[70] D. Campbell, "Downward causation in hierarchically organised biological systems," in *Studies in the philosophy of biology, reduction and related problems*, F.J. Ayala and Th. Dobzhansky, eds. London, Palgrave, 1974, pp. 179–186.

[71] G. Pezzulo and M. Levin, "Top-down models in biology: Explanation and control of complex living systems above the molecular level," *Journal of the Royal Society Interface*, vol. 13, no. 124, p. 20160555, 2016.

[72] U. Lucia, "Thermodynamics and cancer stationary states," *Physica A: Statistical Mechanics and Its Applications*, vol. 392, no. 17, pp. 3648–3653, 2013.

[73] D. Bray, "Molecular networks: The top-down view," *Science*, vol. 301, no. 5641, pp. 1864–1865, 2003.

[74] B.-O. Küppers, *Information and the origin of life*, Cambridge MA: The MIT Press, 1990.

[75] V. Ninkovic, D. Markovic and M. Rensing, "Plant volatiles as cues and signals in plant communication," *Plant, Cell and Environment*, vol. 44, no. 4, pp. 1030–1043, 2021.

[76] R. Vander Meer, M. Breed, M. Winston and K. Espelie, *Pheromone communication in social insects: Ants, wasps, bees, and termites*, New York: Routledge, 2019.

[77] L. Houck, "Pheromone communication in amphibians and reptiles," *Annual Review of Physiology*, vol. 71, pp. 161–176, 2009.

[78] L. Hollen and A. N. Radford, "The development of alarm call behaviour in mammals and birds," *Animal Behaviour*, vol. 78, no. 4, pp. 791–800, 2009.

[79] R. Seyfarth and D. Cheney, "Signalers and receivers in animal communication," *Annual Review of Psychology*, vol. 54, no. 1, pp. 145–173, 2003.

[80] A. Ghysen, "The origin and evolution of the nervous system," *International Journal of Developmental Biology*, vol. 47, pp. 555–562, 2003.
[81] R. Northcutt, "Evolution of centralized nervous systems: Two schools of evolutionary thought," *Proceedings of the National Academy of Sciences*, vol. 1, no. 109, pp. 10626–10633, 2012.
[82] C. Furusawa and K. Kunihiko, "Emergence of multicellular organisms with dynamic differentiation and spatial pattern," *Artificial Life*, vol. 4, no. 1, pp. 79–93, 1998.
[83] J. J. Hopfield, "Neural networks and physical systems with emergent collective computational abilities," *Proceedings of the National Academy of Sciences*, vol. 79, no. 8, pp. 2554–2558, 1982.
[84] J. Maynard Smith and E. Szathmary, *The major transitions in evolution*, Oxford: Oxford University Press, 1997.
[85] E. Jablonka and M. Lamb, "The evolution of information in the major transitions," *Journal of Theoretical Biology*, vol. 239, no. 2, pp. 236–246, 2006.
[86] J. G. White, E. Southgate, J. N. Thomson and S. Brenner, "The structure of the nervous system of the nematode Caenorhabditis elegans," *Philosophical Transactions of the Royal Society of London Series B, Biological Sciences*, vol. 314, no. 1165, pp. 1–340, 1986.
[87] A. Butler and W. Hodos, *Comparative vertebrate neuroanatomy: Evolution and adaptation*, Hoboken, NJ: John Wiley & Sons, 2005.
[88] K. Schwenk, "A utilitarian approach to evolutionary constraint," *Zoology*, vol. 98, pp. 251–262, 1995.
[89] M. Kaiser and S. Varier, "Evolution and development of brain networks: From Caenorhabditis elegans to Homo sapiens," *Network: Computation in Neural Systems*, vol. 22, nos. 1–4, pp. 143–147, 2011.
[90] O. Paulson, "Blood–brain barrier, brain metabolism and cerebral blood flow," *European Neuropsychopharmacology*, vol. 12, no. 6, pp. 495–501, 2002.
[91] M. Caputa, "Selective brain cooling: A multiple regulatory mechanism," *Journal of Thermal Biology*, vol. 29, nos. 7–8, pp. 691–702, 2004.
[92] M. Hatten, "Central nervous system neuronal migration," *Annual Review of Neuroscience*, vol. 22, no. 1, pp. 511–539, 1999.
[93] L. Puelles, "Pattering and cell type specification in the developing CNS and PNS, Volume 1," in *Plan of the developing vertebrate nervous system*, J.L.R. Rubenstein and P. Rakic, eds. Amsterdam, Elsevier, 2013, pp. 187–209.
[94] S. Giménez-Roldán, "Andreas Vesalius and the brain: Limitations of De humani corporis fabrica libri septem and some comments on the matter," *Neuroscience History*, vol. 8, no. 3, pp. 76–86, 2020.
[95] H. Sarnat and M. Netsky, "When does a ganglion become a brain? Evolutionary origin of the central nervous system," *Seminars in Pediatric Neurology*, vol. 9, no. 4, pp. 240–253, 2002.
[96] H. J. Jerison, *Evolution of the brain and intelligence*, New York: Academic Press, 1973.
[97] R. G. Francisco Aboitiz, "The evolutionary origin of the language areas in the human brain. A neuroanatomical perspective," *Brain Research Reviews*, vol. 25, no. 3, pp. 381–396, 1997.
[98] G. Roth and U. Dicke, "Evolution of the brain and intelligence," *Trends in Cognitive Sciences*, vol. 9, no. 5, pp. 250–257, 2005.
[99] M. Raichle and M. Mintun, "Brain work and brain imaging," *Annual Review of Neuroscience*, vol. 29, pp. 449–476, 2006.

[100] S. Genon, A. Reid, R. Langner, et al., "How to characterize the function of a brain region," *Trends in Cognitive Sciences*, vol. 22, no. 4, pp. 350–364, 2018.

[101] M. Hnazaee, B. Wittevrongel, E. Khachatryan, et al., "Localization of deep brain activity with scalp and subdural EEG," *NeuroImage*, vol. 233, p. 117344, 2020.

[102] E. Margalit, K. Jamison, K. Weiner, et al., "Ultra-high-resolution fMRI of human ventral temporal cortex reveals differential representation of categories and domains," *Journal of neuroscience*, vol. 40, no. 15, pp. 3008–3024, 2020.

[103] M. Page, "What can't functional neuroimaging tell the cognitive psychologist?," *Cortex*, vol. 42, no. 3, pp. 428–443, 2006.

[104] G. Rees, "Neural correlates of the contents of visual awareness in humans," *Philosophical Transactions of the Royal Society B: Biological Sciences*, vol. 362, no. 1481, pp. 877–886, 2007.

[105] W. Penfield and T. Rasmussen, *The cerebral cortex of man; A clinical study of localization of function*, London: Macmillan, 1950.

[106] M. Graziano, "Ethological action maps: A paradigm shift for the motor cortex," *Trends in Cognitive Sciences*, vol. 20, no. 2, pp. 121–132, 2016.

[107] W. T. Fitch, "The evolution of speech: A comparative review," *Trends in Cognitive Sciences*, vol. 4, no. 7, pp. 258–267, 2000.

[108] J. Elam, M. Glasser, M. Harms, et al., "The human connectome project: A retrospective," *NeuroImage*, vol. 244, p. 118543, 2021.

[109] M. Rubinov and O. Sporns, "Complex network measures of brain connectivity: Uses and interpretations," *NeuroImage*, vol. 52, no. 3, pp. 1059–1069, 2010.

[110] A. Bessadok, M. Mahjoub and I. Rekik, "Graph neural networks in network neuroscience," *IEEE Transactions on Pattern Analysis and Machine Intelligence*, vol. 45, no. 5, pp. 5833–5848, 2022.

[111] R. Masland, "Neuronal cell types," *Current Biology*, vol. 14, no. 13, pp. R497–R500, 2004.

[112] C. Sherwood and P. Hof, "The evolution of neuron types and cortical histology in apes and humans," in *Evolution of Nervous Systems, Volume 4*, J.H. Kaas, ed. Cambridge, Academic Press, 2007, pp. 355–378.

[113] N. da Costa and M. Kevan, "Sparse reconstruction of brain circuits: Or, how to survive without a microscopic connectome," *Neuroimage*, vol. 80, pp. 27–36, 2013.

[114] M. Kaku, *The future of the mind: The scientific quest to understand, enhance, and empower the mind*, New York, Doubleday, 2014.

[115] G. Knott, S. Rosset and M. Cantoni, "Focussed ion beam milling and scanning electron microscopy of brain tissue," *JoVE (Journal of Visualized Experiments)*, no. 53, p. e2588, 2011.

[116] J. Buhmann, A. Sheridan, C. Malin-Mayor, et al., "Automatic detection of synaptic partners in a whole-brain Drosophila electron microscopy data set," *Nature Methods*, vol. 18, no. 7, pp. 771–774, 2021.

[117] H. Dale, W. Feldberg and M. Vogt, "(1936) Release of acetylcholine at voluntary motor nerve endings," *Journal of Physiology (London)*, no. 86, pp. 353–380, 1936.

[118] K. Kay, "Principles for models of neural information processing," *NeuroImage*, no. 108, pp. 101–109.

[119] J. Eccles, "The mechanism of synaptic transmission," in *Ergebnisse der physiologie biologischen chemie und experimentellen pharmakologie*, K. Kramer, O. Krayer, E. Lehnartz, A. Muralt and H.H. Weber, eds. Berlin Heidelberg, Springer, 1961, pp. 299–430.

[120] S. Lefort, C. Tomm, J. Sarria and C. Petersen, "The excitatory neuronal network of the C2 barrel column in mouse primary somatosensory cortex," *Neuron*, vol. 61, no. 2, pp. 301–316, 2009.

[121] L. McCormick and S. Gupton, "Mechanistic advances in axon pathfinding," *Current Opinion in Cell Biology*, vol. 63, pp. 11–19.

[122] J. Valdes-Aleman, R. Fetter, E. Sales, et al., "Comparative connectomics reveals how partner identity, location, and activity specify synaptic connectivity in Drosophila," *Neuron*, vol. 109, no. 1, pp. 105–122, 2021.

[123] F. Varela, "The re-enchantment of the concrete: Some biological ingredients for a nouvelle cognitive science," in *The artificial life route to artificial intelligence*, L. Steels and R. Brooks, eds. London, Routledge, 1995, pp. 11–22.

[124] G. Chechik, I. Meilijson and E. Ruppin, "Synaptic pruning in development: A computational account," *Neural computation*, vol. 10, no. 7, pp. 1759–1777, 1998.

[125] G. Collin and M. van den Heuvel, "The ontogeny of the human connectome development and dynamic changes of brain connectivity across the life span," *The Neuroscientist*, vol. 19, no. 6, pp. 616–628, 2013.

[126] M. van den Heuvel, K. Kersbergen, M. de Reus, et al., "The neonatal connectome during preterm brain development," *Cerebral Cortex*, vol. 25, no. 9, pp. 3000–3013, 2015.

[127] L. Kozachkov, M. Lundqvist, J.-J. Slotine and E. Miller, "Achieving stable dynamics in neural circuits," *PLoS Computational Biology*, vol. 16, no. 8, p. e1007659, 2020.

[128] B. Hebb, *The organization of behavior: A neuropsychological theory*, New York: Wiley, 1949.

[129] L. Abbott and S. Nelson, "Synaptic plasticity: Taming the beast," *Nature Neuroscience*, vol. 3, pp. 1178–1183, 2000.

[130] T. Nagel, "What is it like to be a bat?," in *The language and thought series*, N. Block, ed. Cambridge MA, Harvard University Press, 1980, pp. 159–168.

[131] C. Shatz, "Impulse activity and the patterning of connections during CNS development," *Neuron*, vol. 5, no. 6, pp. 745–756, 1990.

[132] H. Ko, L. Cossell, C. Baragli, et al., "The emergence of functional microcircuits in visual cortex," *Nature*, vol. 496, no. 7443, pp. 96–100, 2013.

[133] H. Hirsch and D. Spinelli, "Visual experience modifies distribution of horizontally and vertically oriented receptive fields in cats," *Science*, vol. 168, no. 3933, pp. 869–871, 1970.

[134] B. Hochner, "An embodied view of octopus neurobiology," *Current Biology*, vol. 22, no. 20, pp. R887–R892, 2012.

[135] A. Papale and B. Hooks, "Circuit changes in motor cortex during motor skill learning," *Neuroscience*, vol. 368, pp. 283–297, 2018.

[136] C. Yang, N. Luo, M. Liang, et al., "Altered brain functional connectivity density in fast-ball sports athletes with early stage of motor training," *Frontiers in Psychology*, vol. 11, p. 530122, 2020.

[137] A. Heiling and M. Herberstein, "The role of experience in web-building spiders (Araneidae)," *Animal Cognition*, vol. 2, pp. 171–177, 1999.

[138] C. Lee, A. Meltzoff and P. Kuhl, "The braid of human learning and development: Neuro-physiological processes and participation in cultural practices," in *Handbook of the cultural foundations of learning*, N. Suad Nasir, C.D. Lee, R. Pea and M. McKinney de Royston, eds. Routledge, New York, 2020, pp. 24–43.

[139] T. Morgan and K. Laland, "The biological bases of conformity," *Frontiers in Neuroscience*, vol. 6, p. 87, 2012.

[140] E. Jablonka and M. Lamb, "The changing concept of epigenetics," *Annals of the New York Academy of Sciences*, vol. 981, no. 1, pp. 82–96, 2002.
[141] Q. Tan, "The epigenome of twins as a perfect laboratory for studying behavioural traits," *Neuroscience & Biobehavioral Reviews*, vol. 107, pp. 192–195, 2019.
[142] M. Marshall, "The hidden links between mental disorders," *Nature*, vol. 581, no. 7806, pp. 19–22, 2020.
[143] W. Hill, R. Marioni, O. Maghzian, et al., "A combined analysis of genetically correlated traits identifies 187 loci and a role for neurogenesis and myelination in intelligence," *Molecular Psychiatry*, vol. 24, pp. 169–181, 2019.
[144] F. Barlow, "Nature vs. nurture is nonsense: On the necessity of an integrated genetic, social, developmental, and personality psychology," *Australian Journal of Psychology*, vol. 71, no. 1, pp. 68–79, 2019.
[145] V. Ramachandran, "Mirror neurons and imitation learning as the driving force behind "the great leap forward" in human evolution," *Edge*, vol. 69, 2000.
[146] C. Heyes, "Imitation, culture and cognition," *Animal Behaviour*, vol. 46, no. 5, pp. 999–1010, 1993.
[147] L. J. Kirmayer, *Culture, mind, and brain: Emerging concepts, models, and applications*, Cambridge: Cambridge University Press, 2020.
[148] M. Wheeler and A. Clark, "Culture, embodiment and genes: Unravelling the triple helix," *Philosophical Transactions of the Royal Society B: Biological Sciences*, vol. 363, no. 1509, pp. 3563–3575, 2008.
[149] J. Shaules, *Language, culture, and the embodied mind*, Singapore: Springer, 2019.
[150] L. Saidi, V. Perlbarg, Marrelec, et al., "Functional connectivity changes in second language vocabulary learning," *Brain and Language*, vol. 124, no. 1, pp. 56–65, 2013.
[151] K. Sakai, "Language acquisition and brain development," *Science*, vol. 310, no. 5749, pp. 815–819, 2005.
[152] R. Aunger, *Darwinizing culture: The status of memetics as a science*, Oxford: Oxford University Press, 2000.
[153] M. Muthukrishna and J. Henrich, "Innovation in the collective brain," *Philosophical Transactions of the Royal Society B: Biological Sciences*, vol. 371, no. 1690, p. 20150192, 2016.
[154] R. Descartes, *Les passions de l'âme*, Paris: Charles le Clerc, 1728.
[155] B. Spinoza, *Ethica, ordine geometrico demonstrata*, 1677.
[156] T. Hobbes, *Leviathan or the matter, forme and power of a commonwealth ecclesiasticall and civil*, London, A. Crooke, 651.
[157] G. Berkeley, *A treatise concerning the principles of human knowledge*, London, J. Tonson, 1710.
[158] J. Heil, *Philosophy of mind: A contemporary introduction*, London: Routledge, 1998.
[159] J. Dunham, I. Grant and S. Watson, *Idealism: The history of a philosophy*, Abingdon: Routledge, 2014.
[160] D. Dennett, "Facing backwards on the problem of consciousness," *Journal of Consciousness Studies*, vol. 3, no. 1, pp. 4–6, 1996.
[161] C. Frith, R. Perry and E. Lumer, "The neural correlates of conscious experience: An experimental framework," *Trends in Cognitive Science*, vol. 3, pp. 105–114, 1999.
[162] C. Koch and G. Tononi, "The neural correlates of consciousness," *Annals of the New York Academy of Sciences*, vol. 1124, pp. 239–261, 2008.
[163] M. Oizumi, L. Albantakis and G. Tononi, "From the phenomenology to the mechanisms of consciousness: Integrated information theory 3.0," *PLoS Computational Biology*, vol. 10, no. 5, p. e1003588, 2014.

[164] B. Baars, "Global workspace theory of consciousness: Toward a cognitive neuroscience of human experience," *Progress in Brain Research*, vol. 150, pp. 45–53, 2005.
[165] H. Azizi, M. Golshani and K. Nozari, "Foundations of quantum approaches to consciousness," *Philosophical Investigations*, vol. 15, no. 36, pp. 151–170, 2021.
[166] M. De Caro and H. Putnam, "Free will and quantum mechanics," *The Monist*, vol. 103, no. 4, pp. 415–426, 2020.
[167] A. Eddinton, *The nature of the physical world*, New York, The Macmillan Company, 1928, p. 276.
[167a] B. Kastrup, "The universe in consciousness," *Journal of Consciousness Studies*, vol. 25, no. 5–6, 2018, pp. 125–155
[168] N. Bostrom, "Are we living in a computer simulation?," *The Philosophical Quarterly*, vol. 53, no. 211, pp. 243–255, 2003.
[169] R. Badgaiyan, *Neuroscience of the nonconscious mind*, London: Academic Press, 2019.
[170] P. Teilhard de Chardin, "The formation of the noosphere: A plausible biological interpretation of human history," in *The future of man*, Image Books Doubleday, New York, 1959, pp. 149–178.
[171] C. Jung, *The archetypes and the collective unconscious*, London: Routledge, 1959.
[172] G. Hegel, H. Brockmeyer and W. Harris, "Hegel's phenomenology of spirit," *The Journal of Speculative Philosophy*, vol. 2, no. 4, pp. 229–241, 1869.
[173] K. Wilber, "An integral theory of consciousness," *Journal of Consciousness Studies*, vol. 4, pp. 71–92, 1997.
[174] S. Balaratnasingam and A. Janca, "Mass hysteria revisited," *Current Opinion in Psychiatry*, vol. 19, no. 2, pp. 171–174, 2006.
[175] E. Anati, "Prehistoric art and religion," in *Religion and material culture: Studying religion and religious elements on the basis of objects, architecture, and space*, L. Bredholt and J. Tae Jensen, eds. Turnhout, Brepols Publishers, 2017, pp. 103–109.
[176] D. Schaefer, "Do animals have religion? Interdisciplinary perspectives on religion and embodiment," *Anthrozoös*, vol. 25, no. sup 1, pp. s173–s189, 2021.
[177] D. Hume, *The natural history of religion*, Stanford: Stanford University Press, 1956.
[178] E. Scott, "Antievolution and creationism in the United States," *Annual Review of Anthropology*, vol. 26, no. 1, pp. 263–289, 1997.
[179] M. Ruse, *Understanding the christianity–evolution relationship*, Cambridge: Cambridge University Press, 2023.
[180] Gallup International, "Losing our religion? Two thirds of people still claim to be religious," https://www.gallup-international.bg/en/33531/losing-our-religion-two-thirds-of-people-still-claim-to-be-religious, accessed 30-5-2024, 2015.
[181] A. Newberg and E. d'Aquili, "The neuropsychology of religious and spiritual experience," *Journal of Consciousness Studies*, vol. 7, no. 11–12, pp. 251–266, 2000.
[182] J. Bulbulia, "Meme infection or religious niche construction? An adaptationist alternative to the cultural maladaptationist hypothesis," *Method & Theory in the Study of Religion*, vol. 20, no. 1, pp. 67–107, 2008.
[183] S. Blackmore, "Religions as memeplexes," in *The Meme Machine*, Oxford, Oxford University Press, 1999, pp. 187–203.
[184] K. Phillips, A. Beretta and H. Whitaker, "Mind and brain: Toward an understanding of dualism," in *Brain, mind and consciousness in the history of neuroscience*, C.U.M. Smith and H. Whitaker, eds. Dordrecht, Springer, 2014, pp. 355–369.
[185] A. Demertzi, C. Liew, D. Ledoux, et al., "Dualism persists in the science of mind," *Annals of the New York Academy of Sciences*, vol. 1157, no. 1, pp. 1–9, 2009.
[186] C. Littleton, *Gods, goddesses, and mythology*, New York: Cavendish Square, 2005.

[187] E. Holmes, *The science of mind: A philosophy, a faith, a way of life*, New York: Putnam, 1938.

[188] E. Tolle, *The power of now: A guide to spiritual enlightenment*, Novato CA, New World Library, 2004.

[189] K. Goda and M. Kitsuregawa, "The history of storage systems," *Proceedings of the IEEE*, vol. 100, pp. 1433–1440, 2012.

[190] A. Clements, *Principles of computer hardware*, Oxford: Oxford University Press, 2006.

[191] J. Wei, "Thermal management of Fujitsu high-performance servers," *Fujitsu Scientific & Technical Journal*, vol. 43, no. 1, pp. 122–129, 2007.

[192] M. Nowak, J. Plotkin and V. Jansen, "The evolution of syntactic communication," *Nature*, vol. 404, no. 6777, pp. 495–498, 2000.

[193] M. Aubert, et al., "Earliest hunting scene in prehistoric art," *Nature*, vol. 576, no. 7787, pp. 442–445, 2019.

[194] V. Pletser and D. Huylebrouck, "The Ishango artefact: The missing base 12 link," *Forma Tokyo*, vol. 14, no. 4, pp. 339–346, 1999.

[195] V. Pletser and D. Huylebrouck, "Contradictions and narrowness of views in 'The fables of Ishango, or the irresistible temptation of mathematical fiction', answers and updates (in English and in French)," arXiv preprint:1607.00860, 2016.

[196] W. Senner, *The origins of writing*, Lincoln NA, University of Nebraska Press, 1991.

[197] F. Parmentier, "Deciphering the Voynich manuscript: Propositions to unlock research," *Cryptologia*, vol. 46, no. 5, pp. 461–484, 2022.

[198] K. Sugden, "A history of the abacus," *Accounting Historians Journal*, vol. 8, no. 2, pp. 1–11, 1981.

[199] G. Chase, "History of mechanical computing machinery," in *Proceedings of the 1952 ACM national meeting (Pittsburgh)* , New York, Association of Computer Machinery, 1952, pp. 1–28.

[200] J. Essinger, *Jacquard's web: How a hand-loom led to the birth of the information age*, Oxford: Oxford University Press, 2004.

[201] H. Hollerith, "The electrical tabulating machine," *Journal of the Royal Statistical Society*, vol. 57, no. 4, pp. 678–689, 1894.

[202] D. Swade and C. Babbage, *Difference engine: Charles Babbage and the quest to build the First Computer*, London: Viking Penguin, 2001.

[203] G. Boole, *The mathematical analysis of logic*, Cambridge: Macmillan, Barclay and Macmillan, 1847.

[204] A. Turing, "On computable numbers, with an application to the Entscheidungsproblem," *Journal of Mathematics*, vol. 5, pp. 230–265, 1936.

[205] R. Rojas and U. Hashagen, *The first computers: History and architectures*, Cambridge MA: MIT Press, 2002.

[206] G. Ellis and B. Drossel, "How downwards causation occurs in digital computers," *Foundations of Physics*, vol. 49, no. 11, pp. 1253–1277, 2019.

[207] M. Sasikumar, S. Ramani, S. Raman, et al., *A practical introduction to rule based expert systems*, New Delhi: Narosa Publishing House, 2007.

[208] D. King, *Kasparov versus deeper blue: The ultimate man versus machine challenge*, London: Batsford, 1997.

[209] J. Clark, *Why 2015 was a breakthrough year in artificial intelligence*, https://www.bloomberg.com/news/articles/2015-12-08/why2015-was-a-breakthrough-year-in-artificial-intelligence: Bloomberg.com, 2015.

[210] I. Kononenko, "Machine learning for medical diagnosis: History, state of the art and perspective," *Artificial Intelligence in Medicine*, vol. 23, no. 1, pp. 89–109, 2001.

[211] M. Javaid, A. Haleem, R. Singh and R. Suman, "Artificial intelligence applications for industry 4.0: A literature-based study," *Journal of Industrial Integration and Management*, vol. 7, no. 1, pp. 83–111, 2022.

[212] J. Hua, L. Zeng, G. Li and Z. Ju, "Learning for a robot: Deep reinforcement learning, imitation learning, transfer learning," *Sensors*, vol. 21, no. 4, p. 1278, 2021.

[213] R. Young, M. Riedl, M. Branly, et al., "An architecture for integrating plan-based behavior generation with interactive game environments," *Journal of Game Development*, vol. 1, no. 1, pp. 51–70, 2004.

[214] H. Singh, K. Kaur and P. Singh, "Artificial intelligence as a facilitator for film production pProcess," in *International Conference on Artificial Intelligence and Smart Communication (AISC)*, IEEE, 2023, pp. 969–972.

[215] Y. Yoon, T. Guimaraes and G. Swales, "Integrating artificial neural networks with rule-based expert systems," *Decision Support Systems*, vol. 11, no. 5, pp. 497–507, 1994.

[216] M. Hutter, *Universal artificial intelligence: Sequential decisions based on algorithmic probability*, New York: Springer, 2005.

[217] L. Floridi, "AI as agency without intelligence: On ChatGPT, large language models, and other generative models," *Philosophy & Technology*, vol. 36, no. 1, p. 15, 2023.

[218] D. Cotton, P. Cotton and J. Shipway, "Chatting and cheating: Ensuring academic integrity in the era of ChatGPT," *Innovations in Education and Teaching International*, vol. 61, no. 2, pp. 1–12, 2023.

[219] M. Coeckelbergh and D. Gunkel, "ChatGPT: Deconstructing the debate and moving it forward," *AI & Society*, pp. 1–11 https://doi.org/10.1007/s00146-023-01710-4.

[220] J. Searle, "Minds, brains and programs," *Behavioral and Brain Sciences*, vol. 3, pp. 417–457, 1980.

[221] U. Hasson, S. Nastase and A. Goldstein, "Direct fit to nature: An evolutionary perspective on biological and artificial neural networks," *Neuron*, vol. 105, no. 3, pp. 416–434, 2020.

[222] W. McCulloch and W. Pitts, "A logical calculus of the ideas immanent in nervous activity," *The Bulletin of Mathematical Biophysics*, vol. 5, pp. 115–133, 1943.

[223] R. Kohut and B. Steinbach, "Boolean neural networks," *Transactions on Systems*, vol. 2, pp. 420–425, 2004.

[224] E. Bullmore and O. Sporns, "Complex brain networks: Graph theoretical analysis of structural and functional systems," *Nature Reviews Neuroscience*, vol. 10, pp. 186–198, 2009.

[225] W. Baxt, "Application of artificial neural networks to clinical medicine," *The Lancet*, vol. 346, no. 8983, pp. 1135–1138, 1995.

[226] E. Schöneburg, "Stock price prediction using neural networks: A project report," *Neurocomputing*, vol. 2, no. 1, pp. 17–27, 1990.

[227] K. Cios and I. Shin, "Image recognition neural network: IRNN," *Neurocomputing*, vol. 7, no. 2, pp. 159–185, 1995.

[228] D. Pomerleau, "Alvinn: An autonomous land vehicle in a neural network," *Advances in Neural Information Processing Systems*, vol. 1, pp. 305–313, 1988.

[229] H. Miyamoto, M. Kawato, T. Setoyama and R. Suzuki, "Feedback-error-learning neural network for trajectory control of a robotic manipulator," *Neural Networks*, vol. 1, no. 3, pp. 251–265, 1988.

[230] S. Kierner, J. Kucharski and Z. Kierner, "Taxonomy of hybrid architectures involving rule-based reasoning and machine learning in clinical decision systems: A scoping review," *Journal of Biomedical Informatics*, vol. 144, p. 104428, 2023.

[231] E. Duede, "Deep learning opacity in scientific discovery," *Philosophy of Science*, vol. doi:10.1017/psa.2023.8, pp. 1–13, 2023.

[232] D. Castelvecchi, "Can we open the black box of AI?," *Nature News*, vol. 538, no. 7623, p. 20, 2016.

[233] Y. Li, J. Yosinski, J. Clune, H. Lipson and J. Hopcroft, "Convergent learning: Do different neural networks learn the same representations?," in *Proceedings of ICLR 2016*, 2016, p. arXiv:1511.07543.

[234] J. Zerilli, U. Bhatt and A. Weller, "How transparency modulates trust in artificial intelligence," *Patterns*, vol. 3, pp. 1–10, 2022.

[235] J. Burrell, "How the machine 'thinks': Understanding opacity in machine learning algorithms," *Big Data & Society*, vol. 3, no. 1, p. 2053951715622512, 2016.

[236] H. Siegelmann and E. Sontag, "Turing computability with neural nets," *Applied Mathematics Letters*, vol. 4, no. 6, pp. 77–80, 1991.

[237] P. Mantri and J. Thomas, "Design of neural networks," in *IOP Conference Series: Materials Science and Engineering* (Vol. 1174, No. 1, p. 012023), Bristol, IOP Publishing, 2021.

[238] D. Rumelhart, G. E. Hinton, and R. J. Williams, "Learning representations by back-propagating errors," *Nature*, vol. 323, no. 6088, pp. 533–536, 1986.

[239] K. O'Shea and R. Nash, "An introduction to convolutional neural networks," *arXiv*, vol. 08458, no. 1511.

[240] A. Graves, A. Mohamed and G. Hinton, "Speech recognition with deep recurrent neural networks," in *2013 IEEE international conference on acoustics, speech and signal processing*, IEEE, 2013, pp. 6645–6649.

[241] G. Hinton and S. T. Y. Osindero, "A fast learning algorithm for deep belief nets," *Neural Computation*, vol. 18, no. 7, pp. 1527–1554, 2006.

[242] I. Raharjana, D. Siahaan and C. Fatichah, "User stories and natural language processing: A systematic literature review," *IEEE Access*, vol. 9, pp. 53811–53826, 2021.

[243] T. Elsken, J. Metzen and F. Hutter, "Neural architecture search: A survey," *The Journal of Machine Learning Research*, vol. 20, no. 1, pp. 1997–2017, 2019.

[244] Y. Liu, Y. Sun, B. Xue, et al., "A survey on evolutionary neural architecture search," *IEEE Transactions on Neural Networks and Learning Systems*, vol. 25, no. 5, pp. 894–912, 2021.

[245] R. Caruana and A. Niculescu-Mizil, "An empirical comparison of supervised learning algorithms," in *Proceedings of the 23rd international conference on Machine learning*, 2006, pp. 161–168.

[246] J. Arinez, Q. Chang, R. Gao, C. Xu and J. Zhang, "Artificial intelligence in advanced manufacturing: Current status and future outlook," *Journal of Manufacturing Science and Engineering*, vol. 142, no. 11, p. 110804, 2020.

[247] Y. Gao, X. Li, X. Wang, L. Wang and L. Gao, "A review on recent advances in vision-based defect recognition towards industrial intelligence," *Journal of Manufacturing Systems*, vol. 62, pp. 753–766, 2022.

[248] R. Jarvis, "Intelligent robotics: Past, present and future," *International Journal of Computer Science and Applications*, vol. 5, no. 3, p. 23035, 2008.

[249] H. Moravec, *Mind children: The future of robot and human intelligence*, Cambridge MA: Harvard University Press, 1988, pp. 15–16.

[250] L. Steels and R. Brooks, *The artificial life route to artificial intelligence: Building embodied, situated agents*, London: Routledge, 1995.

[251] A. Gupta, A. Anpalagan, L. Guan and A. S. Khwaja, "Deep learning for object detection and scene perception in self-driving cars: Survey, challenges, and open issues," *Array*, vol. 10, p. 100057, 2021.

[252] J. Fossaceca and S. Young, "Artificial intelligence and machine learning for future army applications," in *Ground/Air Multisensor Interoperability, Integration, and Networking for Persistent ISR IX (Vol. 10635, pp. 8–25)*, M.A. Kolodny, ed. Orlando, SPIE, 2018, pp. 8–25.

[253] T. Degris, P. Pilarski and R. Sutton, "Model-free reinforcement learning with continuous action in practice," in *2012 American Control Conference (ACC)*, IEEE, 2012, pp. 2177–2182.

[254] J. Yosinski, J. Clune, A. Nguyen, T. Fuchs and H. Lipson, "Understanding neural networks through deep visualization," *arXiv*, p. 1506.06579, 2015.

[255] O. Gundersen, S. Shamsaliei and R. Isdahl, "Do machine learning platforms provide out-of-the-box reproducibility?," *Future Generation Computer Systems*, vol. 126, pp. 34–47, 2022.

[256] W. Newsome, "Human freedom "emergence"," in *Downward causation and the neurobiology of free will*, N. Murphy, G.F.R. Ellis and T. O'Connor, eds. Berlin, Springer, 2009, pp. 53–62.

[257] S. Wecker, "Computer network architectures," *Computer*, vol. 12, no. 9, pp. 58–72, 1979.

[258] D. Boyd, "Design and self-assembly of information systems," *Interdisciplinary Science Reviews*, vol. 45, no. 1, pp. 71–94, 2020.

[259] T. Zentall, "Imitation by animals: How do they do it?," *Current Directions in Psychological Science*, vol. 12, no. 3, pp. 91–95, 2003.

[260] C. Slobodchikoff, A. Paseka and J. Verdolin, "Prairie dog alarm calls encode labels about predator colors," *Animal cognition*, vol. 12, pp. 435–439, 2009.

[261] M. Adams, *From Elfish to Klingon*, New York: Oxford University Press, 2011.

[262] A. Whiten, "The burgeoning reach of animal culture," *Science*, vol. 371, no. 6537, p. eabe6514, 2021.

[263] A. Vázquez, R. Pastor-Satorras and A. Vespignani, "Large-scale topological and dynamical properties of the Internet," *Physical Review E*, vol. 65, no. 6, p. 066130, 2002.

[264] R. Baheti and H. Gill, "Cyber-physical systems," *The Impact of Control Technology*, vol. 12, no. 1, pp. 161–166, 2011.

[265] R. Arvidson, V. Landa, S. Frankenberg and M. Adams, "Life history of the emerald jewel wasp Ampulex compressa," *Journal of Hymenoptera Research*, vol. 63, pp. 1–13, 2018.

[266] I. Armit, "Violence and society in the deep human past," *The British Journal of Criminology*, vol. 51, no. 3, pp. 499–517, 2011.

[267] E. Urch, "The law code of Hammurabi," *American Bar Association Journal*, vol. 15, pp. 437–441, 1929.

[268] G. Orwell, *Nineteen eighty-four: A novel*, London: Secker & Warburg, 1950.

[269] J. Stratton, "Coronavirus, the great toilet paper panic and civilization," *Thesis Eleven*, vol. 165, no. 1, pp. 145–168, 2021.

[270] E. Weir, "Mass sociogenic illness," *Canadian Medical Association Journal*, vol. 172, no. 1, p. 36, 2005.

[271] M. Burgan, *The Salem witch trials: Mass hysteria and many lives lost, Tangled History*, North Makato MI, Capstone Press, 2019.

[272] T. Fenzl, T. Brudermann, C. Malik and L. Pelzmann, "A mass psychological perspective on financial markets," *European Scientific Journal*, vol. 9, no. 25, pp. 403–426, 2013.

[273] O. Zur, "The psychohistory of warfare: The co-evolution of culture, psyche and enemy," *Journal of Peace Research*, vol. 24, no. 2, pp. 125–134, 1987.

[274] G. Baxter and I. Sommerville, "Socio-technical systems: From design methods to systems engineering," *Interacting with Computers*, vol. 23, no. 1, pp. 4–17, 2011.

[275] E. Frazzon, J. Hartmann, T. Makuschewitz and B. Scholz-Reiter, "Towards socio-cyber-physical systems in production networks," *Procedia CIRP*, vol. 7, pp. 49–54, 2013.

[276] K. Kellogg, M. Valentine and A. Christin, "Algorithms at work: The new contested terrain of control," *Academy of Management Annals*, vol. 14, no. 1, pp. 366–410, 2020.

[277] D. Boyd, "Hybrid information systems: Who is in control?," *Proceedings of the 2021 Summit of the International Society for the Study of Information*, vol. 81, no. 1, p. 109, 2022.

[278] B. Grigorina, "Bias in artificial intelligence," *Smart Cities International Conference (SCIC) Proceedings*, vol. 10, pp. 337–344, 2022.

[279] K. Manheim and L. Kaplan, "Artificial intelligence: Risks to privacy and democracy," *The Yale Journal of Law and Technology*, vol. 21, pp. 106–185, 2019.

[280] S. Larsson and F. Heintz, "Transparency in artificial intelligence," *Internet Policy Review*, vol. 9, no. 2, pp. 1–16, 2020.

[281] C. Stuart-Ulin, "Microsoft's politically correct chat bot is even worse than its racist one," 31 July 2018. [Online]. https://qz.com/1340990/microsofts-politically-correct-chat-bot-is-even-worse-than-its-racist-one/, accessed 30-5-2024.

[282] A. Bouman, M. Ginting, N. Alatur, et al., "Autonomous spot: Long-range autonomous exploration of extreme environments with legged locomotion," in *IEEE/RSJ International Conference on Intelligent Robots and Systems (IROS)*, IEEE, 2020, pp. 2518–2525.

[283] I. Asimov, "Runaround," in *I, Robot (The Isaac Asimov Collection)*, New York, Doubleday, 1950, p. 40.

[284] R. Murphy and D. Woods, "Beyond Asimov: The three laws of responsible robotics," in *Machine Ethics and Robot Ethics*, W. Wallach and P. Asaro, eds. London, Routledge, 2020, pp. 405–411.

[285] W. Saba, "Stochastic LLMs do not understand language: Towards symbolic, explainable and ontologically based LLMs," in *International conference on conceptual modeling*, Cham, Springer Nature Switzerland, 2023, pp. 3–19.

[286] R. Kurzweil, *The singularity is near: When humans transcend biology*, New York: Penguin, 2005.

[287] E. Schwitzgebel and M. Garza, "Designing AI with rights, consciousness, self-respect, and freedom," in *Ethics of artificial intelligence*, S.M. Liao, ed. Oxford, Oxford University Press, 2020, pp. 459–479.

[288] D. Boyd, "Achieving transparency in adaptive digital systems," *New Explorations: Studies in Culture and Communication*, vol. 2, no. 3, pp. 134–149, 2022.

Index

abacus 6, 114
absolute spirit 41
adaptive system 21
alarm call 27
algorithmic information 7
algorithmic transparency 169
Anati, Emmanuel 42
Anderson, Philip 15
anthropomorphism 42
Arabic language 113
architecture 109
argumentation: as linguistic process 108
Aristotle 18, 22
array storage 126
artificial consciousness 172
artificial general intelligence (AGI) 56, 170
artificial intelligence 21
artificial neural network xiv, 57; architecture 59; simulation of 128
ASCII coding system 52
Asimov, Isaac 170
auditory communication 102
authoritarianism 108
autonomous vehicle 57, 61, 132
auxin 72

Babbage, Charles 51
back-propagation 59
Barlow, Fiona 36
Bateson, Gregory 4, 70
bee waggle dance 103
behaviour: coordination of 99; flexibility of 157; responsive 81
Bénard convection cells 18
Berkeley, George 39
Bible 153
binary states: and associated information 122
binary value xv, 9
biochemical process 94
biological competition 144
biological evolution 18
biological neural networks: simulation of 130
biosphere 144
Boolean algebra 51, 75
Bostrom, Nick 40
Braille system 46
brain anatomy 29

Caenorhabditis elegans 28, 88, 92
Cambridge Analytica 169
Campbell, David 22
cancer 23
Caputa, Michal 28
Cartesian dualism 39
caterpillar vs. butterfly 23
Catholic church 108
causation 22; in physical-informational interactions 93
'cells that fire together, wire together' 33, 89
cellular longevity 88
Chalmers, David xiv, 9
Chalmers' Hard Problem 39, 44, 97
Chardin, Teilhard de 41
Chase, George 50
chatbot 168
ChatGPT 56
chess-playing computer 54
Chinese language 113
Chinese whispers 108
choice: as selection process 147
code of conduct 153
Code of Hammurabi 154
codon 25
co-evolution of mental and physical functions 143

collective brain 37
collective unconscious 41
communal consciousness 41
communal mind 160
communication 27, 151
communication technology 37
complex system 21
computational process 9
computer 115; architecture 117; hardware 47; input/output interfaces 121; language 52; network 131
computer programme: design of 120
conflict resolution strategy 162
connectome 30; evolution of 90
conscious reporting 97, 99
consciousness 11; location of 137; non-uniqueness of 97
consumer protection 158
convolutional neural network 59
corporate organization 156
cosmos 14
COVID-19 pandemic 157, 161
creationism 42
crime 153
crystal lattice 22
culture 109; effect on behaviour 36
cyber-physical system 132
cyber-social system 166

da Costa, Nuno 30
data compression 124
debate 109
decision making process 149
Deep Blue supercomputer 54
deep neural network 57
deities 44; and the communal mind 162
democratic political system 159
Descartes, Rene 39
Design process 19
'difference that makes a difference' 70
digital community 132
digital gaming 128
digital technology 117
digital twin 128
digitization of physical phenomena 123
Drosophila melanogaster 32
Duede, Eamon 58

Eddington, Arthur 40
EEG 29
electron microscopy 30
elephant xi
Ellis, George 53
embodiment 142
emergence 14
Emergent Information Theory (EIT) 67
emotion 97
empathy 153
empirical evidence 180
employment law 158
Enlightenment, the 10, 38
environmental regulation 158
epigenetic factor 35
Euclidean dimensions 11, 68
eusocial insect 151
evil 150
evolution: of informational functions 70
evolutionary constraint 28
evolutionary theory xvi
excitable cell 26
excitatory post-synaptic potentials (EPSP) 90
expert system 54
extreme sports 142

farming 109
feline visual cortex: development of 33
finance sector 157
financial market sentiment 161
Floridi, Luciano 3
fMRI 29
free will 145
freedom of thought 155
functional emergence 28, 81

Galilei, Galileo 8
general knowledge 56
general purpose programmable computer 6, 115
genetic information 25
genetics: behavioural effects of 35
genome 19
geometrical volume 86
ghost in the machine xi
global community 152
government 159
grammar 104
graph theory 30

hard problem of consciousness xiii, 3
heaven and hell 10, 44
Hebbian learning 33
Hegel, Georg 41
Heil, John 39
Heßbrüggen-Walter, Stefan 11
hexagonal close packing 16, 86

hierarchical organization 12, 80
higher consciousness 163
Hobbes, Thomas 154, 158
Hollerith, Herman 50
home working 157
Hopfield, John 27
hormonal control system 72
hormone 25
horse-tractor comparison 173
human civilization 152, 159
Human Connectome Project 30
hydrocarbon chemistry 22

idealism 39
identical twins 35
imitation 36, 100
Imitation Game 56
immortality and the soul 44
indoctrination 43
industrial automation 55, 61, 167
industrial production 156
industrial robotics 132
information: definitions of 3; product of physical interaction 71
information dimension 69, 87
information entropy 7
information function: flexibility and adaptability 88
information processing 27, 114
information storage 48
information system: definition 4
information technology 6, 69; requirements 46
information theory 7
information transfer 26; between and within generations 108
informational determinism 146
informational emergence 17, 68, 80
informational specialisation 155
informational tool 166
insulin 25, 72
integrated digital system 63
integrated information theory (IIT) 39
International Business Machines (IBM) 51
internet 62, 131
interneuron 73
inverse non-detectability problem 138
Ishango bone 48
'it from bit' 8

Jagers op Akkerhuis, Gerard 12
James, Glenn 10
Jaquard's loom 50
jellyfish phototropism 76
jewel wasp larva 150
Jung, Carl 41

Kant, Emmanuel 40
Kasparov, Garry 54
Kastrop, Bernardo 40
Kay, Kendrick 31
Keats, John xiii
Korzybski, Alfred 6
Küppers, Bernd-Olaf 25
Kurzweil, Ray 174

Landauer, Rolf 5
language 37; acquisition 106; origins of 105
large language model (LLM) xi, 56, 173
Laws of Robotics 170
legal sector 157
legislation 154
letter symbol: arbitrary relationship with meaning 105
Lincoln, Abraham 159
linear system 21
living organism: dependence on information 4
living system: non-equilibrium state 70
location: of brain function 29; physical vs functional 84
locomotion: diversity of gaits 81

machine code 51, 118
machine design 13
machine learning 21, 55, 169
magnetic bit xiv
Malthus, Thomas 144
'map is not the territory' 6, 83
mass hysteria 41
mass sociogenic illness 161
materialism 39
Maxims of Ptahhotep 153
Maxwell's demon 6
Maynard-Smith, John 27
Mazzocchi, Fulvio 24
mechanical calculating machine 50, 115
medical technology 57
meditation 184
melatonin 73
memetics 37
memory 83
Mendeleev, Dmitri 15
microscope 14
Microsoft Word 118

mirror neuron 36
money 157
moral dilemma 145
Moravec's paradox 61
motor coordination 81
motor cortex 93; training of skills 34
mouse whisker 31
multicellular organism 19, 27
multi-dimensional digital information 127
multidimensionality 85
multidisciplinary approach xii
multidisciplinary team 111
multisensory perception 80, 138
murder 150
murmeration 100
music 109

Nagel, Thomas 33, 185
natural language processing 59
nature-nurture 34, 141
network topology 11, 86
neural architecture search (NAS) 59
neural network 27; intractability 57; thermodynamics 94
neural network simulation: dimensionality of 127
neuron 26; generic stimulus-response 73
neuroscientist xii
neurotransmitter 31, 73
neutral monism 39
New Age spirituality 44
Newsome, William 62
Newspeak 155
Newton, Isaac 38
Newton's laws of motion 47
Nicolelis, Miguel 21
non-detectability 99
non-equilibrium system 19
non-equilibrium thermodynamics 70
non-linear system 145
noosphere 41

obedience of digital systems 175
obsession 142
one-dimensional bit sequence 125
ontogenesis 17
opportunities and threats: in the environment 26
organizational structure 157
Orwell, George 155

Page, Mike 29
panic buying of toilet rolls 161
panpsychism xv
parallel processing 126
parliament 159
Pasteur, Louis 18
peacock tail 143
phase space 10
pheromone 27, 101, 151
philosopher xii
philosophy of mind 38
phoneme: combination to form words 104
physical determinism 145
physical law 145
politics 109
population dynamics 144
pragmatic information 4
prairie dog 102
prediction 83
prehistoric art 42, 48
printing press 49, 114
professional specialism 111
programming language 118
programming skills 120
property dualism 11, 26
proximity: physical vs functional 74
psychiatric disorder 19
psychology 184
punch card 46, 50

qualia xv
quantum indeterminacy 40
quantum mechanics 7
quark 12
quirk 68

radio 49
receptor state 70
recurrent neural network 59
reductionism: limits to 17, 23
reflex 74
reinforcement learning 60
religion 37; origins of 42
religious belief: demographics 43
religious war 163
representation 25
reproductive abstention 142
response diversity 78
responsibility 149
RGB coding system 123
rights of digital systems 174
robotics 55, 60
Roederer, Juan 4
Rosetta space probe xiii

sacrifice 151
Salem witch hunt 161

scaling effect: in emergent systems 16
Searle's Chinese room 56
second law of thermodynamics 6
Second World War 51
self-assembly 18
self-organization 18; of mental functions 141
semiconductor 51
sense organ 26
sensory illusion 138
sensory information: combination of 75
sensory interface 93
sensory perception: location of 137
Shapley, Harlow 14
Simon, Herbert 20
simulation hypothesis 40
single-celled organism 70
skull endocast 29
small world network 84
social conformity 35
social self-organization 162
social skill development 100
social species 107
social structure 100
sociotechnical system 167
software-hardware problem 181
solitary species 107
soul 10
specific value emergence 15
Spinoza, Benedictus de 39
spontaneous generation 18
stochastic neural activity 96
stock trading 57
stratification 13
strong emergence 15, 23
subconscious 40, 98
subjective reporting 184
substance dualism 9, 39, 69
suicide 143
Sumerian proverb 153
superorganism 102, 151
supervised learning 60
supply chain 156
symbol 113
symbolic language 48, 97, 143, 152
synaptic connectivity pattern 32
synaptic junction 31
synaptic plasticity 88
Szathmáry, Eors 27

tally 6
technological evolution 20
telephone 49
telescope 14
television 49
tesseract 85
text: hierarchical structure of 49
thermionic valve 51
thermodynamic equilibrium 20
thermodynamics: of neural networks 34
Tolkien, J. J. R. 105
Tolle, Eckhart 44
tool use 109
top-down causation 22, 34, 53, 94, 120, 141
transistor: physical and informational applications 47
Turing test xiv, 56
Turing, Alan 51
typewriter 114

unconventional computing 55
universal Turing machine (UTM) 51, 115
unsupervised learning 60
US census 1890, 50

Van Gulik, Robert 15
Varela, Francisco 33
Vesalius, Andreas 29
vinyl record 46
virtual reality 128
visual communication 102
visual cortex 79
visualisation of digital information 122
Voynich manuscript 49

warfare 143, 153, 161
wave function collapse 7
waveform sampling 124
weak emergence 15
weaponisation 152
weather forecasting 128
Wheeler, John 8
Wilber, Ken 41
wireless communication 62
word: arbitrary meaning of 105
writing 49, 112

xenophobia 162